Hairdressing
The Foundations

Fourth Edition

Chris Moody

Hairdressing and Beauty Industry Authority Series – related titles

Hairdressing

Start Hairdressing: The Official Guide to Level 1   Martin Green and Leo Palladino

Hairdressing – The Foundations: The Official Guide to Level 2
Leo Palladino with Jane Farr

Professional Hairdressing: The Official Guide to Level 3
Martin Green and Leo Palladino

Men's Hairdressing: Traditional and Modern Barbering   Maurice Lister

African-Caribbean Hairdressing   Sandra Gittens

Salon Management   Martin Green

Professional Men's Hairdressing   Guy Kemer and Jacki Wadeson

Essensuals, Next generation Toni & Guy: Step by Step

Mahogany Hairdressing: Steps to Cutting, Colouring and Finishing Hair
Martin Gannon and Richard Thompson

Mahogany Hairdressing: Advanced Looks

Patrick Cameron: Dressing Long Hair   Patrick Cameron and Jacki Wadeson

Patrick Cameron: Dressing Long Hair Book 2   Patrick Cameron

Bridal Hair   Pat Dixon and Jacki Wadeson

Trevor Sorbie: Visions in Hair   Kris Sorbie and Jacki Wadeson

The Total Look: The Style Guide for Hair and Make-up Professionals   Ian Mistlin

Art of Hair Colouring   David Adams and Jacki Wadeson

Beauty Therapy

Beauty Therapy – The Foundations: The Official Guide to Level 2
Lorraine Nordmann

Professional Beauty Therapy: The Official Guide to Level 3
Lorraine Nordmann, Lorraine Appleyard and Pamela Linforth

The Official Guide to Body Massage   Adele O'Keefe

Aromatherapy for the Beauty Therapist   Valerie Ann Worwood

Indian Head Massage   Muriel Burnham-Airey and Adele O'Keefe

An Holistic guide to Anatomy and Physiology   Tina Parsons

An Holistic guide to Reflexology   Tina Parsons

The Complete Nail Technician   Marian Newman

The Encyclopedia of Nails   Jacqui Jefford and Anne Swain

Nutrition: a practical approach   Suzanne Le-Quesne

The World of Skin Care: A Scientific Companion   Dr John Gray

Safety in the Salon   Elaine Almond

Hairdressing
The Foundations

The official guide to level 2

Fourth Edition

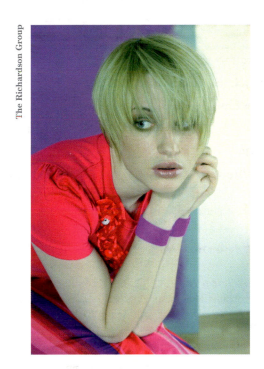

The Richardson Group

Leo Palladino

contribution from Jane Farr

THOMSON ™

City & Guilds

Australia · Canada · Mexico · Singapore · Spain · United Kingdom · United States

HABIA
Hairdressing And Beauty Industry Authority

THOMSON

Hairdressing: The Foundations, Level 2 – fourth edition

Copyright © Leo Palladino and HABIA 2003

The Thomson logo is a registered trademark used herein under licence.

City & Guilds name and logo are the registered trade marks of The City and Guilds of London Institute and are used under licence.

For more information, contact Thomson Learning, High Holborn House, 50–51 Bedford Row, London WC1R 4LR or visit us on the World Wide Web at: http://www.thomsonlearning.co.uk

British Library Cataloguing-in-Publication Data
A catalogue record for this book is available from the British Library

ISBN 1-86152-915-5

First edition published 1991 by Macmillan Press Ltd
Second edition 1995
Third edition 1998

This edition published by Thomson Learning 2003

Reprinted 2003 by Thomson Learning

Typeset by Meridian Colour Repro Ltd, Pangbourne-on-Thames, Berkshire

Printed in Italy by G. Canale & C.

Contents

Hair and skin 1

Client care and consultation 29

Shampooing and conditioning hair 51

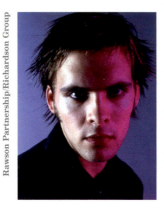

Chris Moody

Ladies cutting

Rawson Partnership/Richardson Group

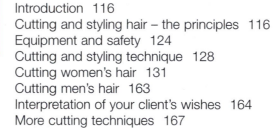

Men's cutting

Lawrence Anthony

Perming

Derrick Mullins, Media Image

Relaxing

Greig Firth

Colouring

Foreword

Ishoka

When HABIA first began to promote the NVQ Level 2 qualification in hairdressing, back in 1989, no one envisaged the phenomenal success that has since been achieved. Within five years the NVQ established itself as the accepted qualification throughout the hairdressing industry. Fundamental to this achievement was the success of Leo Palladino's book *Hairdressing – The Foundations*.

Ever since my first meeting with Leo and our publishers in 1989, HABIA has been an integral part of *Hairdressing – The Foundations*. We are now publishing the 4th Edition. I am delighted that Leo Palladino has actively and consistently updated his original book, in keeping with changes to the qualification and to changes within the industry. This edition has the added benefit of a contribution from HABIA's Jane Farr. Many of you will know Jane in her role as Director of Qualifications & Standards at HABIA. Jane brings a wealth of knowledge and know-how to this new edition. Once you start to read it, you'll see the richness that Jane brings in partnership with Leo Palladino.

Hairdressing – The Foundations was the first book I was involved with at HABIA and I've always liked it. With this edition it has come of age. Thank you Leo and Jane for your insight and creativity.

Alan Goldsbro
Chief Executive Officer
Hairdressing and Beauty Industry Authority

Introduction

Barrie Stephen, Hair Envision

Paul Baker (www.paul-baker-photography.co.uk)

Welcome to the 21st Century a time of changing needs and requirements in the hairdressing industry.

Hairdressing – The Foundations is the official guide for all those studying NVQ/SVQ Level 2 hairdressing. It is based on a number of skills that – when achieved – will help to increase your level of competence in the world of hairdressing.

The work has been streamlined in accordance with the changing needs and standards laid down by the Hairdressing and Beauty Industry Association.

Each chapter represents a unit as required by the NVQ/SVQ syllabus. They may be read as stand alone units or as a total concept. It is not intended that the book is read from cover to cover but dipped into when the need arises.

With the ever changing demands of the hairdressing world it's up to you, as the future of this new era, to make the way forward in this exciting industry.

This guide book contains the theory which will enable you to put it into practice.

Your level of achievement is entirely up to you. You must decide how much effort you are willing to make in order to achieve the status of 'qualified professional hairdresser'

I wish you an exciting and successful path towards your future success in your chosen career.

Leo Palladino

Acknowledgements

The author and publishers would like to thank the following for providing pictures for the book:

American Express, Andrew Collinge, Barclays Bank plc, UK Banking Services - Public Relations, BLM Health, Carol Hayes & Associates, Charles Worthington, Charlie Miller, Charlie Taylor, Cheynes Training, Chubb Fire Ltd, Clinique, Clynol Hair, Comby, Computill Ltd, David Adams, Denman, Depilex/RVB, Derrick Mullings/Media Image, Dr Andrew L. Wright (Consultant Dermatologist, Bradford Royal Infirmary), Dr John Gray (Procter & Gamble), Dr Michael H. Beck (Consultant Dermatologist, Salford Royal Hospitals NHS Trust), Ellisons, Errol Douglas at Neville Daniel, Fire Protection Services, Forfex, Frank Pegg (Volumatic), Freeze Frame Photography, Goldwell (hair cosmetics) Ltd, Hairdressers Journal International, Hairdressing Training Board, HeadQuarters, Indola, Jackie Henry at A Cut Above, Jennifer Taylor (Paress), Jingles International, John Carne, Joshua Galvin Education and Training, Kathryn Longmuir at Ishoka, Lawrence Anthony, Le Noir Salon for designer Touch, L'Oréal, mahogany, Marianne Majerus, Micol Group, National Westminster Bank, Nick Jones Hair Deign, Patrick Cameron, Patricia Livingstone, Paul Baker (www.paul-baker-photography.co.uk), Paul Mitchell Luxury Hiarcare, Ralph Kleeli, Redken, Regis, Richard Thompson, Saks Art Team, Salon Ambience, Schwarzkopf, Sharon Thompson at Luster Products Inc., Sharp, Signs and Labels Ltd, Sminth & Nephew, Sorisa, Splinters, Terence Renati, Vidal Sassoon, Wella Great Britain, Wilkinson Sword.

The author and publishers would also like to thank:

The Controller of Her Majesty's Stationery Office for Crown copyright material, Peter Hickman, John Phelps and all their colleagues, friends and students who were involved in some of the various technique photographs taken for this book. Special thanks to Toni & Guy for their step-by-steps which appear in the 'Cutting and styling hair' chapter.

Martin Green, joint author of Professional Hairdressing and Start Hairdressing! Contributed three chapters to this book.

Every effort has been made to trace all the copyright holders, but if any have been inadvertently overlooked the publishers will be pleased to make the necessary arrangements at the first opportunity.

Special thanks to my wife Della, daughter Corinne and her husband Nigel for their contribution.

Special thanks also, to all those involved at Thomson Learning.

Units / Chapters	G1	G4	G5	G6	G7	G8	H6	H7	H9	H10	H11	H12	H13	H14	H15	H16	H18
1 Hair and Skin			✓		✓				✓			✓	✓		✓	✓	✓
2 Client Care and Consultation			✓	✓	✓												
3 Shampooing and Conditioning									✓								✓
4 Dry Hair										✓				✓			
5 Setting and Dressing Hair										✓	Small section covered						
6 Cutting and Styling Hair							✓	✓									
7 Perming and Neutralising Hair												✓					
8 Relaxing Hair															✓	✓	
9 Colour Hair													✓				
10 Salon Reception		✓															
11 Working Effectively						✓											
12 Health and Safety in the Salon	✓																

Signposting of the Level 2 NVQ/SVQ units covered in this book

Key skill requirements

At the time of going to press, the following are the key skills requirements you may need to complete for your hairdressing Foundation Modern Apprenticeship (FMA) you may also develop skills at a higher level than you require for your FMA. Many of the activities within this book can support you in developing and practicing these key skills. Your tutor or supervisor will guide you towards producing the appropriate sources of evidence to show that you have demonstrated the skills necessary.

All of this material is available from QCA Publications, PO Box 99, Sudbury, Suffolk CO10 6SN. Tel: 01787 884444 or on the website: *www.qca.org.uk/keyskills*

Communication: Level 1

C1.1   Take part in a one-to one discussion and a group discussion about different, straightforward subject.

C1.2   Read and obtain information from two different types of document about straightforward subjects, including at least one image.

C1.3   Write different types of document about straightforward subjects, including at least one image.

Communication: Level 2

C2.1a   Contribute to a discussion about a straightforward subject.

C2.1b   Give a short talk about a straightforward subject, using an image.

C2.2   Read and summarise information from two extended documents about a straightforward subject. One of the documents should include at least one image.

C2.3   Write two different types of document about straightforward subjects. One piece of writing should be an extended document and include at least one image.

Application of Number: Level 1

N1.1   Interpret straightforward information from two different sources. At least one source should be a table, chart, diagram or line graph.

N1.2   Carry out straightforward calculations to do with (a) amounts and sizes, (b) scales and proportion and (c) handling statistics.

N1.3   Interpret the results of your calculations and present your findings. You must use one chart and one diagram.

Information technology: Level 1

IT 1.1   Find, explore and develop information for two different purposes.

IT 1.2   Present information for two different purposes. Your work must include at least one example of text, one example of images and one example of numbers.

Hair and skin

Andrew Collinge Photo: John Swannell

Learning objectives

The following are some of the topics that are covered in this chapter:

- the structure and functions of the skin
- the structure and functions of the hair
- the different types of hair
- possible problems with hair
- general health and lifestyle
- salon hygiene
- hair and skin tests.

Each **client** who walks through the salon door is different, with a unique combination of hair type and colour, skin and **scalp** condition, past history of hair care, and present requirements. It is your job as a professional responsible for giving good client care to examine the hair and scalp, to assess what state it is in, to ask questions and listen to your client's answers, to decide what treatment is necessary and to agree with your client on a course of action.

Just as a doctor needs knowledge of medicine and a reassuring bedside manner, so you need knowledge of hair, the scalp and the skin, and the ability to discuss these with your clients clearly, confidently and tactfully. You also need to be able to recognise any problems and know how to deal with them. For this, you need to have a professional understanding of the bones and muscles that make up the structure of the head and neck. This part of the chapter includes detailed information about these aspects of hairdressing. Take time to read it carefully, to learn about the raw materials you will be working with daily.

The skin

The *skin* is the outer covering of the body. It is a complex and important organ, made up of different layers and containing many parts: oil and sweat glands, hair muscles, blood and lymph vessels, nerves and sensory organs.

The skin has four main functions: protection, temperature control, secretion and excretion, and sensation.

- **protection** – the skin forms a tough, flexible, physical barrier. It keeps excess water out, and body fluids in. The oil and sweat it produces are acid, helping to prevent bacterial growth. **Melanin** pigments in skin help to filter out harmful rays of the sun. In the presence of sunlight vitamin D is produced in the skin which helps to maintain body health.
- **temperature control** – the hair, hair muscles and sweat glands help to maintain the normal body temperature of 37°C. In cold weather, muscles make the hairs stand up, trapping an insulating layer of warm air over the surface of the skin. In hot weather the sweat glands excrete water which evaporates from the skin, cooling the body.
- **secretion and excretion** – oil or sebum is used as a protective covering, waterproofing and lubricating the skin and hair. Waste products such as water and salt are passed out of the body via sweat.
- **sensation** – beneath the top layer of the skin are nerves and sense organs. The many nerve endings are responsible for feelings of heat, cold, pain and touch. These sensations protect the body from harm.

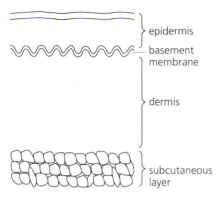

epidermis

basement membrane

dermis

subcutaneous layer

Section through the skin

The epidermis

The skin consists of several layers of different cell tissue. The outermost layer is called the **epidermis**. It has five distinct layers.

- The **horny layer** is the hard, cornified top layer of skin. It is constantly being worn away and replaced by underlying tissue.

- The **clear layer** is transparent and colourless, allowing colour from below to be seen. There is no melanin, but the cells contain **keratin**, the principal protein of hair.

- The **granular layer** lies between the softer living cells below and the hardened dead cells above. It contains granular tissues.

- The **mixed layer** consists of mixed cells. Immediately below the granular layer lie **prickle cells** (spinous cells) which are softer, alive and active. Below these lie the **Malpighian cells**, which contain melanin, the skin colour pigment. (The names **stratum aculeatum**, **stratum spinosum** and **stratum Malpighi** are also used for this mixed layer of cells.)

- The **germinating layer** is the lowest or base layer of the epidermis. It is the site of most active growth. The cells are softer and fuller than those above. The germinating layer and basement membrane connects with the underlying dermis.

The layers of the epidermis

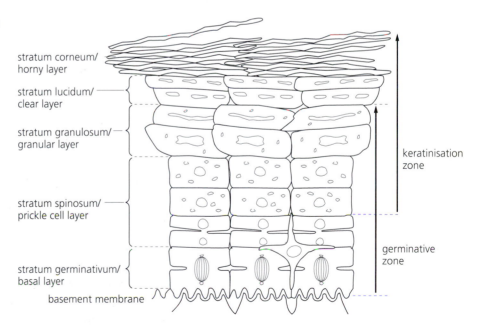

stratum corneum/ horny layer

stratum lucidum/ clear layer

stratum granulosum/ granular layer

stratum spinosum/ prickle cell layer

stratum germinativum/ basal layer

basement membrane

keratinisation zone

germinative zone

The dermis

The **dermis** is the thickest layer of the skin. It is here that the hair follicle is formed. The dermis is made up of elastic and connective tissue, and is well supplied with blood and lymph vessels. The skin

The hair in skin

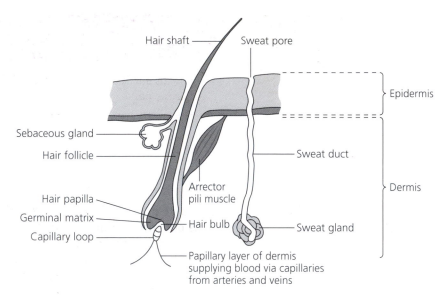

Hair shaft — Sweat pore
Epidermis
Sebaceous gland —
Hair follicle —
— Sweat duct
Arrector pili muscle
Hair papilla —
Germinal matrix —
— Hair bulb
Capillary loop —
— Sweat gland
Dermis
Papillary layer of dermis supplying blood via capillaries from arteries and veins

receives its nutrient supply from this area. The upper part of the dermis, the **papillary layer**, contains the organs of touch, heat and cold and pain. The lower part of the dermis, the **reticular layer**, forms a looser network of cells.

The subcutaneous tissue

The **subcutaneous tissue** lies below the dermis. It is also known as the subcutis, or occasionally as the **hypodermis**. It is composed of loose cell tissue and contains stores of fat. The base of the hair follicle is situated just above this area, or sometimes in it. Subcutaneous tissue gives roundness to the body and fills the space between the dermis and muscle tissue that may lie below.

The hair follicle

Hair grows from a thin, tube-like space in the skin called a **hair follicle**.

- At the bottom of the follicles are areas well supplied with nerves and blood vessels, which nourish the cellular activity. These are called **hair papillae**.
- Immediately surrounding each papilla is the **germinal matrix** which consists of actively forming hair cells.
- As the new hair cells develop the lowest part of the hair is shaped into the **hair bulb**.
- The cells continue to shape the form as they push along the follicle until they appear at the skin surface as **hair fibres**.
- The cells gradually harden and die. The hair is formed of dead tissue but retains its elasticity due to its chemical structure and keratin content.

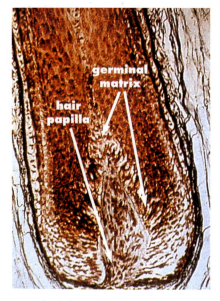

germinal matrix

hair papilla

The hair papilla and germinal matrix

Beverly Cobella

Java for Hair 2002

Activity

Draw an outline of a hair, in its follicle, in the skin. Label the different parts.

Oil

The oil gland, or **sebaceous gland**, is situated in the skin and opens out into the upper third of the follicle. From it oil, or **sebum**, is secreted into the follicle and on to the hair and skin surface. Sebum helps to prevent the skin and hair from drying. By retaining moisture it helps the hair and skin to stay pliable. Sebum is slightly acid – about pH 5.5 – and forms a protective anti-bacterial covering for the skin.

Sweat

A sweat gland, or **sudoriferous gland**, lies beside each hair follicle. These are appendages of the skin. They secrete sweat which passes out through the sweat ducts. The ends of these ducts can be seen at the surface of the skin as sweat pores.

There are two types of sweat gland: the larger, associated closely with the hair follicles, are the **apocrine glands**; the smaller, found over most of the skin's surface, are the **eccrine glands**.

Sweat is mainly water with salt, although other minerals may be present. In abnormal conditions sweat contains larger amounts of waste material. Evaporation of sweat cools the skin. The function of sweat, and thus the sweat glands, is to protect the body by helping to maintain the normal temperature.

The hair muscle

The **hair muscle**, or **arrector pili**, is attached at one end to the hair follicle, and at the other to the underlying tissue of the epidermis. When it contracts it pulls the hair and follicle upright. Upright hairs trap a warm layer of air around the skin. The hairs also act as a warning system – for example, you soon notice if an insect crawls over your skin!

The hair

Many hairdressing processes depend on certain properties of hair. This section introduces you to the structure and chemistry of hair.

The structure of hair

Hairs are fine strands of tissue which appear above the skin surface. They cover most of the body, with the exception of the eyelids, the palms of the hands and the soles of the feet. There are three different types of hair.

- **lanugo hair** – fine, downy hair that covers the body of the unborn child: it is lost just before or around birth.
- **vellus hair** – fine, short, fluffy hair which contains little or no pigment and covers most parts of the body. It can often be seen clearly on the faces of women.
- **terminal hair** – longer, coarser hair, found on the head, on the faces of men, in ears and eyebrows, on the arms, legs and chest, and in the pubic region.

The hair shaft

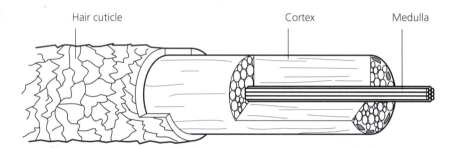

Inside the hair

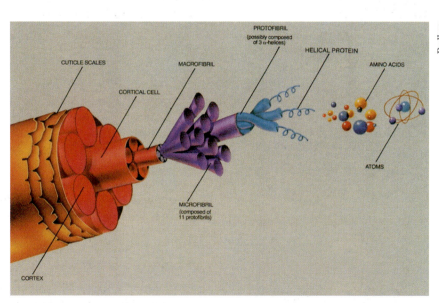

Each hair has the same basic structure. There are three layers.

- **cuticle** – the outer layer of colourless cells, which forms a protective surface to the hair. It regulates the chemicals entering and damaging the hair, and protects the hair from excessive heat and drying. The cells overlap, like rooftiles; if you rub a hair from base to tip it feels smooth, but if you rub it from tip to base it feels rough.

Wella

The hair cuticle

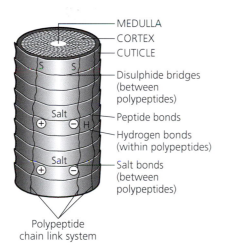

- MEDULLA
- CORTEX
- CUTICLE
- Disulphide bridges (between polypeptides)
- Peptide bonds
- Hydrogen bonds (within polypeptides)
- Salt bonds (between polypeptides)

Polypeptide chain link system

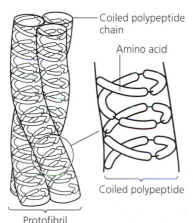

- Coiled polypeptide chain
- Amino acid
- Coiled polypeptide
- Protofibril

Cross-links within hair

- **cortex** – the middle and largest layer, consisting of long spiral chains of cells like springs. Each cell is made of bundles of fibres. These are composed of small bundles of **macrofibrils** which in turn are formed from even smaller bundles of **microfibrils** which are made up of the smallest bundles of **protofibrils** – all long, spiralling, ladder-like chains. The way these fibres and cells are held together determines the strength of hair, its thickness, curl and elasticity. **Pigments** in the cortex give hair its natural colour.
- **medulla** – the central space of the hair. It serves no useful purpose, and is not always present.

Activity

List the functions of the hair and skin. How may these be affected by hairdressing processes, both physical and chemical?

Chemical properties of hair

The bundles of fibres found in the cortex are made from molecules of **amino acids**. There are about twenty-two amino acids in hair, and the molecules of each contain atoms of elements in different proportions. Overall, the elements in hair are in approximately these proportions:

Carbon	50%
Oxygen	21%
Nitrogen	18%
Hydrogen	7%
Sulphur	4%

The amino acids combine to form larger molecules, long chains of amino acids called **polypeptides** or, if they are long enough, **proteins**. One of the most important of these is keratin. Keratin is an essential component of nails, skin and hair: it is this protein that makes them flexible and elastic. Because of the keratin it contains, hair can be stretched and compressed, curled and waved.

In hair, keratin forms long chains which coil up like springs. They are held in this shape by cross-links between chains. The three kinds of link are **disulphide bridges** (sulphur bonds), **salt bonds** and **hydrogen bonds**. Salt bonds and hydrogen bonds are relatively weak and are easily broken, allowing the springs to be stretched out: this is what happens in curling. The normal, coiled form of keratin is called **alpha keratin**; when it has been stretched, set and dried it is called **beta keratin**. The change is only temporary. Once the hair has been made wet, or has gradually absorbed moisture from the air, it relaxes back to the alpha state. Disulphide bridges are much stronger, but these too can be altered, as in perming.

☀ **Activity**

Examine a colleague's hair and scalp. Note the condition of the hair and the skin, the hair length and its colour, and whether the hair has been permed, coloured or given some other treatment.

Physical properties of hair

Hair naturally contains a certain amount of water, which lubricates it, allowing it to stretch and recoil. Hair that is dry and in poor condition is less elastic.

Hair is **hygroscopic**: it absorbs water from the surrounding air. How much water is taken up depends on the dryness of the hair and the moistness of the atmosphere. Hair is also **porous**: there are tiny tube-like spaces within the hair structure, and the water flows into these by **capillary action**, rather like blotting paper absorbing ink. Drying hair in the ordinary way evaporates only the surface moisture, but drying over long periods or at too high a temperature removes water from *within* the hair, leaving it brittle and in poor condition. Damaged hair is more porous than healthy hair, and easily loses any water: this makes it hard to stretch and mould.

Hair porosity

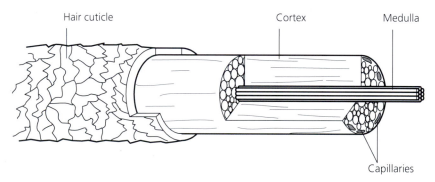

Hair cuticle   Cortex   Medulla

Capillaries

Curled hair returns to its former shape as it takes up water, so the drier the atmosphere, the longer the curl or set lasts. Similarly, curling dry hair is most effective just after the hair has been washed, because although the surface is dry the hair will have absorbed water internally. Blow-styling and curling with hot irons, heated rollers, hot combs and hot brushes all have similar temporary effects.

Hair growth

Hair is constantly growing. Over a period of between one and six years an individual hair actively grows, then stops, rests and degenerates, and finally falls out. Before the hair leaves the follicle the new hair is normally ready to replace it. If a hair is not replaced then a tiny area of baldness results.

The lives of individual hairs vary and are subject to variations in the body. Some are actively growing while others are resting. Hairs on the head are at different stages of growth.

Tip

Hair growth is approximately 12.5 mm per month.

Stages of growth

The life cycle of hair is as follows.

- **anagen** – the active growing stage of the hair, a period of activity of the papilla and germinal matrix. This stage may last from a few months to several years. It is at this stage of formation at the base of the follicle that the hair's thickness, shape and texture is determined. Hair colour, too, is formed in the early part of anagen.

- **catagen** – a period when the hair stops growing but cellular activity continues at the papilla. The hair bulb gradually separates from the papilla and moves further up the follicle.

- **telogen** – the final stage, when there is no further growth or activity at the papilla. The follicle begins to shrink, and completely separates from the papilla area. This resting stage does not last long: towards the end of the telogen stage, cells begin to activate in preparation for the new anagen stage of regrowth.

The new anagen period involves the hair follicle beginning to grow down again. Vigorous papilla activity generates a new hair at the germinal matrix. At the same time the old hair is slowly making its way up and out of the follicle. Often the old and new hair can be seen at the same time in the follicle.

Stages of hair growth

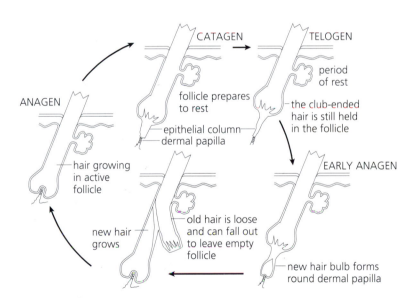

In some animals most of the hairs follow their life cycle 'in step', passing through anagen, catagen and telogen together. This results in moulting. Human hair, however, develops at an uneven rate and few follicles are shedding their hair at the same time. (If all hairs fell at the same time we would have bald periods!)

Regeneration of the hair

The regeneration of hair is influenced by many factors:

- health
- diet
- age
- sex
- hormone balance
- hereditary factors
- climate
- physical condition
- chemical effects
- effects of disease.

Hair types

Hair types

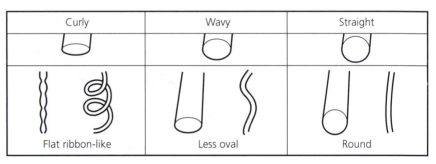

Curly	Wavy	Straight
Flat ribbon-like	Less oval	Round

Human hair is grouped into the following types:

- **Caucasian** (European) – loosely waved or straight hair.
- Black **(Afro-Caribbean)** – tight, kinked, woolly, curled hair.
- **Mongoloid** (Asian) – coarse, straight, lank hair.

The differences between these groups are distinctive, and form an interesting study for forensic scientists.

Hair texture can be either fine, medium or coarse. Some very tightly curled hair varies in texture throughout its length; Afro-Caribbean hair follows this pattern. The fine points can break easily under heat or chemical treatments and this hair type needs special care.

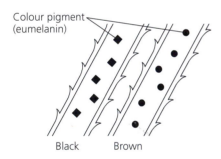

Colour pigment (eumelanin)

Black   Brown

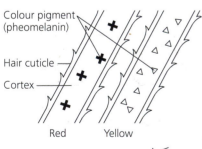

Colour pigment (pheomelanin)

Hair cuticle

Cortex

Red   Yellow

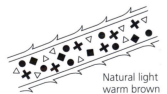

Natural light warm brown

■ Black   ✚ Red
● Brown   △ Yellow

Hair pigments

Hair colour

The **natural colour** of hair depends on the amounts and proportions of pigment (melanin) it contains. Two types of pigment are found in hair: eumelanin and pheomelanin.

- **Eumelanin** gives black and brown colours. Dark ash-brown hair contains a lot of eumelanin.

Charlie Taylor

- **Pheomelanin** gives red and yellow colours. Blonde hair contains relatively little melanin.

White and **albino hair** contains little or no pigment.

Neutralising, colouring and bleaching are chemical processes that act on these pigments to change the hair colour.

Hair condition – possible problems

Hair condition is affected by many factors, not just the external impact of chemicals, physical treatment and the weather but also the internal effects of the client's health and lifestyle.

 Activity

Visit your local chemist or supermarket and list the different hair products that are available. You may be surprised at how many there are. Take note of the prices, the quantities and the names of the manufacturers. Compare this range with your salon's own range of hair products.

External factors

These include all physical treatments, such as:

- combing, brushing, backdressing
- shampooing
- blow-drying/styling
- hot rolling and brushing, crimping or tonging
- all hairdressing processes
- wearing postiche, dreadlocks, etc.

L'Oreal

Careful examination of the hair and scalp is always necessary to check its state and condition. Look at the hair closely; feel the hair's surface and examine the skin of the scalp. Talk to your client, and listen to what is said. Ask them if they have had any problems.

Hair is subjected to many 'normal' treatments, such as shampooing. If badly carried out these can be the main cause of poor hair condition. If necessary, advise your clients on how to care for their hair at home.

Effects of the weather

These include:

- sun, wind, sand, sea and salt
- extremes of climate – hot or cold, dry or humid
- moisture effects on the hair's elasticity or flexibility.

If the effects of the weather are not guarded against, hair condition will inevitably become poor. In extreme weather it is best to keep the hair covered and protected.

Chemical effects

These result from:

- all hairdressing processes, including perming, colouring and bleaching
- swimming in the sea or in pools, if salt or chlorine is left on the hair and the hair is not rinsed thoroughly afterwards
- the use of cosmetics, particularly where manufacturers' guidance is not followed.

If correct procedures are not followed, and the effects are not dealt with, further damage may result.

L'Oreal

General health and lifestyle

The normal or abnormal working of the body has a direct effect on the hair and scalp.

- Good health is reflected in good hair and skin. A balanced diet with plenty of fresh foods contributes to good health.
- Disease, and drugs used in the treatment of disease, take their toll on the hair and skin.
- Genetic factors affecting hair growth determine hair strength and texture.
- The hair of women in pregnancy is usually at its best.
- Deterioration of the hair and skin *after* giving birth is usually due to stress and tiredness.
- If hair becomes a focus of attention it may be pulled, twisted and in general handled too much.

Assessment

Close examination of the hair and skin may reveal the following states or conditions:

- dry/very dry, splitting hair, ends or shafts breaking, dull/very dull appearance
- hair normal, smooth cuticle, shiny, easy to manage
- greasy/very greasy, lank, difficult to control
- dry, splitting ends with greasy roots
- hair forming tight curls

- straight or wavy hair
- chemically processed hair
- lack of elasticity, breaks easily (poor tensile strength)
- poor porosity (absorbs quickly but cannot retain)
- externally coated with chemical deposits from products such as hairsprays.

When you have assessed the hair condition, consider the treatments available to correct it. These are described in Chapter 3.

Diseases

Inside us, and on our skin and hair, we all carry large numbers of **micro-organisms**. These are very small living things; they include **bacteria**, **fungi** and **viruses**. Individual micro-organisms are so small that they cannot be seen with the naked eye: bacteria and fungi can be seen through a microscope, but viruses are too small even for that. However, we may be able to see large numbers, or **colonies**, of bacteria or fungi.

Examples of bacteria

SPHERICAL BACTERIA (COCCI)

Diplococcus
(pneumonia)

Staphylococcus
(pustules, boils, etc.)

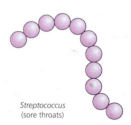
Streptococcus
(sore throats)

ROD-LIKE BACTERIA (BACILLI)

Bacillus tuberculosis
(tuberculosis)

Clostridium tetani
(tetanus)

Bacillus typhosus
(typhoid fever)

SPIRAL FORMS (SPIRILLA)

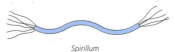
Spirillum

Treponema pallida
(syphilis)

Many micro-organisms are quite harmless, but some can cause disease: these are called **pathogens** (or germs). Flu, for example, is caused by a virus, thrush by a fungus, and bronchitis often by bacteria. Those diseases that can be transmitted from one person to another are said to be **infectious**. The body is naturally resistant to infection: it fights pathogens using the **immune system**. So we may carry pathogenic organisms without necessarily having any disease. And there are many diseases that aren't caused by micro-organisms.

The skin may also provide a home for tiny insects such as lice, and these too can cause disease.

 Activity

Arrange with your trainer a visit to the library or a biology laboratory at your local college. Look at a range of pictures to help you recognise different hair and scalp diseases. Make notes of what you see.

Alternatively, you might be able to visit your local hospital or clinic and get first-hand information about consultation and diagnosis.

Treatment

When you have a disease, the **symptoms** are the signs that you can see or feel that tell you that something is wrong. They are produced by the infection and by the reactions of the body. Symptoms help you to recognise the disease.

Infectious diseases should always be treated by a general practitioner. Non-infectious conditions and defects can often be treated in the salon or with products available from chemists, or by a specialist such as a **trichologist**.

Health & Safety

Find out more about hair and scalp diseases and disorders. There are other textbooks that give more details. When examining clients, make your observations carefully. Check your diagnosis with a trainer or senior stylist.

Salon hygiene

A warm, humid salon can be a perfect home for germs; given nourishment in the form of dirt and dust, they may reproduce rapidly. This is why it is important to keep the salon clean at all times, including clothing, work surfaces, tools and other equipment. A tidy salon is easier to clean, so get into the habit of clearing up as you work. Additional information on hygiene can be found in Chapter 2.

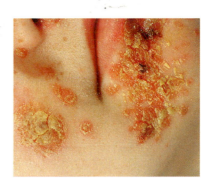

Furunculosis

Dr A L Wright

Sycosis

Dr A L Wright

Impetigo

Dr M H Beck

Bacterial diseases

	Conditions	Cause	Symptoms	Infectious	Treatment
Furunculosis	Boils and abscesses	An infection of the hair follicles by staphylococcal bacteria.	Raised, inflamed, pus-filled spots; there is irritation, swelling and pain.	Yes	By a doctor.
Sycosis	A bacterial infection of the hairy parts of the face.	Bacteria attack the upper part of the hair follicle; this may spread to the lower follicle.	Small, yellow spots around the follicle mouth; burning, irritation and general inflammation.	Yes	Antibiotics, given by a doctor.
Impetigo	A bacterial infection of the upper layers of the skin.	A staphylococcal or streptococcal infection.	First, a burning sensation; spots appear and become dry; honey-coloured crusts form; spots merge to form larger areas.	Yes	Antibiotics, given by a doctor.
Folliculitis	Inflammation of the hair follicles.	A bacterial infection, or chemical or physical actions.	Inflamed follicles. These are a common symptom of certain skin diseases.	Yes	By a doctor.

Viral diseases

Conditions	Cause	Symptoms	Infectious	Treatment
Herpes simplex (cold sore)	A viral infection of the skin.	Possibly exposure to extreme heat or cold, or reaction to food or drugs; skin may carry the virus for many years.	Burning, irritation, swelling and inflammation precedes the appearance of fluid-filled blisters, usually on the lips and the surrounding tissues.	Yes	By a doctor.
Herpes zoster (shingles)	A viral infection of the epidermis and nerve endings.	Perhaps from chickenpox in earlier years; the virus may have lain dormant in the skin before the shingles appears.	Painful blisters appear, often on one side only, of the head or body: sore, inflamed areas result. This may be preceded by a fever. Aching and pain may continue after the condition has cleared.	Yes	By a doctor.
Influenza and the common cold	Viral infections of the body.	Viruses, which attack cells of the body.	Fever, sneezing, aching and the other all-too-familiar symptoms.	Yes	By a doctor, if serious, or with cold-relief treatments from a chemist.
Warts (verrucae)	A viral infection of the skin.	The lower epidermis is attacked by the virus, which causes the skin to harden and the skin cells to multiply.	Raised, roughened skin, often brown or discoloured. There may be irritation and soreness. Warts are common on exposed areas such as the hands or face.	Yes	By a doctor.

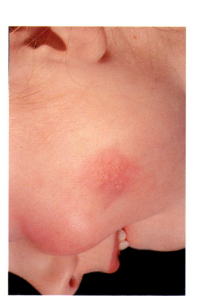

Dr M H Beck

A wart

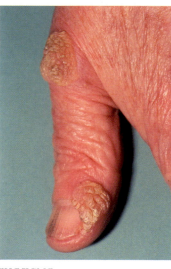

Dr M H Beck

Herpes simplex

Fungal diseases

	Conditions	Cause	Symptoms	Infectious	Treatment
Tinea capitis	Ringworm of the head.	Fungal, vegetable parasite which infects the skin or hair.	Circular areas of grey or white skin, surrounded by red, active rings; hairs broken close to the skin, which looks dull and rough. It is common in children.	Yes	By a doctor.
Tinea pedis (athlete's foot)	Ringworm of the feet.	A fungus attacks the skin between the toes, which becomes soft and soggy. The disease is common among those using swimming pools and not drying their feet thoroughly, and those standing for long periods (including hairdressers).	Soft, sore skin; sometimes bleeding; a bad odour; some irritation.	Yes	By a doctor, or with products from a chemist.

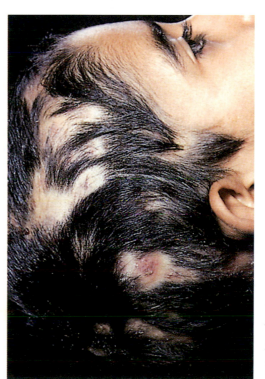

Dr A L Wright

Tinea pedis

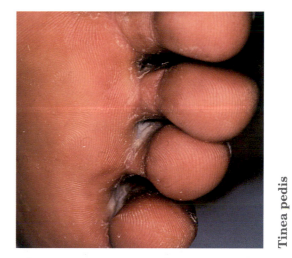

Dr John Gray

Tinea capitis (ringworm)

Diseases caused by animal parasites

	Conditions	Cause	Symptoms	Infectious	Treatment
Scabies	An allergic skin reaction to the itch mite.	A tiny animal mite, *Sarcoptes scabiei*, which burrows through the skin, where it lays its eggs.	A rash in the skin folds, around the midriff and on the insides of the thighs. It becomes extremely itchy at night, there are reddish spots and burrows (greyish lines) under the skin. Scabies is not found on the head or scalp except in children under two years.		By a doctor.
Pediculosis capitis	Infestation of the head by lice.	*Pediculus humanus capitis*, the head louse, attacks the skin and feeds by puncturing the skin to suck the blood; it lays eggs (**ova**) on the hair, close to the skin.	An itchy reaction like a mosquito bite. Some people develop an allergic reaction, with itchy red marks. Lice can be seen by parting the hair; more commonly the eggs (**nits**) or hatched eggs can be seen stuck to the hairs. Live eggs are found close to the scalp. Lice are passed only by actual contact between an infected head and another head.		By a doctor, or with products from a chemist.

BLM Health

A nit (the egg of a louse)

S Lewis

The head louse

Non-infectious conditions of skin and hair

	Conditions	Cause	Symptoms	Infectious	Treatment
Acne	A disorder of the hair follicles and sebaceous glands.	This is not fully understood, but increased sebum and other matter blocks the follicle: the skin reacts to this blockage as though it were a foreign body such as a splinter.	Raised spots or bumps in the skin, commonly on the face and forehead; soreness, irritation and inflammation; severe cases produce cysts and scarring.	No	By a doctor.
Alopecia	Baldness or thinning of hair. **Alopecia areata** is the name given to baldness in circular areas; it is common on the scalp. If the condition continues, these areas join to form **alopecia totalis**, complete hair loss from the scalp. **Alopecia universalis** is complete baldness of the body. **Alopecia traction** is the loss of hair that results from pulling, such as in plucking, rolling, tight curling, brushing, straightening or leaving the hair in tight plaits/pleats for long periods. Areas of thinning hair are commonly to be seen on the front hairline, and the sides.	The hair follicles are unable to produce new hairs to replace the old ones. **Male-pattern alopecia** is baldness found in the teenage years of men and the later years of women; its cause is hereditary, and treatment can be given by the salon, a trichologist or a doctor. **Cicatrical alopecia** is baldness due to scarring of the skin arising from chemical or physical injury. The hair follicles are damaged and permanent baldness results.	Areas of thinning or diffuse hair; in alopecia areata there are small hairs in a pale pink smooth area. These hairs are thinner near the scalp.	No	By a doctor or a trichologist.
Canities	Grey or white hair.	Colour pigment not forming in the new hair.	The presence of white hairs.	No	Colouring

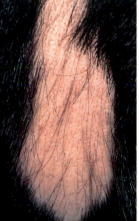

Alopecia areata

Dr A L Wright

Acne

Dr M H Beck

Non-infectious conditions of skin and hair (continued)

	Conditions	Cause	Symptoms	Infectious	Treatment
Eczema; dermatitis	At its simplest, red, inflamed skin.	There are several, with either internal or external factors: it may be due to physical irritation or to an allergic response.	These range from slightly inflamed areas of skin, to severe splitting and weeping areas; there may be irritation, soreness and pain; in advanced stages the underlying skin may become infected.	No	By a doctor.
Dandruff (pityriasis capitis)	Dry, scaling scalp.	Fungal infection, or physical or chemical irritants.	Dry, small, irritating flakes (or scales) of skin; if the scale becomes moist and greasy it sticks to the skin and the condition known as scurf results. Dandruff can be accompanied by **conjunctivitis** (inflammation of the eye) or **blepharitis** (inflammation of the eyelid).	No	By various anti-dandruff medicines and shampoos (see Chapters 3).
Seborrhoea	Excessive greasiness of the skin and hair.	Over-production of sebum, which may be due to physical or chemical irritants.	Very greasy, lank hair, and greasy skin, which makes grooming and dressing of the hair difficult.	No	Regular washing, with a minimum of physical or chemical stimulation; in extreme cases it is best treated by a trichologist or a doctor.
Psoriasis	An inflamed, abnormal thickening of the skin.	Unknown.	Areas of thickened skin, which may be raised and circular; silvery or yellow scales may be present; the skin may be sore, itchy or painful.	No	By a doctor or a dermatologist.

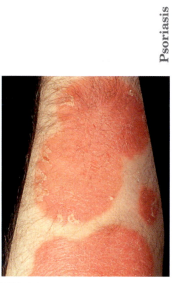

Psoriasis

Dr M H Beck

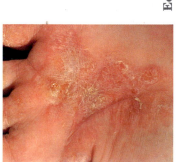

Eczema

Dr M H Beck

Hair conditions and defects

Diseases are not the only kinds of disorder you will meet. There are various conditions of hair that are caused by reactions to physical and chemical processes like backcombing and bleaching. These are non-infectious: they cannot be passed to another person.

There are also defects caused by irregular hair growth. Some are hereditary, and may be shared by members of the same family; others are due to the abnormal structure of hair follicles or to harsh treatment.

Defects of the hair	Conditions	Cause	Symptoms	Treatment
Fragilitas crinium (split ends)	Fragile, poorly conditioned hair.	Harsh physical or chemical treatments.	Dry, splitting hair-ends.	Cutting hair-ends and using conditioners.
Monilethrix	Beaded hair.	Irregular development of the hair when forming in the follicle.	Bead-like swellings and constrictions of the hair shafts; hair often breaks close to the skin.	By a doctor; conditioning may help.
Ringed hair	Alternating white and coloured rings of the hair shaft.	Irregular distribution of pigment during hair formation or regeneration.	Distinct bands of coloured and colourless hair – there may be few or many.	There are few effective treatments other than hair colouring.
Trichorrhexis nodosa	Nodules on the hair shaft, containing splitting sections of hair.	Harsh physical or chemical treatments.	Areas of swelling nodules and lengthwise splitting of the hair.	Cutting at the ends may help, as may conditioning with products such as hair thickeners.

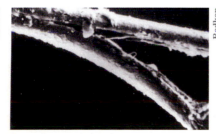

Fragilitas crinium

Monilethrix

Trichorrhexis

Defects of the hair	Conditions	Cause	Symptoms	Treatment
Sebaceous cyst	Swelling of a sebaceous or oil gland.	The sebaceous gland becomes blocked, possibly due to a growth of cells arising from the gland wall.	Bumps, lumps or swellings, 12–50 mm across, on the scalp, soft to the touch owing to fluid content.	Removal of the contents, by a doctor.
Damaged cuticle	Broken, split, torn hair.	Harsh physical or chemical treatments.	Rough, raised, missing areas of cuticle; hair loses its moisture and becomes dry and porous.	By conditioners, thickeners, restructurants and similar products.

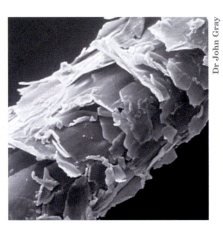

A damaged cuticle caused by backcombing heavily sprayed hair

Damaged hair caused by chemical relaxants

Health risks

You need to be able to recognise skin and hair diseases, and be hygienic in your work. This will help you to avoid catching diseases yourself, or passing them from one client to another.

Two other health risks are also important to hairdressers: you should know about these as well.

AIDS

The **acquired immune-deficiency syndrome (AIDS)** is not itself a disease – it's a condition that makes the body *vulnerable* to diseases. It is these other diseases that may actually lead to death. Because AIDS is often fatal and because there is as yet no known cure, it may seem very frightening. Nevertheless, some fears about

If a tool infected with the blood of an AIDS carrier, such as a razor used for shaving or lining a hairstyle, is used on another client without being sterilised, there is the possibility of cross-infection.

AIDS result simply from misunderstanding. To protect yourself and your clients, you need to understand the condition.

AIDS is caused by a virus known as the **human immunodeficiency virus (HIV)**. This virus attacks the body's immune system and may make it less effective, leaving the body vulnerable to other infections. But some people carry the HIV virus – they are HIV-positive – *without* having AIDS. Anyone who is HIV-positive is potentially able to pass the virus to someone else.

You can become infected only if your body fluids, such as your blood, come into contact with body fluids of someone who is HIV-positive. This most commonly occurs during unprotected sex: condoms help to protect both partners. But this is not the only way – drug addicts who share needles are at risk, and the virus can be transferred through a cut or through broken skin. Remember that infection only occurs through the exchange of body fluids. The virus is sensitive to its surroundings, and cannot live long outside the body (so you can't catch it from a toilet seat, for example). Blood for transfusions is now specially checked to make sure that it does not contain HIV.

Activity

Some people are unnecessarily frightened about AIDS. Others take unnecessary risks. Find out more about this condition. Discuss your feelings about it, and how it should affect your work.

When dealing with a child, examine the hair and scalp for signs of infestation.

Tip

Agreement between the client and senior staff is necessary before a client is referred to a doctor.

Hepatitis B

This infection of the liver is another disease caused by a virus. The **hepatitis B virus (HBV)** is transmitted through infected blood, body tissue fluids and infected water.

The disease is long-lasting and weakening, and can be fatal. Successful treatments are available, but the virus is very resistant and is said to last a long time outside the human body. Good hygiene is therefore essential. Disinfection, sterilisation and the use of detergents and bleach for washing surfaces is thought to help.

Inoculation is available to protect against HBV. It should be seriously considered by all those who may be at risk, including hairdressers, beauty therapists, electrolysists and manicurists.

You should also now be able to recognise infections and diseases of the hair and scalp. It's important to avoid **cross-infection** – carrying an infection from one person to another – so remember these points:

- Make sure you are free of infection yourself, and that your hands are clean.

- Examine the client's hair and scalp before beginning any hairdressing treatment. Divide the hair so that you can see the scalp. Feel the hair for roughness.
- If you find signs of disease or infection, do not carry out any hairdressing but ask a senior hairdresser to give a second opinion. If they agree with you, the senior will then tell the client tactfully, and suggest a visit to the doctor as soon as possible.
- If you notice the infection when you have already started hairdressing, finish what you are doing and then consult with a senior. Allow the client to leave as soon as possible, without coming into contact with others.
- Sterilise all equipment and disinfect the area where you were working.
- Stay quiet and unflustered, so as not to cause anxiety to other clients.

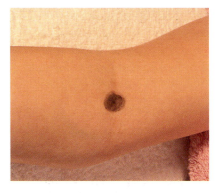

Skin test

Testing the hair and skin

There are various tests you can make to help you diagnose the condition of your client's hair. These tests will help you decide what actions to take before applying hairdressing processes. Results of tests should be noted on the client's record card. Skin allergies are considered in Chapter 9.

Hair and skin test chart

Type of test	*What does it test?*	*When to carry it out*	*How to carry it out*
Skin test (also known as the predisposition test, patch test or Sabouraud–Rousseau test)	The reaction of the skin to a chemical product	Prior to colour services when the colour contains para dyes or when you mix colour with hydrogen peroxide. Carried out 24–48 hours before the service	A small amount of colour to be used is mixed with hydrogen peroxide and applied to the clients skin. See chapter 9.
Strand test	The resultant colour on a strand or section of hair	During a colouring service while colour is processing and developing	During the colour development remove the colour from strands of hair with cotton wool or the back of a comb to see if the colour is developing evenly. If it isn't more processing time is needed or in some cases more colour may need to be applied. See chapter 9.

Type of test	*What does it test?*	*When to carry it out*	*How to carry it out*
Test cutting	The amount of processing needed and the effect it will have on the hair	Prior to a colouring, straightening, relaxing and bleaching service	Cut a small section of hair from the back of the head so that it is not noticeable. Apply the chemical i.e. mixed up colour and apply it to the test cutting. Keep checking the development of the colour on the cutting and making notes on the resulting colour and effect on the hair condition. See chapter 9.
Test curl	The perm lotion strength, size of rod to be used and the development time needed for a perm	Prior to perming	Wind, process and neutralise one or more small sections of hair. Select sections that can be easily hidden and in areas where the hair may be resistant, delicate or damaged. See chapter 7.
Curl check or test	The development of the curl	During perming	Unwind a perm rod at intervals pushing the hair back towards the head to check the 'S' shape curl development. This should happen throughout the development to stop over processing and damaging the hair. See chapter 7.
Incompatibility test	Chemicals already on the hair that could react adversely with a new product	Prior to colouring or perming	Place a small sample of hair in a mixture of 20 parts hydrogen peroxide (6%) and 1 part ammonium hydroxide. If the mixture bubbles, heats up or discolours do not carry out the service. See chapters 7 and 9.
Elasticity test	How much the hair will stretch and then return to its original position	Prior to chemical services	Take a hair or a couple of strands of hair between your fingers holding them at the roots and the ends. Pull the hair between the two points to see if the hair will stretch and then return to its original length. If the hair breaks easily it may be that the cortex is damaged and using chemicals could cause the hair to break. See chapters 7 and 9.

Hair and skin test chart (continued)

Type of test	What does it test?	When to carry it out	How to carry it out
Porosity test	The hair's ability to absorb moisture or liquids	Prior to chemical services. If the hair cuticle is torn or damaged absorption may be quicker and less processing may be required. If the cuticle is smooth and tightly packed, it may be more resistant to the passage of products entering the hair.	Rub strands of hair between your fingertips to feel how rough or smooth it is. See chapters 7 and 9.

Activity

Carry out each of the tests listed in this section. Take careful notes of each result. Make sure that you list exactly what is done, the time taken, and the materials used. Use part of the hair sample as a 'before' example, to be compared with the 'after' result. Keep these carefully in your notebook or folder.

Tip

You need to know
- when?
- how?
- where?
- why?

these tests need to be made, and the consequences of not doing so.

Activity

Make a list of what might happen if procedures are not carried out correctly.

Negative results of tests may indicate that care is needed when giving the service as planned, or even that it should not be given at all.

Other factors that may limit or affect the services given include adverse conditions of the skin, hair or scalp, incompatibility of a product, the presence of a hairpiece (or the consequences of wearing one), a condition that justifies referral, such as a suspected infection or infestation, or a condition of which the diagnosis is doubtful.

Assignments – Hair and skin

With the help of your colleagues, practise examining hair and the scalp, testing hair and the skin. Keep notes of any problems and difficulties you come across. Then answer the following question for your folder.

- List the hair and skin tests that you can use. State when and why each test should be applied and how you record the results of them.

For you to find out

Investigate the process of analysis and diagnosis of diseases and defects of the hair and skin. Exercises can be simulated by working with your colleagues. Use your textbooks, drawings, sketches, photographs and other means of illustration. Both audio and video recorders can be helpful. Then answer the following questions. Record all your answers for your folder.

1 What do the words 'analysis' and 'diagnosis' mean?

2 Outline the stages of examining the hair and scalp. What are you looking for? How do you record the results?

3 List the symptoms of the various conditions. List the causes of each disease. How does this information affect the work to be done?

4 List the hair and skin tests that can help you decide what can be done for your client. How do you compile the results? What do you do with them?

5 What are the different hair types, hair textures and hair conditions? Describe these, and try to illustrate them. How do they affect hairdressing services?

6 Draw a hair and the skin in cross-section. Label the different parts. List the effects that hairdressing services (chemical and physical) may have on the hair and skin.

Preparing for Assessment

In preparing for your assessment on hair and skin the following checklist may be useful. Check that you have covered and now fully understand these items:

- Recognising the differences between hair types, states and conditions
- Considering the effects of chemicals on 'virgin' (untreated) and treated hair
- Differentiating between diseases, conditions and defects of the hair and scalp
- Testing hair and scalp for suitability for the different chemical treatments
- Dealing with a client when test results indicate that their request for a service cannot be carried out safely.

By reading this chapter, carrying out the above assignments and meeting the requirements in preparing for assessment you will have worked towards the key skill requirements in Communication Level 1 (C 1.1) (C 1.2) (C 1.3) and Level 2 (C 2.1) (C 2.2) (C 2.3).

If you have used a computer to complete your assignment or activity you will have worked towards the key skill requirements in Information Technology Level 1 (IT 1.2).

Client care and consultation

2

Mahogany

Learning objectives

The following are some of the topics covered in this chapter:

- preparing your work area ready for your client
- preparing your client for a service
- how to communicate
- identifying what the client wants
- advising your client on services and products.

Introduction

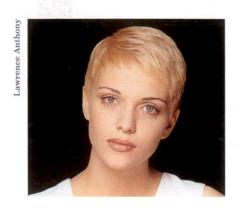

Lawrence Anthony

Client care is essential to your success as a hairdresser. It is an important part of all that you do for your client whilst they are in the salon. Consulting with your client to determine their ideas and requirements and making suitable recommendations based on the information received and the results of your analysis of their hair, skin and scalp will enable you to meet all your client's hairdressing needs. Like most skills, client care and **consultation** has to be learned, and this requires thought and study. Additional information on consultation can also be found in each chapter covering specific hairdressing services.

Hygiene – the science of health

Regis

Salon

Regis

Salon

Clients expect the salon to be clean. They expect towels to have been washed and brushes cleaned and they take it for granted that good **hygiene** is maintained.

You are as responsible as every other member of staff for maintaining the highest standards of cleanliness and hygiene at all times, to safeguard both clients and staff from infection.

Cross-infection – the passing of disease from one person to another – may follow unhygienic use of washbasins, cups, tools, and so on. If you take sensible precautions the salon can be kept as clean as possible and the risk of cross-infection can be minimised.

- Use only clean towels and gowns for each client
- Wash combs and brushes before sterilising or disinfecting them.
- Use 70 per cent alcohol, or alcohol wipes, for cleaning tools.
- Keep floors and surfaces clear, tidy and clean.
- Maintain good personal and general hygiene – wash your hands regularly, and clean cups and mugs thoroughly.

Many clients are too embarrassed to complain, and are reluctant to do so, when they encounter problems with hygiene or hairdressing service. Ideally the need should not arise, but in case it does, always encourage clients to let the salon know what is wrong.

! Health & Safety

It is when the salon is busiest that the greatest care needs to be taken. Don't let your standards of cleanliness drop, however rushed you may be.

General hygiene

In the salon, as long as you take sensible precautions there should be no risk to you or your clients. It is essential that you are thorough in sterilising all equipment, particularly that used for electrolysis, ear piercing and tattooing. Good hygiene, correct disinfection, and protection of any cut or open skin will reduce the dangers not just of HIV/AIDS and hepatitis B but of all infectious diseases.

- Keep any cuts and open skin wounds covered.
- Wash your hands regularly.
- Clear away spilt blood from all surfaces, and apply bleach, detergent or a disinfectant. Wear rubber gloves.
- Always clean and sterilise tools before using them on clients.
- Use only sterile, disposable razors or needles on, or in, the skin.
- Wrap any blood-soaked materials carefully and place them in a special covered bin.
- Arrange removal and disposal of suspect materials by the local health authority.

Personal health and hygiene

Hairdressing is a personal service industry. It relies solely on the profits generated from the sales of services, products and treatments to clients. Every member of staff has a role within the task of establishing and then maintaining a satisfied clientele.

Initially, your clients will judge your personal and professional standards by the way in which you present yourself. Remember, hairdressing is an image-conscious industry. We strive to provide a high quality service that gives clients well-cut, well-styled and well-groomed hair, so that they feel pleased and confident and have greater self-esteem. What confidence could you provide them with if you turned up for their appointments with stained overalls, unkempt hair and dirty hands and nails?

Hands and nails

Your hands should always be perfectly clean. Dirt on your hands and under your nails will harbour bacteria. By spreading germs you could infect other people. Your hands need washing not only before

A safe, hygienic salon

work, but several times throughout the day. Where hands regularly come into contact with water or detergents, the skin may lose its moisture, become dry and crack. Cracked, broken skin allows germs to enter and infection may follow. To prevent this from happening you should regularly moisturise your skin after washing. If your hands are often in water (for example, in shampooing or conditioning), you may find it helpful to use a **barrier cream**. Barrier creams cover the skin with an invisible barrier which greatly reduces the penetration of hairdressing cleansing and conditioning agents. (Many trainees have given up hairdressing after developing the skin condition called **dermatitis**, in which the hands become sore, cracked, itchy and red. At this stage work becomes painful and medical advice should be sought.)

Long nails not only trap dirt underneath, but also can cause discomfort to clients. In certain hairdressing procedures it is quite possible that longer nails could even scratch or damage the skin. This risk of spreading infection and disease can be prevented by keeping nails short and neat. Clean, well-manicured nails without splits or tears are hygienic and safe.

The body

Taking a daily bath is necessary to remove the build-up of sweat, dead skin cells and surface bacteria. Skin in areas such as armpits, feet and genitals has more sweat glands than elsewhere, and the warm, moist conditions in these areas provide an ideal breeding ground for bacteria. Regular washing is therefore essential if 'BO' (body odour) is to be prevented.

Antiperspirants will reduce underarm sweating. These products contain astringents, which narrow the pores that emit the sweat and cool down the skin. Alternatively, deodorants may be used. These products will not reduce the amount of sweating but can mask any odour by killing the surface bacteria with antiseptic ingredients.

 Activity

Certain jobs require personal protective equipment. Find out from your supervisor what jobs in your salon require special equipment. List the jobs, and any relevant equipment that must be used.

The mouth

Unpleasant breath is offensive to clients. Bad breath (halitosis) is the result of leaving particles to decay within the spaces between the teeth. You need to brush your teeth after every meal. Bad breath can also result from digestive troubles, stomach upsets, smoking and strong foods such as onions, garlic and some cheeses.

Personal appearance

In addition to personal cleanliness, your personal appearance is also an important factor. The effort you put into getting ready for work reflects your pride in the job. It is all right for you to have your own individual look, provided that you appreciate and accept that there are professional standards of dress and appearance that must be followed – a sort of personal code of practice.

Clothes

Clothes or overalls should be clean and well-ironed. It is sensible to wear clothes made from fabrics that are suitable not only for your intended work but also for the time of year. Clothes that are restrictive or tight will not allow air to circulate around your body and will prevent you from keeping cool and fresh; they could lead to uncomfortable perspiration or possibly BO. Apart from the clothes that other people see, remember that a daily change of underwear is essential.

Shoes

Kay McIntyre

Wear shoes that have low heels. They should be smart, comfortable and be made of materials suitable for wearing over long periods of time. Remember that hairdressing involves a lot of standing and your feet can therefore get tired, hot, sweaty and even sore. It is worth wearing shoes that allow your feet to 'breathe', as ventilated feet remain cool and comfortable throughout the working day.

Hair

Your hair reflects the image and expected standards of the salon in which you work. It should be clean, healthy and manageable. Don't let long hair fall over your face, as this will obstruct good communication with the clients and your poor body language may give them the wrong message.

Jewellery

Only the minimum of jewellery should be worn in the salon. Rings, bracelets and dangling necklaces will get in the way of normal day-to-day duties and will make the client uncomfortable. In many hairdressing operations, such as shampooing and conditioning, jewellery can catch and pull at the client's hair as well as provide unhygienic crevices for dirt and germs to lurk in.

Posture

Bad posture will lead to fatigue or even longer-term injury. Adopting the correct posture is essential for trainee and competent hairdresser alike. An incorrect standing position will put undue strains on both muscles and ligaments, as well as giving your clients an impression of an uncaring, unprofessional attitude towards work.

Posture fatigue will occur when a part of the body is out of line with another part immediately below. Hairdressers have to be on their feet a great deal, therefore adopting a good posture is a requirement of the job. You will achieve correct posture when your head, shoulders, upper torso, abdomen, thighs and legs distribute your body's weight in a balanced, equally proportioned way, over feet that are positioned forward and slightly apart. Dropping a shoulder will shift your body's weight over one foot. This will cause curvature of the spine, applying strains on muscles and ligaments, as well as exerting pressures on the intervertebral discs in your spine. This will at least be uncomfortable and at worst dangerous, possibly starting a longer-term back problem or injury.

Your posture whilst sitting should be restful. Your back should be supported all the way down. This does not mean that chairs must have a continuous back or have contoured, moulded panels, but that your sitting position should provide your body with support so that the pelvis and not the base of the spine takes the body's weight. Avoid sitting with crossed legs, as this will restrict blood circulation. It will result in numbness and a sensation of 'pins and needles'.

Preparing clients

Tip

If a client's clothes are stained, make sure this is noted. Clothes may be returned to the salon for cleaning. Alternatively the client may have this done themselves and send the bill for the salon to pay.

Gowning the client

Once a client has arrived for an appointment and you have taken care of their coat and belongings, find out what services have been requested or booked in advance and prepare the client accordingly.

Gowning and protecting

- Remember to check that the chair is clean.
- Place tissue or a towel over the client's collar and shoulders.
- Place a suitably sized **gown** in position, and secure it.
- If shampooing, place a thicker towel over the shoulders.
- If cutting, use cottonwool, tissue or a cutting cape in place of a thicker towel.
- If colouring or bleaching, use dark towels, plastic capes and special tint coverings.
- Make sure all the client's clothes are covered and all materials are secured so that they remain in place.
- Do not tuck in absorbent materials – they act like sponges. Liquids can seep through and damage clothing.
- Make sure nothing falls between the client and the chair back.

Preparing the hair

Hair needs to be free from tangles, hairspray and other materials before it can be worked on. Prepare the client's hair as follows:

1 Loosen the hair by teasing it apart with your fingers.
2 Using a wide-toothed comb or **rake**, start combing the hair points and gradually work upwards to the scalp.
3 Proceed from the neck and sides to the top front.
4 Remove tangles and backcombing without pulling, scratching or breaking the comb.
5 Brush the hair smoothly and firmly, without jerking the client's head.
6 Start brushing at the hair points and gradually work upwards to the scalp.
7 Once the hair is free of tangles, brush in different directions to loosen it.

Combs and combing

Combs come in many shapes and sizes. They may be of vulcanised rubber, tortoiseshell, ivory, wood, metal, bone, horn or various types of plastic. Some combs are made of synthetic material, but these are apt to give rise to electric charges on the hair (static) and make the hair 'flyaway'.

Always use good-quality combs. Poor-quality combs may break, tearing the hair and scalp. This could result in infection: a broken comb is difficult to clean and so may carry germs.

When using a comb, hold it correctly to avoid straining it or the hair:

- hold the comb firmly, with your middle fingers on one side and thumb and little finger on the other
- hold it so that your fingertips cannot slip to the teeth points
- hold it upright – do not flatten or drag it
- use a raking action, without tugging
- work from the points to the roots (if you start combing at the roots you will produce more knotting, and a painful few minutes for your client)
- support the client's head to prevent discomfort.

Brushes and brushing

Brushes are made from a variety of materials. Good brushes are made from natural bristles, such as those of pigs. Others may be wire, plastic or rubber. They are designed for various purposes, such as dressing or clearing loose hair, so choose the correct type of brush for the job in hand.

Health & Safety

All towels, and ideally all gowns, should be freshly laundered. If a gown has to be reused, make sure no part of it comes into contact with the client's skin.

Tip

Choose a comb that is unbroken, flexible, well balanced, non-flammable, resistant to chemicals, and easy to clean. It should have widely spaced teeth, and have no mould marks or sharp edges.

Combs

Brushes

 Activity

With your trainer, arrange a visit to a hairdressing supplier. Take note of the types of brushes and combs available. You may also be able to collect brochures of reception furniture – these would be helpful in designing the ideal salon – or use a computer to extract information from manufacturers' websites such as:

Denman – www.denmanbrush.com

Goldwell – www.goldwell.com

Wella – www.wella.co.uk

L'oreal – www.loreal.co.uk.

By completing this activity you will have worked towards the key skill Information Technology Level 1 (IT 1.1).

For preparing hair, use a firm, tufted brush which takes out tangles. For dressing hair, use a short, tufted brush. Generally, for thick, coarse hair a short natural bristle or nylon-tufted brush is suitable for salon use. For soft, thin hair a longer bristle may be kinder. The brushing action stimulates and distributes natural oil – this is best achieved with a soft bristle brush. Hair styling requires a variety of brushes, but the personal choice of a brush is finally determined by its weight, length, size and comfort in use.

Brushing should be a smoothing, stroking action – never harsh scrubbing. Two brushes may be used with a rolling wrist action, one following the other.

 Activity

Use your practice blocks to develop the correct action in combing and brushing. First use one brush and your hand; then two brushes, one in each hand.

!

Health & Safety

Use only good-quality tools which are not likely to damage the hair, and apply them gently and correctly. If you accidentally tear the scalp with a broken brush or comb, report this at once to your trainer or senior. They will try to stop the bleeding, clean with water, apply a clean dressing and seek medical advice.

 Tip

Nylon tufts can be harsh on hair if used too often. Natural bristle brushes are kinder to hair.

A good brush will penetrate and grip the hair, and allow you to place the hair where you want it.

Cleaning tools

- Clean tools after use.
- Never use tools on another client without cleaning and sterilising them first.
- Remove loose material from combs and brushes, wash and disinfect them, then dry them. Disinfectant cabinets may be used after drying.
- Always rinse liquid disinfectants from tools with plenty of water, otherwise they may irritate the client's skin.

Comby brush

- Don't leave metal tools in liquid disinfectants or disinfecting cabinets for hours. They will spoil and become pitted.
- Always check the manufacturer's instructions before using liquid disinfectants or disinfecting cabinets.

What is meant by client care?

Client care means what it says: caring for your client, looking after them and making sure that they are comfortable, satisfied with the service and safely attended. This begins when the client enters the salon and continues until they leave. Helping the client with managing their hair at home is a part of client care. So too is making your expertise available to them to ensure that when they leave they will be really happy with the appearance of their hair.

Looking after clients before and during services

- Check that all protective coverings – towels, cutting collar and so forth – are accurately placed.
- Collect together all tools, equipment and products to be used so that the client's services are not constantly interrupted.
- Reassure the client that their belongings are safe.
- Explain the processes that are taking place as you go along.
- Indicate how each process is progressing, what is to follow, and how long it may take.
- During any lengthy process, offer the client reading materials, access to the telephone or writing materials. This could be a good time to ask them to complete a salon questionnaire.

Maintaining client goodwill

A client's trust and goodwill are enhanced by clear **communication**, and the manner in which you communicate with them. Leaving misunderstandings unexplained can undermine a great deal of careful, thoughtful work. The following points may be of help.

- Telling the client the reasons for delays or disruptions in services can be reassuring; leaving your client wondering what is happening is the last thing to create goodwill!
- Learn to recognise the cultural differences and needs of your clients. Different races and religious creeds have different requirements, and you must be able to understand them. Ask your seniors for help and advice about this.

Ishoka

- Your client will feel more comfortable if they are confident that you are looking after them and their personal belongings carefully and reliably. Simply putting their possessions on a chair in reception and leaving them there is not acceptable – the client is sure to feel anxious about them.
- Discuss regularly how the service is progressing with your client. This will reduce tension and uneasiness.
- You can also help to maintain client confidence by being prepared to enlist the aid of other competent staff if necessary.

 Activity

Look up the words 'goodwill' and 'trust' in a dictionary. Make a note of the meanings given there, and keep it in your folder.

 Activity

Describe ways in which you would ensure the client's confidence while dealing and giving the services the client requests.

After services

- Ensure that the client's clothes are not stained or covered with loose hairs.
- Complete record cards for the services completed. Include any comments made by the client regarding the services they have received.
- Make sure that all the client's belongings are returned to them before they leave the salon.
- Offer to arrange the client's next appointment, and make sure that they have the salon's telephone number and address for future use.

Consultation

For client care to be fully effective an initial consultation is essential. This applies to both new and existing clients. The importance of consultation with your clients cannot be overemphasised.

Consultation – a meeting at which advice is given and taken – consists of talking to the client, listening to them so that you can establish their needs and jointly negotiating a suitable course of action. You will be expected to exchange views, and to discuss with them just what is to be done with their hair. You, the professional, already know a lot about hair in general, but your client is more familiar than you are with their own hair and how it behaves. Listen to what your client tells you, and find out what they have in mind. They may ask for a service which you know will not lead to a satisfactory outcome, and this requires careful consideration. Work should only proceed after you have carefully determined what is required, achieved your client's understanding and agreement, and confirmed that their requests are suited to their own wishes and to the services given in your salon.

Consultation includes the following:

- determining exactly what a client wants before and during the application of hairdressing services
- questioning and observing and using visual aids such as magazines and colour charts to determine the services and products required
- testing where necessary to ensure safe practices and the client's well-being (see Chapter 1)
- noting and taking account of any limiting factors, such as adverse hair, skin or scalp conditions, the presence of incompatible chemicals, hair that is in a poor state, the use of hair pieces or added hair such as extensions and so on (see Chapter 1)
- accounting for the client's use of hairpieces and deciding how these might affect the services she has requested
- referring a client where necessary to a senior member of staff for further action, advice and guidance
- ensuring the client agrees to the services being carried out
- making further information available if the client is still uncertain
- assuring clients of complete confidentiality by keeping their individual records private
- communicating effectively to ensure understanding.

Communication

Good communication between you and your client is one of the most important aspects that will determine your success as a hairdresser.

Most hairdressers are good communicators. The relationship between stylist and client is built on quality of service, professional advice, trust, support and a listening ear. Good communication ensures productive and effective action. On the other hand poor communication can lead to misunderstandings, misinterpretation and mistakes.

Activity

With a colleague, take turns at being the client or hairdresser in the consultation process. Notice the kinds of remark or question that gain most information, and note how one question may lead to another.

By completing this activity you will have worked towards the key skill requirement Communication Level 1 (C 1.1) and Level 2 (C 2.1).

There are a number of different ways in which we communicate:

Oral communication

Speech is used to pass on information and to ask questions. There are three types of questioning:

- Open – these require the client to give information. They begin with the words, what, who, which and when
- Probing – these are used to find out more information to investigate further
- Closed – these questions tend to give a yes or no answer and very little information.

You will have informal conversations chatting with your client during the service and more formal conversations greeting your client, during consultations or giving instructions to colleagues.

Talking and listening to your client is one of the most important parts of the hairdressing service. It will enable you to find out what the client wants and if they have any problems with their hair. You need to listen closely to what they are saying and ask questions to clarify any areas you are not sure about. You also need to ask open questions about their hair to ensure you get enough information to make judgements, explore ideas and give opinions such as:

- What don't you like about your current style?
- What would you like to change?
- How often do you wash your hair?
- How much time each day do you spend styling your hair?
- What type of products do you use on your hair at home?

Tip

If further processes or products need to be used ensure that the client agrees to the additional costs that may be involved.

Activity

With colleagues, practise asking different types of question. Ask your trainer to explain the difference between 'open' and 'closed' questions. This activity will help you to meet parts of the key skill requirement Communication Level 2 (C 2.1).

Written communication

A client record card is an ideal means of providing written communication about the client and the services carried out. It will clearly indicate:

- The client's name
- Client's contact details
- The services carried out
- The products used
- Test carried out and the results
- The price of the service
- The date of the service
- Timings involved in any chemical service
- The name of the stylist who carried out the service, and
- Any other information that will help ensure the client receives continuous good service.

Tip

Record all client information. Ensure that it is easy to retrieve.

Tip

If you don't consult with your client correctly and communicate with them effectively – and treat everything they tell you as confidential – you are likely to end up with a dissatisfied client. The client may even decide not to come back to the salon.

 Activity

Explore the use of the computer for the storage of all client details. Useful website addresses include

Computill: www.computill.com

xn corporation: www.xn.corp.com

By completing this activity you will have worked towards the key skill requirement Information Technology Level 1 (IT 1.1).

A client record card

CLIENT RECORD CARD			
Name:	Address:		
Telephone numbers: Home: Work:	Date first registered:	Age group ☐5–15 ☐16–30	
	Stylist:	☐31–50 ☐50+	
Hair condition:	Scalp:	Skin type:	

Date	Services and products used	Remarks/price charged	Stylist

Using the record card as part of your consultation with the client will enable you to ask knowledgeable questions about their last visit to the salon and the service they had. When completing a record card, if it is not done on a computer, make sure your handwriting is clear and easy to read. Put as much information on the card as possible to make sure that another stylist would understand exactly what had been done to the client's hair – what products were used or bought, the results of any tests that had been done and any suggestions for following visits to the salon. Another good example of providing written communication for a member of your team would be a memorandum (or memo).

Written communication: a memorandum

Memorandum

TO: John

FROM: Linda

DATE: 1/10

SUBJECT: Staff absence

Jayne will not be in for the rest of the week as she has a virus. Please could you reschedule her appointments, and advise all clients accordingly

Thanks.

Body language

As well as using words, we express our interest and attitudes by non-verbal communication – our eye contact, posture and general body positioning. So it is very important that we convey the right *message*, particularly when dealing with clients and potential customers.

Eye contact – maintain eye contact when talking to the client. Where possible, maintain the same eye level as the client; for example, when you carry out a consultation with a client and they are seated, sit beside or opposite them. Standing over or above your client and looking down will convey a feeling of authority, or as if you are trying to assert control. This is intimidating and definitely the wrong signal to send to a client.

Distances – people have a 'comfort zone', a space around the body within which they feel at ease. Within a close, intimate relationship shared proximity may be welcome, but *uninvited* invasion of this space is at least uncomfortable, at its worst menacing or threatening.

Posture/body positioning/gestures – volumes have been written on this subject alone and the psychology of body language is far too complex to address in a few paragraphs. But following certain obvious rules can help us convey the right message and impression.

- Slouching in the salon looks really unprofessional.

- Folded arms – crossing the arms on the chest is a protective gesture and suggests a closed mind or a show of defensiveness.

- Open palms – as a gesture supporting explanation or information, with hands at waist height, palms upwards, this indicates that the person has 'nothing to hide'. This is interpreted as openness or honesty.

- Scratching behind the ear or rubbing the back of the neck while listening indicates that the listener is uncertain or doesn't understand.

- Talking with your hand in front of your mouth may lead the listener to believe that you are not being honest. You are hiding yourself by your gestures.

These forms of communication are only indications of feelings and emotions. In isolation, they may not mean anything at all. Taken together, however, they can convey a very clear message. Make sure that you show the appropriate signals; be – and look – interested, keen, ready to help and positive. Above all, show that you can listen.

 Activity

Use role-play with a colleague to experiment with non-verbal communication. See if you can interpret what is or isn't being said!

Dealing with difficult clients

As discussed above, good communication is important. It will help you to deal with many different situations. Not all clients are easy to get along with or to extract information from, some clients may be angry because they have been waiting for a long time for their appointment or are unhappy with the style you have just given them. Some clients may find it difficult to explain what they want or not understand what you are asking. As a stylist it is your job to stay calm and deal with each situation in a professional way.

Angry client

Stay calm, listen to the client, let them explain why they are angry, use open friendly **body language** and maintain eye contact, keep your speech clear and low when asking questions or giving information to clarify the situation. If you are not in a position to deal with the problem make sure you get someone who can – this may be a senior stylist or the manager. Never ignore the client; they are angry for a reason and usually the situation can be sorted out.

Confused client

Not all clients know what they want when they book an appointment or understand what you are suggesting for their hairstyle. Make sure that you give the client time to talk to you and ask questions. Listen to them, maintain eye contact, use open body language and gestures such as nodding your head or open palms to confirm you are listening and ready to support your client. Use simple explanations and questions to extract information. Use visual aids such as style books or colour charts to help you. Reaffirm you clients' understanding by asking open questions and giving reassurance.

Dealing with complaints

It is not easy to deal with an unsatisfied client – you will need all your skills of tact and diplomacy. Remember that a client has every right to expect the services agreed and paid for. If the salon is at fault, mistakes must be put right.

It can be difficult to decide what is reasonable or unreasonable. Whatever your personal feelings, try to remain calm, polite and understanding. Arguing back will probably make the client more angry and is not good for the salon's image. A satisfied client is good business!

If you notice a mistake, don't try to pretend it hasn't happened. Put the situation right before the client leaves the salon. If a client approaches you with a complaint, you should:

- Deal with the client pleasantly and politely
- Discuss the nature of the client's complaint
- Analyse the complaint carefully and sympathetically
- Discuss the complaint with a senior staff member before suggesting corrective action
- Agree with the client what is to be done
- Carry out the correction then and there, or agree a convenient time for the client to return
- Record the complaint and the action taken.

If the complaint is serious – such as hair breaking off after a perm, or hair becoming discoloured after tinting – it may be difficult to put right. Give all the details to your employer, who will warn the salon's insurers, as the client has legal right to claim **compensation**. With tact it may be possible to avoid this by agreeing a course of corrective action and refunding money paid.

Tip

Don't be too hurried in trying to put a problem right – you might make a bad situation worse. Always remain calm and give careful consideration to the problem, making sure the client understands and agrees to any cause of correction action.

Activity

Collect information about different software systems that can be used in the salon. Review how they differ from one another and how a reception area would benefit by becoming computerised.

This activity will work towards key skill Communication Level 2 (C 2.2).

Consulting and diagnosing techniques

Chris Moody

Examining the hair

In every consultation with a client there are certain things you must attend to.

- Listen to what the client tells you.
- Find out what clients want – their desires or requests.
- Question the client courteously, so that you get useful information on which you can base accurate decisions.
- Observe the client carefully and thoroughly during the examination.
- Ensure that the client is comfortable and at ease throughout the consultation.

Here are some of the questions you can ask yourself:

- Is the hair dry, brittle or breaking?
- Is it extremely greasy?
- Is the hair too short or uneven?
- Is there too much frizz or perm from previous treatment?
- Is there variation in synthetic colouring?
- What have been the effects of physical processes, such as crimping or tonging?
- What have been the effects of chemical processes, such as perming or colouring?
- Have incompatible chemicals been used, such as home hair treatments that leave metallic salts which might react with hydrogen peroxide during bleaching?

Diagnosis like this may tell you whether hair will stand up to processes such as perming. (Further aspects of hair, such as hair growth quantity and movement, are considered in Chapter 6.)

 Activity

List other questions that might be asked of your client.

Client aftercare

Aftercare and subsequent salon services include

- advising clients on how to manage new styles
- passing product knowledge on to the client, together with manufacturers' recommendations for aftercare

- discussing the possible effects that salon services might have on the client and their hair in the future, particularly those involving treatment with chemicals
- prompting and encouraging clients to ask about salon services about which they are unsure
- guiding clients to adopt safe practices, such as combing and brushing hair correctly, or avoiding swimming without hair protection (which can affect coloured and bleached hair)
- promoting the client to use products and practices that will benefit them and keep their hair in good condition
- recording carefully all the services the client receives in the salon, so that they can be readily identified if the client asks for a repeat treatment.

 Activity

Collect individual manufacturer's product and technical services information. This can form the basis for giving useful advice to your clients. You can find additional information from manufacturer's websites, e.g. www.wella.co.uk and www.loreal.co.uk. By completing this activity you will have worked towards the key skill Information Technology Level 1 (IT 1.1).

Promoting services and products

Your salon will want you to promote services and products to your clients. It not only gives your client a choice of what you can offer so that they do not go to another salon but also helps to improve the salon's business. Most salons have guidelines and procedures for recommending and selling additional salon services and retail products so that they meet the requirements of consumer and retail legislation.

Consumer and retail legislation

The Consumer Protection Act 1987	This Act follows European directives to protect the buyer from products that do not reach a reasonable level of safety.
The Consumer Safety Act 1978	This Act reduces the possible risk to consumers from any products that may be potentially dangerous.
The Price Act 1974	This Act states that prices of products have to be displayed so that consumers are not given a false impression of their value.
Trades Descriptions Act 1972	This Act states that products should not be falsely or misleadingly described in relation to its quality, price, fitness or purpose, by advertisements, displays, orally or through descriptions. Since 1972 it is also a requirement to label a product clearly so that the consumer can see where the product was made.

The Resale Prices Act 1964 and 1976	This Act states that manufacturers can supply a recommended price, but the seller is not obliged to sell at the recommended price.
The Sales and Supply of Goods Act 1994	This Act states the seller must ensure that the goods on sale are: of a satisfactory quality – defined as the standard that would be regarded by a reasonable person as satisfactory having taken into account the description of the goods, the price and any other relevant circumstance. Reasonably fit – the seller must ensure that the goods are able to meet what the seller claims they do.

Most salons will offer promotions on services or products to increase business; as a stylist it will be part of your role to tell your clients about any promotion that is taking place. You may also have a regular target to meet selling retail products as part of your job and may be given a percentage of the sale as an incentive. As a hairdresser you have an excellent opportunity to advise your clients on the services and products available in the salon during the consultation and throughout their time in the salon. Selling is a recommendation of a service or product that will meet your client's needs. The best advice is based on listening to what your client needs and clarifying their concerns. After you have listened to your client's concerns, you can offer advice and solutions, be it a perm, a colour service or a styling product. By recommending services or products you are giving professional advice that will gain you the respect of your client and their continuous support.

How to promote services and products

As a professional stylist you need to know what the salon has to offer your clients. You will need to learn about all the services and products available and how much each one costs. Imagine you have a client who is booked in for a cut and blow dry – whilst carrying out the consultation you discuss with the client the condition of the hair. The client's hair is very dry and brittle. You suggest to your client that it would benefit the hair to have a conditioning treatment prior to the cut. You explain to the client how the treatment will work, what benefit it will have on the hair and how using the product at home on a regular basis will improve the condition, make it shine and look healthy. By giving this advice to your client you are providing the professional service the client is seeking.

The selling process

Selling can be divided in to three steps and is a sequence that is used when giving a good consultation.

1   Finding out the client's needs – by using your communication skills listen to your clients to find out how well they can manage

their hair at home, ask questions about the type of products and tools they use.

2   Giving advice – After listening to you client suggest ideas of an additional service that may help them create the look they are after. Use visual aids such as stylebooks to help you explain and show the client what you mean. If you are suggesting a product explain how it will help achieve an effect the client wants to achieve. Explain in simple straightforward language how the product works, how much product is needed to create the effect and how much the product costs. Give the client time to ask questions and be honest in your answers. If the product will not do what you say it will and the client buys it, on their next visit to you they may not be happy and will probably not trust you when you suggest other products or services. If the client is not interested in buying a product or service do not carry on with the sale, as this will only make the client feel uncomfortable or angry.

3   Gaining an agreement – confirming with your client the service to be done or the products to be used or sold.

How to recognise a buying signal:

- Your client is interested in what you are saying
- They ask questions about the product or service
- They touch, smell or try the product
- They ask you to explain how a product works
- They ask how much it costs.

How to recognise a client not interested in buying a product or service:

- They will change the conversation
- Become distracted by other activities
- They will tell you that they are not interested.

Things to remember:

- Your guidelines for retailing products
- Your responsibility under the Sales and Supply of Goods Act
- Know every thing there is to know about your salon's products and services
  - The features of a product – What it contains and how it works
  - The benefits of a product – What it will do for the client's hair
  - The cost of a product or service
- Give an honest balanced view about the products and services on offer and how they will benefit your client
- Do not push your client in buying something, you may lose not only the sale but also your client.

Selling products

Remember when recommending products to your clients to use the product as an aid. Let the client hold the product as you explain how it works and what it can do. Show the client how much product is needed by demonstrating how to use it. Explain how long the product will last and how much it costs. Clients will appreciate the advice you give. You are the professional – they come to you for your skill, knowledge and expertise. Make sure you give them the best advice on all you and your salon has to offer.

 Activity

Make a list or table of the retail products in your salon. For each product write down

- the features of the product e.g. leave in conditioner used for dry hair, protects the hair and leaves cuticle smooth, contains moisturisers.
- the benefits of the product e.g. quick to use, detangles the hair and leaves it full of bounce and shine.
- the difference between your other retail products and how much it costs.

By completing this activity you will have worked towards the key skill requirement Communication Level (C 1.2) and Level 2 (C 2.2).

If you have used a computer you will have worked towards the key skill requirement Information Technology Level 1 (IT 1.2).

Assignments – Client care and consultation

A practical activity

With the help of your colleagues, practise the different processes of client care, such as consultation, preparing the client and their hair, questioning a client, examining hair and scalp, and so on. Keep notes of any problems and difficulties you come across. The use of audio and video recorders is invaluable; keep copies of your tapes if you can. Then answer the following questions. Record your answers for your folder.

1 What is client consultation? Why is it necessary?

2 List the questions that need to be asked during a consultation. How do you record the consultation process?

3 Make a list of your salon's services and the prices charged for them. List any other sales or services you know of.

4 What are the processes of client and hair preparation? Why are they necessary?

5 What is meant by the words 'goodwill', 'trust' and 'confidentiality'?

Assignments – Client care and consultation (cont.)

For you to find out

Investigate the different types of verbal and non-verbal communication that you use in your job as a hairdresser, to ensure you deliver good client care. You can simulate activities by working with your colleagues.

Then answer the following questions.

Record all your answers for your folder

- Explain the difference between verbal and non-verbal communication

- Describe the verbal and non-verbal communication methods you and your client would use when:
  - Carrying out a consultation
  - Selling products to your client
  - Explaining to your client that a service can not be carried out
- Outline the stages of the sales process. What buying signals you look for.
- Explain the importance of being patient and using a courteous manner.

A case study

Your salon has decided to take on a new range of products, which can be used for most of the services offered to clients. Outline what you need to do

- to understand what the products can do and what they have to offer – their advantages and disadvantages
- to satisfy yourself of their suitability for your different clients

- to best present these new products to your clients
- to begin to understand how the different services and products are finally priced.

What might you do if the clients began to complain of the results of these new products?

Preparing for Assessment

In preparing for your assessment on client care the following checklist may be useful. Check that you have covered and now fully understand these items:

- consulting with clients before any services are applied
- identifying clients' wishes and requirements'
- referring clients to others
- identifying factors that limit services and choices of product

- preparing clients for an agreed service – the time the service takes, the price charged and the aftercare required
- communicating effectively, reassuring the client that goodwill, trust and confidentiality are maintained in your salon
- maintaining accurate records of information – and understanding how it should be used. When you feel that you are ready to be assessed, talk to your trainer and arrange a suitable time.

By reading this chapter, carrying out the above assignments and the case study, and by meeting the requirements in preparing for assessment you will have worked towards the key skill requirements in Communication Level 1 (C 1.1) (C 1.2) (C 1.3) and Level 2 (C 2.1) (C 2.2).

Shampooing and conditioning hair

3

Carol Hayes and Associates

Learning objectives

The following are some of the topics covered in this chapter:

- **understanding shampoos and shampooing**
- **selection of products**
- **chemistry of shampoos**
- **how shampoos work**
- **shampooing techniques**
- **acidity and alkalinity**
- **hair conditioners**
- **hair treatments**
- **massage techniques.**

Introduction

Shampoos and shampooing, conditioners and conditioning, are important parts of good hair care, and indeed the basis of it. Whether shampoos and conditioners are sold for you to use in the salon or for clients to use at home, their application requires thought and care. They affect most of the physical and chemical applications in hairdressing.

There is a wide range of shampoos and conditioners, especially designed for use on the hair and scalp. The chemistry involved is not simple. Much time, effort, money and research is spent on designing and making professional products so that they can benefit the user's hair and be safe to use. Always follow the manufacturer's guidance for their use, since only the maker can be fully aware of their composition and effects.

Shampooing – the principles

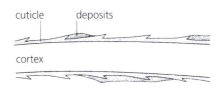

Dirt on the hair cuticle

Shampooing is the important procedure of cleaning both the hair and the scalp. Shampooing removes dirt, grease and any other matter that coats the hair and scalp. This is essential in preparing the hair for other services: if any deposits remain in the hair after shampooing, they may interfere with the service you are carrying out – for example, they could block perm chemicals or leave the hair too greasy to blow-style.

Good shampooing can be both physically and psychologically soothing, relaxing and enjoyable. Make sure your client is comfortable throughout. Poor shampooing technique may irritate your client, and lead to general dissatisfaction.

Preparing to shampoo

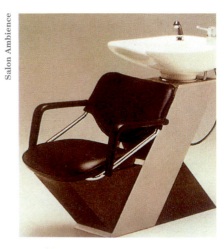

Equipment

- Discuss with the client what you are going to do.
- Select suitable protective clothing – gowns and towels.
- Analyse the condition of the hair and scalp, examining it carefully. Consider the service to follow. Ask questions, such as 'What products do you use at home?', 'How often do you shampoo your hair?', 'How do you style your hair?'
- Report immediately to a senior member of staff any signs of abnormality (infection or injury) such as redness, sores, swelling or irritation. Serious injury and some infectious diseases indicate that no hairdressing service should be carried out (see Chapter 1).
- Consult with the client throughout. Make sure the client knows the price to be paid for any special treatments used, and agrees to your choice of shampoo.
- Indicate how long shampooing will take – about five minutes – and what is to follow.

Choosing a shampoo

Shampoos come in various forms, including creams, semi-liquids and gels. There are different shampoo bases (the substances that form the bulk of the shampoo), and some are kinder and gentler on hair and skin than others. The balance of the various shampoo ingredients is important, for example the detergent content in shampoos for greasy hair is higher than in those for normal or dry hair. So too is their ability to deal with different hair types and conditions.

Shampoos may be named after the ingredients contained in them, such as 'lemon shampoo' for its lemon essence or citric acid content. Herbal, vegetable and other natural products are popular.

Choosing the right shampoo for the hair condition and following service is important. If the wrong shampoo is used the hair could become difficult to handle, flyaway, static, feel dry and brittle or look dull. If the shampoo doesn't remove all the styling products that have been on the hair, it could interfere with or block a chemical service.

Popular shampoos

Shampoo ingredients	Effect on the hair
Jojoba	A light non-greasy plant-based oil, which has a good moisturising effect on dry hair
Coconut	Contains an emollient, which helps dry hair regain its smoothness and elasticity
Camomile	Used on greasy hair to give brightness and shine
Rosemary	Used on normal hair, reduces scale on the scalp, is an antiseptic and is stimulating
Soya	Contains a moisturiser for normal hair
Oil	Contains pine, palm, almond, and other oils used to smooth and soften dry hair and scalp
Egg	Egg white is used on greasy hair (it emulsifies the grease) the egg yolk is used on dry hair
Medicated	Helps maintain the normal state of the hair and scalp. Contains antiseptics such as juniper which is helpful if the scalp is scaly
Treatment	Variety of shampoos each used to deal with a specific problem, such as dandruff or excessive greasiness: they usually contain cetrimide, selenium sulphide or zinc pyrithione.
Pre-perm	Used before perming: contains ingredients that ensure the hair surface is clear of all products that could interfere with the perm action.

Shampoos

Making the right choice – the needs of the hair

The right choice of shampoo depends on several factors.

- **Type, texture and condition of hair** – fine hair requires a shampoo that will not degrease it or make it too fluffy. Choose a shampoo that will add body, or consider using a hair thickener. Coarse hair requires a shampoo that will tend to soften it and make it more pliable. Thick hair requires a shampoo that will penetrate and make good contact with all of the hair and the whole scalp. (See page 63 for a discussion of products designed to deal with hair in poor condition.)

- **Frequency of shampooing** – if hair is washed once or more daily, choose a shampoo specially designed for frequent use.

- **Water quality** – if the water used in the salon is hard (see page 60), soap-based shampoos will tend to form scum. Use soap-free shampoos. In soft water areas most types of shampoo can be used.

- **The function of the shampoo** – is it intended to colour, tone, condition or just cleanse the hair?

- **Hair treatments planned** – what are you going to do with the hair later? Some shampoo ingredients (lanolin is an example) coat the hair shaft. This would prevent cold perm lotions from working, for instance. In this case you would need to use a pre-perm shampoo. Pre-perm shampoos not only cleanse the hair and scalp but also remove natural oil (sebum) that coats the hair to protect it. If the oil remains on the hair it may cause a barrier for the perm lotion to penetrate the hair cortex, therefore affecting the final result of the curl produced.

 Activity

When visiting a chemist or hairdressing wholesaler, note the shampoos that are recommended for frequent use (once or more daily).

Which types of shampoo does your salon use? Which does it sell for home use?

Mahogany

How shampoos work

The object of shampooing is to clean the hair by removing dirt, grease, skin scale and sweat, plus any hairspray, gel, mousse, dressing cream, etc. Water alone cannot dissolve and rinse out all these substances to leave the hair in a suitable condition for processes such as blow-styling, setting, perming or bleaching.

Shampooing involves rubbing the head with shampoo and water to enable the cleaners to surround the hair and dirt particles. Using large amounts of shampoo is unnecessary and wasteful. A small amount, thoroughly spread and massaged into the scalp, is just as effective.

 Activity

Use a shampoo containing soap with hard water. Note the scum that forms.

Then use an acid rinse. Notice how the scum is cleared from the scalp and hair.

Types of shampoo

- **Soap shampoos** – these are not generally used in salons nowadays. They cleaned the hair, but formed scum deposits on the hair and skin when used with hard water. These coated the hair and made it lank. Citric acid (from lemon juice) and acetic acid (from vinegar), made into rinses, were used to remove the scum.

- **Soapless shampoos** – these are now popular in most salons. They are effective in both hard and soft water, and do not leave scum deposits. The early soapless shampoos were very harsh and removed too much grease from the hair and skin. They also produced static electricity, which made the hair flyaway. These faults have now been largely overcome.

- **Synthetic detergents (surface-active agents, surfactants)** – the bases from which soapless shampoos are made. An example is triethanolamine lauryl sulphate, commonly known as TLS.

Detergents

By itself, water does not spread thoroughly over the hair and scalp. This is because water molecules are attracted together by weak electrical forces. These have their greatest effect at the water surface, creating what is known as **surface tension**. On hair, water by itself tends to form droplets. The **detergent** in shampoo reduces surface tension, allowing the water to spread easily over the hair and scalp, wetting them. Detergents are, in other words, **wetting agents**. Shampoo is anionic detergent.

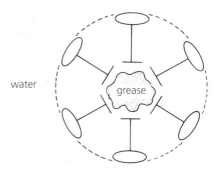

Detergent molecules surrounding grease

water

grease

A detergent molecule

Each detergent molecule has two ends. One end (the **hydrophilic** one) attracts water molecules; the other (the **hydrophobic** one) repels them, and instead attracts grease. Detergent molecules lift the grease off the hair surface and suspend it in the water. The suspension is called an **emulsion**. The dirt is held by the grease, so as the grease is removed, the dirt loosens too. The emulsion and loose dirt can be rinsed away with water, leaving the hair clean. Therefore a good shampoo should contain a good wetting agent, a good emulsifier and should rinse out of the hair easily to leave it manageable and shiny when dry.

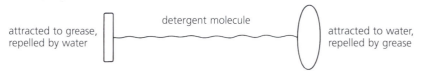

attracted to grease, repelled by water

detergent molecule

attracted to water, repelled by grease

Shampooing technique

Health & Safety

Remove rings, wrist watches or bangles when shampooing to avoid moisture or shampoo building up on your skin, which could become sensitised.

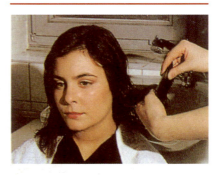

Disentangling the hair

Wella

Shampooing: water flow

Apart from cleaning the hair, shampooing can affect the client's mood. Hands and fingers used too lightly or too harshly may irritate, as may missing out parts of the head. Be thorough in all your hand and finger movements.

Shampooing method

1 Protect and care for the client throughout the process.
2 First prepare the hair by combing and disentangling it. Ensure that long hair is off the face and neck. Do not let it become tangled.
3 Check that the client is comfortable, especially the position of the head.
4 Run the cold water first, then mix hot water into the cold. Test the water mixture and temperature on the back of your hand. After lifting the spray, and before applying it to the client, test the water temperature again.
5 Check the water flow and pressure. Do not allow water to flow down the neck or on to the face.
6 Keep one hand between the head and the water spray – you will then be aware of any temperature changes.
7 Thoroughly wet the hair: avoid wetting the client.
8 Ensure that the hair, particularly if it is long, is controlled and directed into the water stream.
9 Apply shampoo, first into the palm of your hand. Distribute it evenly over the hair and scalp. Use as little shampoo as is necessary, or most of it will be wasted.
10 With clawed fingers, massage the scalp in a circular manner. Cover the whole scalp – be sure to avoid missing any part.
11 Rinse the hair thoroughly, again checking the water temperature and pressure.
12 If there is still product on the hair or the hair is not washed frequently, apply more shampoo and repeat the process.

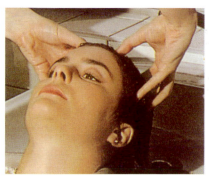

Shampooing: finger positions

13 Finally, rinse all traces of lather from the skin and hair making sure the water flow is directed down the hair to help smooth the cuticle.

Massage techniques

There are three types of massage movements you can use when shampooing: **effleurage** (stroking), **pétrissage**, **rotary** (circular), and **friction** (rubbing).

1 Begin shampooing with smooth effleurage movements. Spread products evenly.
2 Continue with firm but gentle rotary movement:
   - Let your fingertips glide over the scalp. Lift your hands periodically to avoid tangling the hair.
   - Move your hands towards each other – up from the sides to the top and down across the nape area.
   - Move your hands in decreasing circles around the head to make sure you cover the scalp fully.
3 Use lighter, plucking, friction movements to stimulate the scalp gently.
4 Finally, use soothing effleurage movements to complete the shampooing process.

Tip

Effleurage – gentle, stroking movement used when shampooing and conditioning.

Rotary – quick, circular small, firm movements used when shampooing.

Friction – quick, rubbing movement used when shampooing.

Pétrissage – slow deep circular kneading movement used when conditioning.

Shampooing: finger movements

Tip

Hard, straight-line massage movements should be avoided, because they cause discomfort to the client.

Wella

While shampooing

- Make sure the client is comfortable at all times.
- Check massage movements, water temperatures, water flow and pressure, and the client's position.
- Work hygienically. This is good practice at all times; it also reassures your client who can then relax and enjoy the hairdressing processes.

After shampooing

1 Turn off the water flow. Return the spray head to its place.
2 Lift the hair from the face. Wrap it with a towel, and gently remove any surplus water remaining in the hair.
3 Reposition the client comfortably.
4 Check that all shampoo, dirt and grease has been removed and that the skin and hair are clean. (Your assessor or trainer will be specially looking to see whether the hair and skin *are* clean after shampooing.)
5 At this stage you may apply conditioner if this is required. The hair should now be ready for combing and the processes that follow.

Do's and don'ts

- Give your complete attention to the client.
- Never use unwashed linen on another client.
- Ensure that towels and gowns are clean, in place, and not too tightly secured.
- Use sensible hygiene to prevent cross-infection and to safeguard health generally.
- Do not allow shampoo to come into contact with the client's eyes.
- Direct the water flow away from the client to avoid wetting their clothes and face.
- Comb the hair after shampooing, without tugging or pulling it. Comb from points to roots starting at the nape of the neck.
- As soon as you have finished, clean the part of the salon where the shampooing was carried out. Remove dirty, used towels. Replace shampoo containers. Make sure the chair is left clean.
- Always turn off the water – do not allow water to run continuously between washes. This soon empties the hot water tank. By turning water off when it is not in use you avoid delay, waste and higher costs.
- Always rinse your hands after shampooing. Do not allow shampoo to remain: it might cause dryness and soreness (dermatitis). Gently pat your hands dry – never scrub them with a towel.

!

Health & Safety

Remove any shampoo from the eyes with plenty of cool, clean water.

After shampooing

Patting the hands dry

Health & Safety

Raising a client from a forward washing position too quickly can make them feel dizzy. Allow a little time before moving them to another position.

Do not let the hair fall over the client's eyes when moving.

When using a back wash, do not put excessive pressure on the back of the neck as this will be very painful and may lead to a reduction of blood flow to the brain.

Remember that, apart from chilling and scalding your client, water that is too hot or cold can cause shock. Always check the water temperature before applying the water.

Tip

Always record the products used on the client record card so that you know which to use, and those not to use, in the future.

Activity

With colleagues, shampoo each other's hair. Compare the shampoo actions used with long and short hair.

Massage the scalp. When the hair is long, notice the position of your hands. How often do you lift the hands from the head to avoid tangling the hair?

Water for shampooing

Salons use a lot of water – about 10–20 litres for each wash. It is therefore important that there is a constant supply of both hot and cold water. Anything that interferes with the salon's plumbing and drainage systems may cause delay and financial loss. Don't leave hot taps running longer than necessary, or you could soon empty the hot water tank, or if you have a direct water heater i.e. a boiler that heats the water as it passes through, leaving the hot tap running will increase the salon's electric or gas bills.

Cold water reaches the salon via a main supply pipe from the road: if necessary this can be disconnected using a stopcock. Cold water is stored in a tank. Some is heated (using gas, electricity or oil) and this hot water is stored in a second tank.

Waste water leaves the salon via outlet pipes to the drains. Beneath each basin is a waste trap. This has two functions. First, it holds water and stops gases and smells from the drains reaching the salon. Second, it collects hair and debris, making the pipes less likely to block. If an earring, for example, falls through the plughole, you can retrieve it by undoing the trap.

Tip

Prolong the life of your equipment by keeping it free from limescale.

Hard and soft water

There are two types of water, hard and soft. The area in which you work or live will dictate whether the water coming out of the tap at the backwash is hard or soft.

Hard water is water that contains calcium and/or magnesium salts. If these are not removed, they react with chemicals in soap (sodium stearate) to form an insoluble scum (calcium or magnesium stearate). So soap shampoos should not be used with hard water, without using special rinses afterwards. Soapless shampoos are now almost always used, and these do not form scum in hard water.

The chemicals in water determine whether it is permanently or temporarily hard. This affects the products and equipment used. Permanently hard water contains calcium and magnesium sulphates. These cannot be removed from the water by boiling. Temporarily hard water contains calcium and magnesium hydrogencarbonates (bicarbonates). Boiling temporarily hard water changes these into the carbonates, which are insoluble and so separate out of the water. These form a hard deposit of fur, or **limescale**, in steamers, kettles, hot water pipes, shower heads and sprays. Limescale can be removed using special descaling solutions.

Soft water is water that is free from calcium and magnesium salts. Soft water may be supplied direct by the local water authority, or it may be hard water that has been softened by a special softening process. Soft water does not form scum when used with soap, nor does it form limescale when it is heated.

Activity

Find out where the main electricity switch and the water stopcock are, and how to turn them off.

If a tank or pipe bursts, turn off *both* the electricity *and* the water. Until you have done so, don't touch light switches or electrical devices – you might be electrocuted.

Activity

Find out if the water in your salon is hard or soft. If it is hard, is it permanently or temporarily hard?

Acidity and alkalinity: the pH scale

Shampooing, like other chemical actions, can affect the surface of the skin. You should consider how acid or alkaline the skin surface will be left after shampooing.

APPROXIMATE pH VALUES OF VARIOUS SUBSTANCES

Acid	0.1–6.9
Alkali	7.1–14.0
Neutral solution	7.0
Normal hair/scalp	4.5–5.5
Pre-perm shampoo	7.0
pH-balanced Shampoo/ conditioner	4.5–5.5

The **pH scale** measures acidity or alkalinity. It ranges from pH 1 to pH 14. **Acids** have pH numbers below 7. **Alkalis** have pH numbers above 7. **Neutral** substances have a pH close to 7. The *higher* the pH number, the more *alkaline* the substance; the *lower* the pH number, the more *acid* the substance.

The normal pH of the hair and the skin's surface is 4.5–5.5. This is referred to as the skin's **acid mantle**. The acidity is due in part to the sebum, the natural oil produced by the skin.

An important skin function is the protection of the underlying tissue (see Chapter 1). The skin does this by acting as a barrier, preventing liquid loss from inside, and keeping excess liquid outside the body. It also protects the body from infection. An acid skin surface inhibits (slows down) the growth of bacteria, and makes them less likely to enter the skin. If the acidity of the skin is reduced – if the pH rises above 4.5–5.5 – infections are more likely. This may happen if the pH is not adjusted after chemical hairdressing processes such as perming.

The pH can be measured using **pH papers** or Universal indicator papers. **Litmus papers** will tell you whether something is acid, alkaline or neutral.

The pH scale

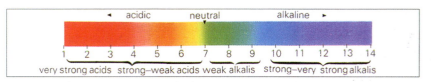

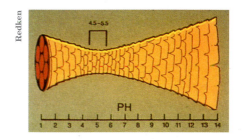

How pH affects the hair

If hairs are placed in an alkaline solution they swell, and the cuticle lifts. In slightly acid solution the cuticle is smooth and the hair is soft; in strong acid, however, it begins to break down.

Activity

Keep a 'product knowledge' book. Record the shampoos and conditioners you use. What are their active ingredients? What pH does each have? (You can use indicator papers to find out.) What are the effects on your clients' or your own hair?

How would you advise your clients about choosing a shampoo?

Conditioning – the principles

Caring for your client's hair and keeping it in good condition is the basis of good hairdressing. If the hair is torn and breaking, or the surface cuticle rough and splitting, the appearance will be dull and uninteresting. It may lose its elasticity and shape and the curl will be difficult to hold. Control too becomes difficult. If you ignore poor condition and apply further harsh treatments, you may cause more serious damage.

IMJ Hair Studio for L'Oreal

The client

- As a first step, consult the client. Ask what has been done and what has been used on the hair. If this is a regular client, check the record card for past history.

- Examine and analyse the hair and scalp closely. Assess the condition and extent of any damage to the hair.

- From what you can see, identify any problems – porous hair, loss of elasticity, cuticle peelings, split ends, dryness, greasiness and so on. Try to find the reasons for these faults.

- Advise the client – what can be done, what treatments are available, which products to use and the possible benefits.

- Agree with the client on the course of action to be taken. Make sure that the cost of the services you agree is understood and is acceptable.

- Make sure that the client is aware of the need for more than one treatment, application or process of conditioning.

- Emphasise the need for correct home care. Offer advice and suggest ways in which the client can help improve the condition of their hair.

- Advise on retail products available that they can use at home – (see Promoting products in Chapter 2).

Tip

Acid products close the hair cuticle.

Alkali products open the hair cuticle.

Choosing a conditioner

Soft Sheene Carson Professional

The best **conditioners** protect hair so that it does not lose its natural condition, or help chemically treated hair to maintain or improve its condition. They have the following general effects:

- the hair cuticle is smoothed
- hair tangling is reduced
- broken areas of the cuticle or cortex may be repaired
- the hair surface reflects more light, producing a gloss or sheen
- surface acidity/alkalinity is balanced.

Conditioners may also be used to deal with particular problems:

- some allow the cortex to attract water – these are called **humectants** and **moisturisers**.

- others allow the cortex to retain moisture – these are called **emollients**

- some counteract the effects of oxidation (chemical reactions which take place during processes like colouring or bleaching) – these are called **antioxidants**.

Conditioners

Soft Sheene Carson Professional

Conditioners

Mahogany

The following are some of the conditioners used:

- control creams, dressings, oils, hairsprays, gels
- reconditioning rinses, emulsions, humectants
- acid and alkaline rinses
- restructurants and protein builders
- antioxidants
- pH balancers (after shampooing, colouring, etc.)
- gels, mousses (foams for setting, dressing, etc.)
- hair thickeners (for conditioning and building fine hair).

Types of conditioner

There are several different types of conditioner. Some remain on the surface of the hair, others penetrate the cortex. Some may be both surface *and* penetrating in their action. Both surface and penetrating conditioners may be combined with **bactericides** and **fungicides** to help stop the growth of bacteria and fungi on hair and skin.

Surface conditioners

Surface conditioners add gloss and help to make the hair manageable. They do not enter the hair but remain on the surface and smooth the surface by coating it. Some also neutralise the effects of chemical processes such as colouring and bleaching.

Commonly used surface conditioners include:

- dressing creams and oils
- reconditioning creams and lotions
- acid or rehabilitating rinses.

These may be applied before, during or after treatments. They may contain some of the following ingredients:

- lanolin
- cholesterol
- vegetable and mineral oils
- fats and waxes
- lecithin
- citric, acetic and lactic acids.

Penetrating conditioners

Penetrating conditioners enter the hair shaft by capillary action – the passage of materials through the tiny cellular spaces within the hair. Penetrating conditioners are designed to repair the chemical structure of fibres within the cortex which have been damaged or affected by previous hairdressing processes. These types of conditioner can also smooth the hair cuticle and make the whole hair structure much stronger. They may contain the following ingredients:

Tip

Protective conditioners, when used before chemical applications, even-out hair porosity.

Tip

Corrective conditioning products used prior to direct heat minimise cuticle damage.

- quaternary ammonium compounds
- sulphur compounds
- protein hydrolysates (individual amino acids and very short lengths of polypeptides, see p. 7), which strengthen the hair
- humectants, which hold water in the hair
- emollients, which soften tissue and hair
- moisturisers, which help to retain moisture.

How conditioners work

Modern conditioners achieve their effects by chemically balancing the hair structure. They also counteract the effects that chemical and physical processes have on the hair. This applies particularly to the alkalinity or acidity of the hair's surface. The electrical and chemical properties of substances in conditioners help them to adhere to or combine with the hair.

Materials which are chemically attracted to the hair structure are called substantive conditioners. The newer hair thickeners, hair builders, restructurants and protein hydrolysates combine with the polypeptide chains within the hair, and create extra crosslinks. This builds up the hair, and in some cases actually thickens it.

Protein hydrolysates are produced by a chemical reaction involving protein breakdown and the addition of water. They may be obtained from animal and other proteins. They are used in conditioners which strengthen and moisturise the hair.

Conditioning treatments

Conditioning treatments may be applied:

- to correct some hair states – dryness or greasiness, for example
- to counteract the effect of hairdressing processes
- as 'before' or 'after' treatments
- to soften and smooth tight curly hair or coarse hair
- to maintain healthy hair
- to maintain a healthy scalp.

Dandruff

Dandruff, or **pityriasis capitis**, is caused by the overproduction of skin cells. It appears as small, very fine, white, loose scales. These may irritate the scalp to varying degrees; they are also unsightly when they fall on to the shoulders, and may cause the sufferer anxiety. If the scales stick to the skin small patches of dry skin may result: these can cause inflammation.

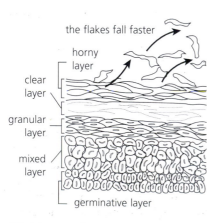

the flakes fall faster

horny layer

clear layer

granular layer

mixed layer

germinative layer

Flaking scalp

Activity

With colleagues, examine and assess each other's hair condition before and after conditioning. Compare the effectiveness of different products and methods, and record your results.

Conditioning treatments

Goldwell

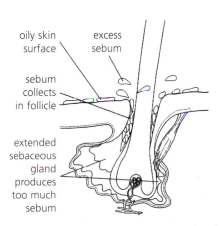

Treatment

Dandruff is commonly treated at home. Treatment may include special shampoos, lotions or creams derived from tar, sulphur or zinc pyrithione. Recent reports suggest that fungicides may be helpful.

Special shampoos are usually sufficient, but particularly serious cases may require daily applications of anti-dandruff lotions or creams. If these are not effective, advise your client to see a doctor or trichologist.

It is important that you do not handle the hair roughly, and that you reduce scaling that might irritate your client's eyes. Although dandruff is not thought to be infectious, you should still take all the usual measures for hygiene to prevent any possible cross-infection.

Greasy hair

Greasy hair, or seborrhoea, is caused by grease from the sebaceous glands. These may be overstimulated by too much combing or brushing, or by too much hand or vibration massage. The use of greasy or oily products adds to the problem.

Treatment

Excessive grease must be removed by regular washing with balanced shampoos. Ammonium hydroxide, borax and astringent lotions may be used to correct excessively greasy conditions. Astringent lotions cause the skin to contract slightly, temporarily reducing the output of grease. If fungi or bacteria are irritating or stimulating the skin and causing the grease to be produced, fungicides and bactericides may be helpful, as may alkaline rinses.

!

Health & Safety

When treating dandruff or greasy hair, try one product at a time. Give it time to work before trying something else.

oily skin surface

excess sebum

sebum collects in follicle

extended sebaceous gland produces too much sebum

Greasy scalp

These deal with the grease that is present: as with other problems, it is also important to identify the causes and deal with those too if possible.

Other hair conditions

- **Fragilitas crinium (split ends)** – treat with substantive conditioners or restructurants, and by cutting.
- **Damaged cuticle** – treat with products such as protective conditioners, restructurants or rehabilitating creams.
- **Trichorrhexis nodosa** – treat with protein hydrolysates or substantive conditioners.
- **Dry, brittle, broken, over-processed hair** – treat with rehabilitating creams, moisturisers, restructurants or protein hydrolysates.

These conditions (also discussed in Chapter 1) may be caused by bad grooming, sleeping in rollers and curlers, wearing postiche too long, using poorly made combs and brushes, bad perm winding, chemical over-processing, and overexposure to sun, wind and the like. Explain to your client the cause of the condition and encourage them to deal with the causes of the problem.

Where possible, cutting should be used to remove the worst areas of hair splitting.

Before and after processing

Where the cuticle has been damaged, the hair cortex becomes too porous, like a sponge, soaking up any chemicals applied to the hair. Older hair is more likely to be damaged than newer growth. The porosity must be reduced before hair can successfully be permed or coloured.

Pre-perm treatments consist of lotions or creams that make porosity uniform throughout the hair, so that perm lotion will be taken up evenly. Pre-colouring treatments have a similar function, 'filling' or repairing areas of the cuticle. Use only conditioners that have been specially designed for use before chemical hairdressing processes, because these allow other materials to pass through to the hair – they are **permeable**. Conditioners that have not been designed to do this may form a barrier and make a process such as perming ineffective. Before using any conditioner, always check the manufacturer's instructions.

After processing, hair may need further treatment. For example, the hair's normal state is slightly acid: many processes use alkaline solutions, so an acid conditioner may be needed at the end to correct the pH. Acid balancers and antioxidants help to remove surplus chemicals such as hydrogen peroxide, and to smooth the hair cuticle and keep it manageable.

Mark Hill

Maintaining a healthy condition

Keeping hair in good condition requires the regular use of conditioners to reduce the effects of harsh chemical and physical treatments.

Many poor hair states are caused by ignoring the basic principles of good hairdressing and grooming – cleaning and rinsing the hair correctly, carrying out processes as recommended, and handling the hair gently will all help to ensure good hair condition. Conditioners will keep healthy hair looking good and help in styling.

 Activity

In your 'product knowledge' book, keep records of the different conditioners and treatments you use, and their effects on the different heads of hair. Don't forget those you use on your own hair!

Other treatments

The following treatments (with or without conditioners) may usefully be applied to the hair and scalp:

- massage
- steamers
- accelerators
- rollerballs
- radiant heat
- oil treatments, shampoos and applications.

Massage

Massage is a method of manipulating the skin and muscles. It may be applied by hand or machine, for example a vibro machine or high-frequency machine. In the salon you will apply massage to the scalp, neck and face only.

Effects of massage

These include the following:

- improved blood flow to the skin – the redness this produces is called **hyperaemia**
- stimulation and soothing of nerve endings
- improved muscle tone, assisting normal contraction and relaxation

Effleurage

Pétrissage

Friction

Tip

Use a timer for accuracy when you are giving massage.

- removal of congestions or fatty lumps or adhesions in the skin
- improved removal of waste matter from the skin surface
- stimulation of the skin and of appendages such as hair follicles
- improved functioning of cells in the skin, including their nutrition, diffusion within them, and their ability to secrete substances.

There are several hand massage movements. Those of special interest to hairdressers are effleurage, pétrissage, tapotement, vibration and friction.

Effleurage – a smoothing, soothing, stroking action, performed with firm but gentle movements of the hands and fingertips. You use it before and after the most vigorous movements. It improves skin functions, soothes and stimulates nerves and relaxes tensed muscles.

Pétrissage – a deeper, circular kneading movement, used to break down adhesions or fatty congestions in the skin. It assists the elimination of waste products and the flow of nutrients to the tissues of skin and muscles. It is usually used during conditioning treatments.

Tapotement – a stimulating tapping or patting movement – a rapid, gentle beating applied with the hands and fingertips. Tapotement is used to stimulate nerves, restore muscle tone, and free the skin of fatty deposits. It is *not* recommended for scalp massage – it is mainly used on the body, on the hands and, lightly, on the face.

Friction – a rubbing movement applied with the fingertips in a light, flicking, gently plucking action. It is used on the scalp when applying lotions or during shampooing.

Vibration – a shaking movement, similar to friction but deeper. Light vibrations are soothing, heavier ones are more stimulating. These movements may be imitated by vibratory machines, commonly called 'vibros' and mainly used on the body. They *may* be used on the scalp, but only gently and carefully.

Points to remember

- Massage is only beneficial when applied in a quiet atmosphere. Keep noise and discussion to a minimum.
- Avoid hard, jerky, heavy movements to the scalp or head – these can only cause your client discomfort.
- Complete massage should not take longer than 15 minutes. Overstimulation might cause a headache, muscle fatigue or other problems.
- Do *not* give massage if there are any **contraindications** – inflammation, breaks in the skin, spots, rashes or signs of disease, or if the client is undergoing medical treatment.
- Do *not* give massage if the client has recently had a perm or colour.

Tip

All massage movements should be rotated to avoid discomfort to the client. Avoid tangling the hair, particularly when massaging long hair.

Applying scalp massage

Scalp massage stimulates grease production and loosens skin, scale and dirt from the pores, so it is best given before shampooing. If the scalp or hair is very dirty, shampoo before *and* after massage. The duration of the massage depends on the client. Some people can stand more stimulation than others; older clients, for example, may be more sensitive.

A spirit-based massage lotion may help your hands and fingers to grip the skin surface. Remember that discussion between you and the client during massage will cause muscle tension to return, destroying the benefit of the massage.

Providing hand massage

1   Seat your client comfortably, with suitable protective garments.

2   Use effleurage first. Draw your fingertips firmly, but not too hard, over the head. Your hands should move from the front hairline down to the nape and shoulder tops.

   Repeat this several times. Make sure that the whole scalp is covered in this way. This soothes the skin surface and the underlying structures, relaxing the client.

3   Next use pétrissage. Apply this lightly but firmly: hard, fierce movements may rupture small blood vessels and cause discomfort.

   With the fingertips, feel through the hair to the scalp, and gently rotate the scalp over the skull. To achieve and maintain the correct balance, pressure and movement, claw the fingers and move them towards the thumbs. Slowly and gently cover the whole scalp, without exerting too much pressure. Use the small fingers, particularly on the temples.

4   Finally, use effleurage again: this removes excess blood brought to the scalp.

5   Allow your client to sit quietly for a while, to enjoy the effects of the massage.

Wella

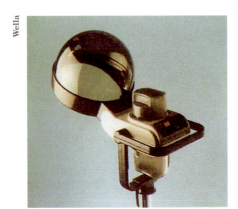

A steamer

Steamers

Steamers are commonly used to apply moist heat to the skin and hair. They may be used before or during conditioning.

When you place the steamer over the client's head, steam is able to flow around the hair, which expands and softens. This helps conditioners to pass through the cuticle and enter the cortex of the hair. Conditioning products may be placed in the water reservoir and applied, with steam, to the hair. Steamers are beneficial when colouring and bleaching as they halve the normal processing time.

To achieve satisfactory results, always check the manufacturer's instructions before using the steamer.

Tip

Use distilled or deionised water in steamer kettles to prevent limescale build-up.

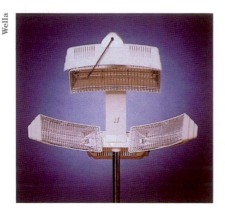

An accelerator

A rollerball

Tip

Check electrical equipment is working correctly before using it on your client.

Activity

Place a dry hair practice block (or samples of very dry hair in poor condition) under a steamer, and steam for several minutes. Note how much more resilient, or elastic, the hair becomes.

Accelerators

Accelerators use radiated light and dry heat. They are useful for deep penetration of conditioning products. Like steamers, they help the hair to absorb conditioners and so reduce the processing time.

Rollerballs

The rollerball is a kind of accelerator, using infra-red heat and also offering a fan. The source of the heat moves continually, preventing 'hotspots'. Hairdressing processes can be carried out while it is in use. The rollerball can be used while perming, colouring or treating the hair, or simply to dry it.

Radiant heat and infra-red lamps

Like accelerators, radiant heat and infra-red radiation are used to irradiate the head and hair. The shorter rays of infra-red and radiant heat penetrate deep into the skin. Accelerators are used to activate certain chemical processes or to heat the hair before conditioning.

Scalp massage using electrical equipment

Scalp massage can be performed using either a vibro massage machine or a high-frequency machine.

The vibro or vibratory machine is an electrically operated massager designed to produce vibratory movements similar to pétrissage and friction movements of hand massage.

The vibro machine usually has a number of attachments:

- A spiked rubber-pronged applicator for use on the scalp
- A soft rubber sponge for use on the face
- A hard rubber applicator for use on nerve endings and stimulation.

How to use a vibro massager

The vibratory machine is controlled by both hands: one holds the machine firmly while the other controls its direction.

Health & Safety

Jewellery should be removed or covered before the massage commences as they may cause irritation through sparking of electricity where skin contact is made.

Vibratory machine and applicators

- Use before shampooing as the movement will loosen scale and grease
- Apply circular movements on the scalp or in straight movements from the forehead to the neck
- Lift the machine from the head at regular intervals to prevent the hair over tangling
- The spiked attachment is used directly on the scalp
- The harder rubber attachment is often used over your fingers to protect the clients scalp
- The massage treatment should not last longer than 15 minutes
- Do not put added pressure on to the machine – the machine's weight is sufficient

How to use a high-frequency massager

High frequency is the term given to an electrical current produced by a high-frequency portable generator which produces a high voltage and low current strength.

There are two methods of applying high-frequency massage: direct and indirect.

The direct method consists of applying glass electrodes to the skin. These include:

- A round glass bulb for use on the bare areas of the face or scalp in a rotary action
- A glass comb or rake for use on the hair on the head, passing through the hair upwards towards the crown.

Before applying any electrode to your client you should touch it until it is placed on the scalp. This prevents sudden sparking of the current between the electrode and the skin. The recommended time for using each electrode is 3 minutes.

The indirect method is applied by your client holding a metal bar or saturator in their hands. When the current is switched on it is directed on to the scalp by your hands. As your fingers touch the client's skin the electrical current flows from the machine to your client through the bar they are holding to your fingers. You can then massage the scalp.

The current should be low for the first treatments and only increase when your client's tolerance increases and they become more comfortable with the treatment. Total treatment time can also be increased but should not exceed 12 minutes.

When not to use high frequency

High-frequency massage should not be carried out if:

- There are signs of inflammation
- Evidence of skin disorder
- The client is receiving medical treatment

- Electrodes or other parts of the machine are cracked or damaged
- You are near water.

Oils

Oils are useful for conditioning very dry, overbleached or overprocessed hair.

Oil applications or treatments

These consist in the use of a vegetable oil (such as olive or almond oil) directly on the hair and scalp. Use a brush or cottonwool to apply the oil.

1   Preheat the oil to a comfortable temperature. Never use hot oil, as this is dangerous and could burn. Alternatively, apply heat to the hair using hot towels, heat lamps, a steamer or an accelerator, before or after applying the oil.
2   Allow the oil to remain on the hair for 5–15 minutes. During this time you could apply a vibro massage.
3   Remove the oil from the head, first applying soapless shampoo: the shampoo combines with (emulsifies) the oil, and can then be rinsed off with water. Do not apply water first – it would prevent the shampoo from combining with the oil, so that after rinsing there would still be oil coating the hair and skin.

Oil shampoos

Oil shampoos contain conditioning agents and emollients or tissue softeners. They are pH-adjusted; they regulate the acid balance of the hair (see page 60–61).

1   Use oil shampoos similarly to oil applications, heated as described above. You may apply hand or vibro massage while shampooing.
2   Remove the shampoo by rinsing with water, lathering, and finally rinsing the hair.

Chris Moody

Conditioning and hair care products

- After conditioning, the hair should be smooth and shiny, and the cuticle should have been repaired. It should look and feel better.
- The hair should be more pliable, more elastic and more resilient. Setting and styling should hold longer.
- The hair should be tangle-free.
- Apply chemical processes only after careful testing – assess the condition thoroughly first.
- Read manufacturers' instructions carefully before applying conditioners or using equipment.

- Make sure the hair is towel-dry before applying conditioners. Excess water could dilute them and reduce their effectiveness.
- Help your client to improve the home management of their hair – advise on home treatments that will help to maintain the improved condition. Recommend the correct retail products your salon has on offer – see Chapter 2 – and when to return to the salon.
- For future reference, note on the client's record card details of conditioning treatments given.
- Make sure that the client is satisfied with the condition of their hair, and so will feel encouraged to return to the salon again.

 Activity

Look through the salon's client records. Note those of any clients who have been ill. Have these clients experienced any ill effects after having hair processes such as perms and tints?

Product summary

Many types of product are available – choose one to suit the hair's state.

Shampoos	Jojoba	For dry hair
	Soya	For normal hair
	Lemon	For greasy hair
	Medicated	For various hair types
Setting and shaping agents	Setting lotions, gels, mousses, glitz, glaze, gloss, and wax	Used to hold or coat the hair when it is wet
	Plastics and PVP	Leave a film on the hair, help to wet the hair, resist the effect of moisture, reduce static electricity and help hair to hold its style longer
	Cationic detergents and cetrimide	Keep hair pliable, help repair damaged hair, reduce static and add shine
	Plasticisers, emollients and moisturisers	Combine the features of other styling and shaping agents

Hair thickeners and builders	Cationic detergents	Give body to the hair
	Protein hydrolysates	Attach to the hair and thicken it
Conditioning rinses and agents	Lemon juice (citric acid)	Remove soap scum
	Humectants	Smooth the cuticle, make it easy to comb the hair and counteract alkaline effects
	Vinegar (acetic acid)	Removes soap scum, reduces alkaline effects, smooths the hair surface and helps to ease combing
	Beer or champagne	Adds body and smooths the cuticle
	Cream rinses and mousses	Helps ease combing and brushing
	Cetrimide	Used after chemical processing, aids damaged cuticles, smooths the hair surface, acts as antioxidant and pH balancer
Restructurants	Rinses, creams, gels, mousses made from quaternary ammonium compounds, protein hydrolysates, protein from soya and keratinous products	Penetrate and aid damaged hair, repair and fill the hair structure, soften hair, smooth the cuticle, add shine, make the hair pliable and able to hold a shape and thickens fine hair
Antioxidants	Rinses, lotions and creams	Used after bleach and colours to stop oxidation and neutralise alkalis
pH balancers	Rinses, lotions and creams	Used after chemical processing to counteract oxidation
Dressings	Control creams, vegetable and mineral oils, gels and gloss	Smooth the hair surface, soften the cuticle, retain moisture, add shine and are a dressing aid
Hairsprays	Shellac (hard coating), plastic (pliable coating)	Resist moisture helping to retain the style/shape/curl and can help smooth the cuticle

Health & Safety

Dipping your fingers into containers is unhygienic. Use a spatula or a tissue, once, then discard it.

Two-in-one technology

Products that combine both a shampoo and a conditioner – '2 in 1' are effective and popular. A chemical in the shampoo forms a molecular lattice, on which the conditioner is suspended. The hair is washed, when it is rinsed, the water breaks down the lattice and releases the conditioner. Further washing removes the conditioner.

Assignments – Shampooing and conditioning hair

A practical activity

The process of selecting suitable shampoos and conditioners is important. In the beginning it helps to work with your colleagues to establish a procedure which will elicit all the facts on which to base choice. Work through the following sequence:

1   Examine each other's hair and scalp. Note down what you see.

2   List the questions you might ask, such as: 'What has the client been using? What have been the results? Why is the client not satisfied? What problems has the client had?', and so on.

3   Determine the state of hair and skin.

4   Note down carefully the different conditions present.

5   Consider the range of products available. What are their advantages and disadvantages?

6   What hairdressing services have been previously carried out for the individual? What is intended to be carried out next?

When you have established a reliable process of selection, extend it to meet the requirements of your clients. Be methodical and compile your notes so that further information can be added or changes made.

For you to find out

Investigate all the sources of information you can find that deal with shampoos, shampooing, conditioners and conditioning. Use your libraries, local stores and chemists' shops to find out what is available, particularly for home use. Product knowledge sessions with your wholesalers and manufacturers can be very helpful for studying products for salon use. Don't forget to look at trade publications and manufacturers' websites before answering these questions.

1   What shampoos are there available? What are the differences? List the ranges. Note their contents and prices.

2   What conditioners are there available? What are the differences? List the ranges. Note the contents and prices.

3   How are they applied? Is any special equipment required?

4   How do the different shampoos and conditioners work?

5   What is 'detergency'?

6   Outline a shampooing method. Name the massage movements used.

7   How does water affect shampooing?

8   What is the pH scale? How does it affect shampooing?

A case study

A client of yours has extremely dry hair, breaking at the points. It is unruly and unmanageable. Describe how you would proceed to deal with this client.

Work through the following sequence, writing down the outcome of each step.

1 Find out what has been used on the hair. (Use your question list.)

2 Find out what physical or chemical hairdressing processes have been applied.

3 Determine the type, texture and condition of the hair throughout its length.

4 Decide which products to use, and explain to the client why you are proposing to use them. Agree on what is to be done, how long it will take and how much it will cost.

5 Note the results and effects produced. Keep notes for your folder and record card.

6 Ensure that treatment is continued by advising the client what to use, and how to use it, at home.

7 Examine hair and scalp carefully on subsequent visits and amend the treatment if necessary.

8 Add any further information that you think is necessary and discuss with your trainer.

Preparing for Assessment

In preparing for assessments on shampooing and conditioning hair, the following checklist may be useful. Check that you have covered and now fully understand these items:

- analysing different hair conditions
- applying suitable examination and consultative techniques
- selecting from a range of suitable shampoos, conditioners and treatments
- applying good shampooing and conditioning techniques
- understanding the massage movements and when they should or should not be applied
- compiling and applying product knowledge
- maintaining accurate and careful records of information
- applying any further information you think necessary.

When you feel that you are ready, talk to your trainer and arrange a suitable time for your assessment.

By reading this chapter, carrying out the above activities, assignments and the case study, and by meeting the requirements in preparing for assessment you will have worked towards the key skill requirements in Communication Level 1 (C 1.1) (C 1.2) (C 1.3) and Level 2 (C 2.1) (C 2.2).

If you have used a computer to complete your assignments or activities you will have worked towards the key skill requirements in Information Technology Level 1 (IT 1.2).

Drying hair

Mahogany

Learning objectives

The following are some of the topics that are covered in this chapter:

- equipment/tools and product
- styling aids
- blow-drying
- scrunch-drying
- blow-waving
- hand or finger drying
- dealing with complaints.

Introduction

After shampooing, cutting, colouring, perming or relaxing your client's hair, you need to consider how the hair is to be finished. Does the hair require positioning or placing? Should it be left to dry naturally? Other options that should be considered are:

- setting the hair into shape and drying under a hood dryer using a variety of techniques, such as pin-curling, rollering or fingerwaving; techniques of this kind are described in Chapter 5
- blow-styling, using a variety of techniques
- heat-moulding, using a variety of techniques and tools to dry and shape the hair are described in Chapter 5
- towel-drying or blow-drying the hair and then applying a heat-moulding technique to shape it.

Whichever method you use to dry the hair, the following points also require consideration:

- applying the different forms of drying and shaping to a variety of hair lengths and shapes – above or below the shoulders, layered lengths and so on
- determining the important factors influencing the finished shape, such as the client's hair cut or style, their hair growth patterns, hair texture and structure, and whether it is curly, wavy or straight
- application of hair cosmetics and aids to drying and shaping, such as setting/finishing sprays, gels or mousses.

Study this chapter together with Chapter 5, Setting and dressing hair, and Chapter 6, Cutting and styling hair.

Richard Thompson, Mahogany

Blow-shaping

Drying hair to shape and creating a finished look

Tip

Don't let the hair to be styled dry out. Keep it moist during the styling process to ensure a smooth, balanced finished shape.

Drying hair – the principles

Drying hair is the process of styling wet hair while blow-drying it. Using a hand-held dryer, you use a variety of techniques to create different effects. While directing heated air on to the wet hair, you mould the hair with brushes, combs or your fingers, positioning it to fit the style for which it has been cut. Chapter 5 explains changes to the hair structure which occur during drying and setting.

Like other methods of setting wet hair (see Chapter 5), blow-styling works by changing the hair's structure. Wet hair can stretch, adding up to 50 per cent to its length. Heat softens it: the weaker links

Tip

If the hair is left to dry naturally it takes the shape of natural growth patterns (see page 121), which need to be fully considered.

between the polypeptide chains (the hydrogen bonds and salt bridges) are broken, allowing the keratin to stretch and change from its alpha to its beta form. While hair is wet, and heat is applied, it can be moulded into a chosen shape.

The styled shape is only temporary, though – as the hair gradually absorbs moisture from the atmosphere, it returns to its original state. Combing styled hair with hot water returns the hair to its natural form straight away.

Equipment/tools/products

Health & Safety

All tools and equipment should be tested periodically by a qualified electrician. The tests should be recorded (with dates) and the equipment should be clearly labelled.

- **The hand-held dryer** is the most important piece of equipment you need. There is a wide range of models to choose from. The dryer should have adjustable speeds and temperatures, and be designed for long periods of use. It needs to be light and easy to hold, and to have controls positioned where they are easy to reach when in use. There should be a means of attaching it safely to the bench when not in use.

- **Hand dryer attachments** – such as nozzles and diffusers – are available (see page 84–85). Using the dryer without a nozzle or diffuser allows for a wider directed air flow.

A hand-held infra-red dryer

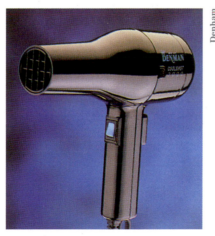

A hand-held dryer

Hand-held dryer and styling brushes

Activity

At your wholesaler's, look at the different types of hand-held hairdryer. Professional models are designed to be used continuously in the salon. Compare these with the hairdryers in the shops, which are designed for home use. Clients often ask which is the best dryer for home use: what would you say?

Health & Safety

Metal combs retain heat and can burn the skin.

Tip

Always dry the roots first, before the middle and end lengths of the hair. If you don't do this, the hair won't lie in the direction of the style you intend.

Styling products

- **Brushes** are probably the most important items after blow-dryers. A firm, stiff, bristle or plastic brush is required. This will help you to grip, direct and control the hair. (Soft brushes are suitable only for finishing.) Half-round plastic brushes are used for general shaping. Larger types are best used on long hair, smaller for short-to-medium hair. A range of smaller roller brushes on which to form shapes is also required. Different brushes are necessary for particular shapes.

- **Combs** should be professional and heat-resistant. The comb you will use most will have both widely spaced and narrowly spaced teeth.

Activity

Various different attachments for hairdryers are made. What are they, and what do they do? Check the manufacturers' instructions, and practise handling these attachments.

Styling aids

Blow-styling, setting, styling and dressing can be usefully aided by using some of a large variety of products. Most hair cosmetic manufacturers feature them. Some are physically designed to give added support to the hair shapes, so as to retain style as long as possible. Others have a chemically bonding action with the internal hair structure, which both retains moisture and resists the effects of excess moisture on newly shaped hair styles. Yet others combine both physical and chemical attributes that enhance hair shaping and styling.

There are aids available to meet most needs. Product knowledge will help you select the correct one for your client. The aids in the following list may contain **plasticisers** to enfold and support the hair, moisturisers to retain or resist moisture (see page 62), protective **screeners**, silicone **shiners**, **sun carers** and so on.

Tip

There are so many recent developments in style aids that you will need to visit manufacturers and wholesalers regularly to maintain and update your product knowledge.

Health & Safety

Always check tools and equipment before use to make sure that they are safe to use.

Activity

Collect information on the different drying and styling products available – set out a chart/table to describe what the product is, when it is used and how to use it.

If you use a computer to produce your chart/tables, you will have worked towards the key skill requirement Information Technology (IT1.2).

- **Blow-styling aids** protect the hair from excessive heat, increase the length of time for which the hair shape is held, and give body to the hair. There are different strengths – firm hold, extra hold, medium hold, ultra, ultimate and so forth – for different hair conditions and texture types. Different products are sold for use before, during and after blow-styling.

- **Dressing aids** give sheen, shine, gloss or glitz to the hair. Gels, oils, silicones, mousses, foams and waxes may be used to reflect light and to enhance a healthy-looking head of hair.

- **Setting aids** enhance the hair's elasticity, help the hair to keep its spring and bounce, and allow it to stretch easily. Volume/styling/body-building mousses, soft-shaping gels, sprays and styling creams, cetrimide conditioners and finishing hairstyle sprays are all commonly used.

- **Protectors** shield the hair from the harsh effects of exposure to the sun – for example, sunscreeners, sun care sprays and ultra-violet filters and gels.

- **Curl enhancers** enable the hair to retain curl or wave formation longer and include perm enhancers, maximum-curl retainers and volume, movement and shape revitalisers.

Blow-styling technique

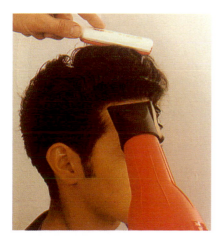

Blow-styling

The technique you choose will be determined by the hair texture, the quality and quantity of hair, the style to be produced, and the cut. The most suitable hair for blow-styling is firm, thick, coarse hair. There are now a number of styling aids – thickeners, setting mousses and gels – which are designed to give direction to the hair. Fine, fluffy hair requires the help of one of these if you are to obtain successful results.

Whether the client's hair is curly, wavy or straight, whether the length is above or below the shoulder, whether it is layered or is cut to give a one-length look, the techniques in the following list can be adapted for both ladies and men's hairstyles.

- **Blow-waving** – shaping the hair into waves, using directed heated air from a dryer, and combs, brushes or your hands. It achieves natural, soft fullness (see page 84).

An Airstyler – dries, smooths and shapes the hair in a single process

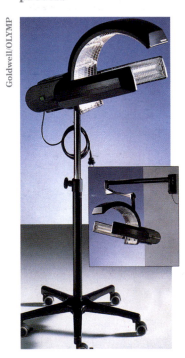

A heat lamp

- **Blow-drying** – simply drying the hair with the hand-held dryer. It is usual to blow-dry hair into a chosen shape, or in a required direction (see below)
- **Scrunch drying** – gripping and squeezing clumps of hair, while directing heated air into the hand. The process yields a casual, ruffled, moulded shape (see page 83).
- **Finger or hand drying** – lifting, teasing, pulling and directing hair with the fingers or hands. Casual, soft and full shapes can be achieved. Billowing fullness is perhaps the chief effect.
- **Blow-combing** – drying and shaping using a comb, or a comb attachment fixed to the hairdryer. It is a kind of blow-drying, and achieves shape and direction.
- **Blow-stretching or straightening** – a means of smoothing, unkinking or straightening the hair. A variety of brush shapes and sizes may be used (see page 85).

Blow-styling consists of first shampooing the hair, then softening it with a dryer or heated lamp, and finally moulding it into shape using a blow-dryer. It may be dressed, if required, when the hair has cooled.

Natural drying – leaving the hair to dry naturally – may be chosen, depending on whether the cut and the style are suitable. Natural drying may be assisted by the heat of the sun, infra-red lamps, accelerators, rollerballs or other equipment.

Preparing hair for blow-styling

1   Shampoo and towel the hair dry, then comb out any tangles.
2   Cut the hair into style.
3   Apply a suitable blow-styling aid, such as mousse, gel or lotion, if required.
4   Section the hair – the longer the hair, the more sections you will need.
5   Clip long hair out of the way and re-section it as required.
6   Position and grip the hair with a brush, a comb or your fingers to control it.

Blow-drying

You can start blow-drying at any part of the head. On long hair it is best to dry the lower, underneath sections first. With practice you will achieve a continually moving brush technique, with the lift and control required. Do not allow the top sections, which are still wet, to fall on to the lower, previously dried ones: this spoils work done and wastes time. Clip wet hair well out of the way.

Blow-styling works best on coarse hair. Fine hair may quickly become overheated and overdried. When dealing with short hair, take care not to blow it out of line. The air stream should be directed the way the hair is intended to lie. Short hair may be best rolled on to a circular brush, allowed to cool, and combed or dressed into position.

Tip

Remember that dryers blow out and suck in air. Ensure that the client's hair, your clothes or towels are not sucked into the dryer, which could get blocked.

Tip

Blow-drying against the natural growth direction achieves maximum lift.

Peter Hickman

John Phelps

Scrunch drying

Which tool or technique you use depends on the style effects required. For full, soft effects use large, round brushes. For more bounce and curl, use smaller brushes. Fluffy effects may be achieved with open bristle brushes. A general method is as follows:

1   Towel-dry the hair. With hands and fingers loosely stroking and lifting the hair, remove any excess moisture. Apply mousse or blow-drying aids, if required.

2   Cleanly divide small sections of hair. The angle to lift the hair is determined by the fullness required. Lift the hair to allow the heated air to penetrate the section. For one-length, bobbed shapes, take sections horizontally or diagonally. For swept-back shapes, use vertical sections.

3   It is important to work methodically and cleanly. Make sure that the hair not being dried is clipped up, so that it cannot get in the way.

4   Place the sectioned hair on to the brush with the thumb or fingers. When the hair is firmly in position on the brush, begin directing heated air on to it – first on one side of the section, then on the other. With the brush, direct the hair section away from the head so that the root ends are thoroughly dried. Do not wind the brush right down – allow space for the hair to be dried. Keep the brush moving as the heated air is passed repeatedly over the section, winding the hair up and down to allow the warm air to penetrate the hair fully. Make sure each section is fully dry before passing on to the next.

5   Allow the hair to cool before removing the brush – when warm, it is still soft.

6   For maximum lift, hold the hair section well up from the scalp. Keep the dryer close to the hair but moving, and directed away from the scalp. This action should be for short periods of time. Generally, hold the dryer about 30 cm from the hair – do not hold the dryer or direct the air flow too close to the scalp, as the heat from the dryer will burn your client's scalp. For wedge shapes, blow air through the hair section as the hair is allowed to flick from the brush in a combing, lifting action.

Scrunch drying

1   Prepare the hair for blow-drying by removing excess moisture with a towel, or hood drying the loose hair.

2   Run the fingers through the hair and lift it from the scalp. As you lift it, grip it firmly. Direct the heated air into your hand just before closing your grip. Hold the hair firmly and continue drying.

3   To see the effect produced, tousle the hair by shaking it. It is important to follow the shaping process in the mirror.

4   Continue to direct the hot air into the palm of the hand, to prevent discomfort. Repeat the process of blow-drying, gripping the hair, and lifting hair sections, to increase volume and shape.

5   Work from side to side. Make sure each section is dry before proceeding to the next.

Providing the shape is carefully studied, a full, lightly tousled effect can be produced by this method.

John Phelps

Finger drying

Andrew Collinge. Photo: John Swannell

Tip

The depth of the wave or the height of the crest is determined by the angle the hair is combed.

Health & Safety

Do not try to blow-wave when the hair is too dry or wet. Keep the airstream moving, to prevent discomfort.

Hand or finger drying

This is similar to scrunch drying, but uses hands and fingers to lift, mould and shape the hair. It gives a wider, looser, billowing fullness.

Activity

Select three textured practice blocks of different hair and blow-style each in a very full style. Leave them in the salon where they can absorb atmospheric moisture. Note how long the different textures of hair hold their shape and position.

Blow-waving

A method of waving using a comb or brush, carefully directed heated air, and a series of shaping movements is often used when styling men's hair. Position the hair into a crest formation and direct heated air through a nozzle attachment. Control the waves by comb or brush movements in relation to the hair position. Repeated combing or brushing is required to shape the hair.

1   Begin at the front hairline and follow the hair's natural movements.

2   With the wide-toothed end of the comb, make a backward, slightly turning movement, gripping the hair and holding it in a wave-crest shape.

3   Direct warm air on to the trough below the crest. The airstream should be opposite to the direction of the comb holding the hair. The airstream should be at half strength, or the hair will be blown away from the comb.

4   Movements of both hands must be coordinated and repeated. Continually move the dryer along the hair. This directs the heat evenly and avoids burning the scalp.

5   The second crest is formed similarly to the first. Direct the airflow along the line the hair is intended to lie. This produces the required line and shape. When you reach the hair ends, position them in line with the waves formed.

6   Use of the coarse end of the comb allows air penetration and speeds the process. For finishing, use the fine end. A smooth finish can be obtained by lightly blowing through a net stretched over a frame.

Blow-drying tools

Apart from the variety of brushes and hand-held dryers, the diffuser and nozzle are particularly useful.

The diffuser fits over the end of the hair dryer and distributes an even flow of warm air. It reduces a strong air flow to a gentle one, and is used for finishing styles. It is ideal for producing soft, casual, ruffled, natural curl looks. It can be used on various hair lengths.

The nozzle is intended to concentrate the hot air flow on to a specific area. It is ideal for blow-waving, as it allows the air to be directed at the troughs and crests of the wave shapes.

Electrically heated styling irons or tongs are often used to finalise a dried hair shape. The hair is rolled and held in place long enough for the heat to soften the hair. The irons are then slid out to leave a smooth rolled shape, similar to that produced by rollers. The various angles and directions into which the hair is placed determines the final style.

Electrically heated hot brushes and heated rollers are available in several sizes. They are applied to the dried hair in a similar manner to styling tongs. They are popular in many salons, and a great many clients use them at home.

BaByliss

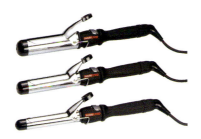

Heated brushes and tongs

 Activity

Collect three types of hairspray and try them out on fine and coarse hair. Position the hair on a practice block or sample so that the hair is sprayed in an upright position. Over the next few days, note which is quickest in absorbing moisture from the atmosphere.

Blow-stretching or straightening

This involves the technique of stretching the hair rather than waving it. The aim is to straighten and smooth the hair lengths. Use larger, round brushes under or on sections of hair, and turn them to grip and slightly stretch the hair. This technique produces soft, slightly lifted shapes on very short hair, and sleek straightness on long hair. The brush size must be varied to suit different lengths of hair. Use a hand-held dryer, as in blow-drying, and direct the heated air on to the stretched hair. This technique is equally suitable for women's and men's hairstyles. You may also use heated combs for straightening hair.

John Phelps

Blow-stretching

 Tip

Make sure the filter on the hairdryer is cleaned regularly – if blocked it could damage the dryer.

Don't hold the dryer too close to your body. If you do it will pick up fluff from your clothes, which may block the filter.

Don't rev the dryer motor – this eventually causes it to overheat and fuse.

Health & Safety

Use only professional tools.

Ensure that all electrical equipment is in good order.

Never use electrical equipment with wet hands – you might be electrocuted.

Never use faulty equipment.

Work comfortably. Avoid continually twisting or stretching your body.

Maintain high standards of hygiene.

Test the heat of the dryer before applying it to the hair – you may cause discomfort to your client or damage to the hair. If the air is too hot for the skin, it is too hot for the hair.

Direct hot air away from the scalp.

Do not keep the dryer in one place too long.

When straightening, never overstretch the hair.

Do not attempt to shape hair when it is too wet.

Tugging and pulling the hair may cause breakage.

Use suitable blow-styling aids, such as lotions and creams, to protect the hair from overheating.

Do not blow-style hair that is in poor condition.

Blow-drying and shaping: a summary

Length/texture	*Tools*	*Techniques*	*Effects/results*
Short; tight/very curly/fine/medium/coarse	Small round brushes to form roller shapes to grip/smooth/straighten	Blow-drying	Smoother, looser, more wavy
Short; curly/wavy, medium/coarse	Small/curved round brushes with/without diffuser	Finger drying, scrunch and blow-waving	Fashion, natural, casual
Short, one-length looks	Small; curved, vent brushes	Blow-combing/scrunch/natural/finger drying, blow drying	Casual, spiky, flat or lifted
Medium-length/below-nape, above-shoulder; loose curl/wave, medium/coarse (most versatile)	Curved/half-round/vent/flat/circular/small/medium brushes	Blow/finger drying scrunch	Tight, loose, curled, wavy, straight, ruffled, casual or set
Long, below-shoulder, one-length bobs; wavy/straight, medium/coarse	Large/flat/circular brushes	Finger/natural drying, blow drying (beware of snagging long hair)	Lifted, or flowing, smooth or straighter
Layered looks, varied lengths; slightly wavy, medium/coarse	Variety: round, curved, vent/circular etc.	Finger/hand/scrunch drying	A variety of tousled natural, casual, ruffled looks

Notes

1 Short and medium-length hair that is slightly wavy and of medium-to-coarse texture is probably ideal for blow-drying techniques.

2 Varying the dryer speed gives you better control of the hair, particularly longer hair.

Dealing with complaints

For safe drying/styling:

- Check all tools before use
- Handle tools as recommended
- Store all electrical tools as directed
- Report any damage as soon as possible.

If your client does not like the style you have produced, the following may help:

- Take steps to rectify the complaint as soon as possible.
- Try to see the client's point of view and be sympathetic in your response.
- Explain that the new style requires time to adapt to.
- Honestly justify what you believe is correct and suitable.
- Do not talk the client into something that you do not believe is suitable.
- Do not allow the client to leave with a poor shape or style.
- It is relatively simple to rectify a blow-style by redressing, resetting, wetting the hair and blow-drying it again.
- Exercise tact, understanding and courtesy throughout.
- Most clients do not like to express displeasure and may become distressed. Be aware of this, and make sure your client really is satisfied.

See also Chapter 2.

Assignments – Drying hair

A practical activity

Using your practice blocks, hair switches or models, experiment by applying the different blow-styling and heat-moulding techniques. Note the differences produced on the different hair textures and densities. Use photographs, sketches and video taping to capture the 'before' and 'after' effects. Then answer these questions.

1 What happens to the hair structure during blow-styling? Make sketches where possible.

2 What effects do the different hair-drying techniques produce? List these.

3 List the best drying techniques to use on hair of different lengths. Consider, for example, below-shoulder-length hair, layered lengths, one-length styles and as many others as you can. Keep your list in your folder.

4 How do you choose which products to use on the different hair types? How do you know that they will be suitable? What questions would you ask? List these.

5 Your client is considering changing from setting to blow-styling. What advice would you give? List the points that you would put to your client.

For you to find out

Investigate the variety of hair cosmetics that are available for blow-styling, heat-moulding and setting. Check in your local stores and chemists' shops for information on home use products and check manufacturers' websites for information. Check how these compare with products used in your salon: compare prices, effects, package sizes and so forth. Then answer these questions. Keep your answers in your folder.

1 How could you present a new hair cosmetic to your clients? How could you prove its suitability.

2 How would you explain the effects of the different hair cosmetics used for blow-styling and shaping? List these, and keep your list for reference.

3 List the differences between the various hair cosmetics.

4 What after-care advice do you give your clients regarding hair-drying to shape and the use of hair cosmetics? List the points that you can make.

A case study

Your client has fine hair which has previously been set. They feel that this is old-fashioned and would like to change to blow-styling.

1 How do you deal with this? Briefly outline and list the points that you would make.

2 If blow-styling would not suit your client, how could you explain and justify the alternatives you propose?

3 How would you deal with the aftercare required? What do you propose?

4 List the products, equipment and tools that you would require to meet your client's wishes.

5 What problems might arise? List the precautions to be taken.

Preparing for Assessment

In preparing for assessment on drying hair the following checklist may be useful. Check that you have covered and now fully understand these items:

- checking a client's previous hairdressing history
- discussing the possible limitations of hair type, condition and so on
- determining a suitable blow-style, and agreeing it with the client
- explaining the techniques and movement sequences

- ensuring that the equipment used is safe
- applying suitable hair cosmetics
- anticipating problems that might arise
- being familiar with the precautions that need to be taken
- ensuring cleanliness of all tools
- completing short or long hair styles in the given salon time.

When you feel that you are ready, talk to your trainer and arrange a suitable time for your assessment.

Tip

You can update your knowledge of drying/styling by:

- reading the trade press
- attending trade events
- taking part in training events
- talking with colleagues

By reading this chapter, carrying out the above activities, assignments and the case study, and by meeting the requirements in preparing for assessment you will have worked towards the key skill requirements in Communication Level 1 (C 1.1) (C 1.2) (C1.3) and Level 2 (C 2.1) (C 2.2).

If you have used a computer to complete your assignments or activities you will have worked towards the key skill requirements in Information Technology Level 1 (IT 1.1) (IT 1.2).

Setting and dressing hair

Chris Moody

Learning objectives

The following are some of the topics covered in this chapter:

- setting – what it is and what it does
- techniques and methods
- dressing – what it does
- shapes and styles.

Introduction

Chris Moody

Setting and dressing hair are important hairdressing techniques.

Setting is the process of placing tension on the hair (stretching it) at various points along its length. Setting hair, wet or dry, involves curling, rollering, waving, twisting, pinning, clipping, positioning, placing and fixing it. This gives hair spring, body, volume and direction, achieved by the structural changes brought about by the altered tension. Blow drying uses the same principle but gives the hair a softer, less structured look.

Dressing blends the set movements and the directions of the hair, and finalises the style. Dressing can also be carried out as a service in its own right, particularly when dressing long hair into plaits or braids.

Setting – the principles

Tip

Hair positioned and secured when wet will retain its shape when dry. In the end, you will get the shapes that you form.

Tip

Root direction determines hair flow.

Like blow-styling, setting is a method of forming wet hair into shape. Hair can also be moulded dry. Setting is used to produce a variety of looks and can make hair straighter, curlier, fuller, flatter or more wavy.

Setting involves placing wet hair in chosen positions, and holding it there while it dries into shape. You may roll the hair round curlers, secure it with clips or pins, or simply use your fingers. Once dry, you complete the process by dressing the hair with brushes and combs. Hair that has been set is called a **pli**. Wet pli or first pli refers to wet hair in position after setting, dry pli or second pli refers to each after being dried and dressed. This term comes from the French *mis-en-pli*, meaning 'put into set'.

Hair must be controlled effectively, using initiative and a creative interpretation of the client's wishes, taking into account the same factors you consider when you are cutting or styling (see Chapter 6).

Dexterity – skilled, competent hand and finger movements, achieved after much practice – enables you to attain both effective control and shape variety.

As with other techniques, setting produces only a temporary change in hair structure. The pli will be lost as moisture is absorbed by the hair. Various setting aids are available which slow down this process, holding the shape longer (see page 93).

 Activity

Using sketches or photographs, compile a style book. Collect those styles that appear to you to be suitable and complementary to the wearer. Also collect hairstyles that are totally *unsuitable*, and note why you think this is. Discuss these styles with your colleagues and tutors.

Setting hair: different lengths

Different effects can be produced by different techniques:

- Increasing volume – adding height, width and fullness, by lifting bases when rollering or curling.
- Decreasing volume – producing a close, smooth, contained or flat style by pincurl stem direction, or by dragged or angled rollering.
- Movement – variation of line, waves and curls, produced by using differently sized rollers, pincurls or finger waving.

Different techniques are used for hair of different lengths:

- Longer hair (below shoulders) requires large rollers, or alternating large and small rollers, depending on the amount of movement required.
- Shorter hair (above shoulder) requires smaller rollers to achieve movement for full or sleek effects.
- Hair of one length is ideal for smooth, bob effects.
- Hair of layered lengths is ideal for full, bouncy, curly effects achieved by, say, barrel or clockspring curls (see page 97).

> **! Health & Safety**
>
> Repeated combing, particularly with hot combs, can cause hair to break.

> **! Health & Safety**
>
> Always check the temperature of a heat appliance to ensure your client does not get uncomfortably hot.

Different techniques can also be used to improve the appearance of hair of different textures:

- fine, lifeless hair can be given increased body and movement
- lank hair can be given increased volume and movement
- coarse, thick hair requires firm control
- very curly hair can be contained and made smoother, and its direction varied
- the volume of unruly hair can be decreased.

Setting can also be used to relax naturally curly hair. Relaxed hair effects can be produced by wrapping hair or by using a large roller.

Temporary or physical relaxing

The temporary methods of relaxing hair include the following:

Tip

When rollering long hair, take care to avoid tangling it.

- placing large rollers in wet hair and drying
- wrapping wet hair around the head and drying
- using heated rollers
- using heated irons or tongs
- blow-drying or stretching
- using hot combs
- applying hot brushes
- pressing – hard and soft.

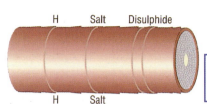

Normal unstretched hair bonds

Tip

The terms hard press and soft press are used to describe the amount of curl reduction imposed on the hair. In *hard press*, most of the curl is removed; in *soft press*, about half the curl is relaxed.

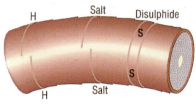

Stretched broken bonds

!

Health & Safety

Do not press hair that is in poor condition. Wait until it has been conditioned.

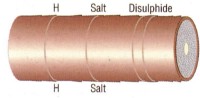

Water/moisture returns links to normal.

Setting – what it does

Hair is both flexible and elastic. As hair is curled or waved, it is bent under tension into curved shapes. The hair is stretched on the outer side of the curve and compressed on the inner side. If it is dried in this new position, the curl will be retained. This happens because when hair is set the hydrogen bonds and salt bonds between the keratin chains of the hair are broken (see page 7). The linking system is moved into a new temporary position. (The stronger disulphide links remain unbroken, this is known as beta keratin.)

Hair, however, is **hygroscopic** – it is able to absorb and retain moisture. It does so by capillary action: water spreads through minute spaces in the hair structure, like ink spreading in blotting paper. Wet hair expands and contracts more than dry hair does, because water acts as a lubricant and allows the link structure to be repositioned more easily. So the amount of moisture in hair affects the curl's durability. As the hair picks up moisture the rearranged keratin chains loosen or relax into their previous shape and position. Hair in its natural unstretched state is known as alpha keratin. This is why the **humidity** – the moisture content of air – determines how long the curled shape is retained.

Goldwell

Tip

The keratin bonds of unstretched hair are in alpha position. Keratin bonds of stretched hair are in beta position. This is the basis of cohesive and temporary setting.

The condition and the porosity of hair affect its elasticity. If the cuticle is damaged, or open, the hair will retain little moisture, because of normal evaporation. The hair will therefore have poor elasticity. If too much tension is applied when curling hair of this type it may become limp, overstretched and lacking in spring. Very dry hair is likely to break.

The client

- Prepare your client by carefully gowning them and making sure they are comfortable. Remove damp towels and any loose cut hair before setting commences.
- Talk with your client about what you are going to do next. Discuss the final effect you are aiming for. Pictures of styles in magazines and style manuals may be useful – explain how you are going to dress the hair to suit your client's face shape. (See the section in Chapter 6 on choosing a hairstyle).
- Examine the hair again – check the natural direction and movement, the effects of previous perming, and the condition of the hair. Whether a given style is suitable will depend on its texture and condition.
- Agree with your client what you will do. Estimate how long it will take and what it will cost.
- Analyse the techniques you will need.
- Discuss any setting aids you plan to use (see below) – your client may have personal preferences.
- Assemble the tools you will need, so that they are to hand as you carry out any rolling or pinning.
- Advise your client on how to manage the style at home.

Setting aids

Setting aids

When you have towel-dried and combed your client's hair, and before you start work on the pli, you may decide to apply one of a range of setting aids. These products help to hold hair in shape, maintain the curls and waves, and thus make the set last longer. They include lotions, sculpting creams, mousses, gels, glitz, waxes, sprays, moisturisers and hair thickeners; some setting aids also add glaze, glitter, shine or colour to the hair. They contain **resins** or **plastics** (polymers such as **PVP** and **PVA**). These soften the hair, allow shapes to be formed, prevent flyaway effects and coat the hair with a fine plastic film which slows down the absorption of moisture.

When applying setting aids, remember the following:

- If the hair is too wet, the setting aid will become diluted and will be less effective.
- If the hair is too dry, it will become sticky and difficult to manage.

Tip

Each technique creates its own effects. Learn these, to make yourself adaptable.

- Don't apply too much. Apart from being wasteful, it will make the hair sticky.
- Apply setting aids evenly. Massage or comb them through the hair to make sure each hair is completely covered.
- Protect your client's face – chemicals can be irritating to the skin and harmful to the eyes.
- Always follow manufacturers' instructions

 Activity

On your collected hair samples or the practice block, try out the effects of different setting lotions, mousses, gels and creams, using fine, medium and coarse hair. Note the appearance and the feel of the hair, and how long the styles last.

Curling technique

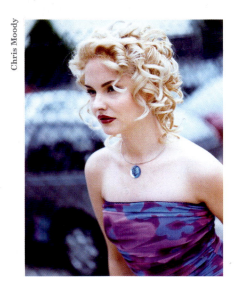

Chris Moody

A curled dressing

Curls are series of shapes or movements in the hair. They may occur naturally, or be put there by hairdressing – chemically by perming, or physically by setting. Curls add bounce or lift to the hair, and determine the direction in which the hair lies.

Each curl has a **root**, a **stem**, a body and a point. The **curl base** – the foundation shape produced between parted sections of hair – may be oblong, square, triangular and so on. The shape depends on the size of the curl, the stem direction and the curl type. Different curl types produce different movements.

You can choose the shape, size and direction of the individual curls: your choice will affect how satisfying the finished effect is, and how long it lasts. The type of curl you choose depends on the style you're aiming for – a high, lifted movement needs a raised curl stem; a low, smooth shape needs a flat curl. You may need to use a combination of curl types and curling methods to achieve the desired style – for example, you might lift the hair on top of the head using large rollers, but keep the sides flatter using pincurls. Think about this when designing the pli.

Tip

Evenly tensioned curls produce even movements. Twisted ones produce difficulties.

Rollering

There are various sizes and shapes of **roller**. In using rollers you need to decide on the size and shape, how you will curl the hair on to them, and the position in which you will attach them to the base.

- Small rollers produce tight curls, giving hair more movement. Large rollers produce loose curls, making hair wavy rather than curly.

Curl parts

Curl types

Curl bases

Roller setting: wound

Roller setting: completed effect

Tip

If you're not sure which size of roller is best, use smaller ones – if necessary you can brush out too tightly curled hair later. Loosely curled hair will drop more easily, so you may not achieve the style you were aiming for.

- Rollers pinned on or above their bases, so that the roots are upright, produce more volume than rollers placed below their bases.
- The direction of the hair wound round the rollers will affect the final style – do you want the hair to flick upwards or turn under?

Hair rollers/wavers

Health & Safety

Don't position metal clips or pins on the scalp itself. They will get hot when you dry the hair, and may burn the skin.

Never allow a pin to pierce the skin. Watch what you are doing!

Securing rollers

Pinning rollers

Tip

More tension is required when rollering coarser hair. Chemically treated hair, and very fine hair, require little tension.

Tip

Curled or rollered hair will kick out if kinked.

Rollering method

1. Begin at the point from which the curled hair is to flow, at a place that is comfortable for the client and convenient to work from.

2. Section the hair to avoid unwanted divisions after setting and drying. Use a tailcomb with which you can divide and control the hair easily.

3. Cleanly comb a section of hair – no longer nor wider than the roller size being used – straight out from the head.

4. Place the hair points centrally on to the roller. Use both hands to retain the hair section angle and keep the hair points in position.

5. As you turn the roller, 'lock' the hair points against the body of the roller. Then wind down the hair and roller evenly. Don't move the hair from side to side when winding: if you do, the hair will slip out.

6. As you work, make sure that any fine, wispy hair is included on the roller. Don't overstretch the hair – this could make the hair break or become limp.

7. Place the wound roller centrally on to the sectioned base to achieve the full height effect. Secure the wound roller by pinning through it to prevent unwinding.

8. If you are using pins to secure the rollers, make sure you don't pierce the client's scalp, or disturb hair that has already been wound.

Common faults

- If you don't secure the wound roller carefully on its base you may get a dragged or flat effect, without the volume you had intended.
- If the hair sections are too big or too small, you will find it difficult to blend the curls when dressing.
- Don't allow roller pins to scratch the skin. It is better to pass them through another roller.
- Longer hair requires a large roller, unless very tight effects are required. Large rollers in short hair make control difficult and the effects produced are weak.
- Dragging hair from either side of the roller produces divisions which will not dress out easily.
- If you bend back the hair points you may cause '**fish-hooks**'.
- Twisting hair as you roll it will distort the movement of the hairstyle.
- Working untidily can lead to sloppy rollering, which in turn causes dressing problems and distorts the movement directions of the final style.

Activity

Practise setting a circle of curls. This will help you to achieve control of stem directions.

Barrelspring curl

Clockspring curl

 Activity

Practise setting one row of curls with stems to the left, the next with stems to the right, and the third with stems to the left. Dry in position, then brush the hair and blend the curls. You should have achieved a wave shape.

Pincurling

Pincurling is the technique of winding hair into a series of curls which are pinned in place while drying. The two most common types of curl produced in this way are the barrelspring and the clockspring.

- **The barrelspring curl** has an open centre and produces a soft effect. When formed, each loop is the same size as the previous one. It produces an even wave shape and may be used for reverse curling, which forms waves in modern hairstyles. In this, one row of pincurls lies in one direction, the next in the opposite direction. When dry and dressed, this produces a wave shape.
- **The clockspring curl** has a closed centre and produces a tight, springy effect. When formed each loop is slightly smaller than the previous one. It produces an uneven wave shape throughout its length. It can be suitable for hair that is difficult to hold in place.

 Activity

Set the hair of your practice block in rollers. As you place the rollers, ensure that you form a brick-like pattern with no partings. Set another block, placing one roller level with the next where possible. When dry, brush out both blocks and note the difference between them. The second block will have harsh divisions or partings which are difficult to dress out.

Pincurling method

The following method of curling can be used for curls that are tight or loose, big or small, and for even and uneven shapes.

1. Neatly section the hair and comb cleanly through it. (The section size is determined by the effect required.)
2. Hold the hair in the direction in which it is to lie after drying and dressing.
3. Hold the hair, at mid-length, in one hand, using the thumb and forefinger, with the thumb uppermost. Using the thumb and finger on the other hand, with the thumb underneath, hold the hair a little way down from the hair points.

4   Turn the second hand to form the first curl loop. The hand should turn almost completely round at the wrist.

5   On completion of the first loop, transfer the hair to the finger and thumb of the other hand.

6   Form a series of loops until the curl base is reached. The last loop is formed by turning the curl body into the curl base. The rounded curl body should snugly fit into the curl base.

7   Secure the curl without disturbing its position on its base. Use clips or pins.

This curling method can be used to produce either barrelspring or clockspring curls. The curl loops may be formed either larger or smaller, as required. It can be used whether you are right- or left-handed.

Common faults

- Tangled hair is difficult to control – comb the hair well before your start.
- If the base size is too large, curling will be difficult, particularly if the hair is short.
- If you hold the curl stem in one direction but place it in another, the curl will lift.
- If you don't turn your hand sufficiently you will find it difficult to form loops.

Curl variations

Roller, stand-up and barrel pincurls are similarly formed. Each has its stem directed up from the head, which produces height and fullness.

- **The stand-up pincurl** is formed on an oblong base – longer than it is wide – and has an open centre and a lifted base. These curls produce high, soft, casual, loose shapes. Their main advantage is individual direction and shape.
- **Roller curls** are similar to stand-up curls but do not have the individual shape and movement produced by separate curls. The main difference between these curls is the tension used, and their size.
- **The barrel pincurl** is formed on a smaller base than that used for rollering. Variation in stem direction produces interesting shapes. The curl is formed from its points, or held in the centre and the points placed on to the base. A clip retains the lifted base and curl position. Barrel pincurls are normally wider than stand-up pincurls, and narrower than roller curls.

Stand-up pin curls

Roller curls

Barrel pincurl

 Activity

Try securing some pincurls with hairpins, some with setting clips, and some with hairgrips. When dry, dress each of them and note the differences produced.

Curl body directions

Curl body directions

A flat curl may turn either clockwise or counter-clockwise. The body of a clockwise curl moves to the right, like the hands of a clock. The counter-clockwise curl moves in the opposite direction. Roller and stand-up pincurls are formed with their stems directed up from the head.

Make sure that you place the hair carefully to get the curls going in the right direction for the style you have chosen.

Reverse curls

Using alternate rows of clockwise and counter-clockwise barrelspring curls, you can create a wave shape. Double rows of reverse curls – two rows clockwise, then two rows counter clockwise – produce larger waves. Wave size is determined by the hair length and the curl size, and by the use of single or double rows.

Health & Safety

Never place clips or pins in your mouth – this is unhygienic and dangerous.

Never place tailcombs in your pocket – they may pierce the body when you bend over.

Never work on a wet, slippery floor.

Always use clean, sterile tools, towels and equipment, to avoid cross-infection.

Activity

List the movements and directions produced by the different types of curl.

Activity

Using three separate blocks, form, dry and dress three different curl types. Look carefully at the different effects and consider how you might use each kind of curl in your designs for setting.

Drying a pli

The pli is usually dried using a hood dryer, carefully lowered to cover the set head of hair.

Wella

A hood dryer

1   Make sure the client is comfortable.

2   Set the dryer to a temperature that suits the client. Most dryers have thermostatic controls, but it is a good idea to check with the client from time to time. Fine hair should be dried at lower temperatures. If the temperature is too hot it will become uncomfortable for your client and will physically damage the hair unnecessarily.

3   Drying will take about 20–30 minutes. The thicker the hair, the longer the drying time. The dryer may have an automatic timer which reminds you when the time is up.

4   Allow the hair to cool fully before removing pins, clips and so on. If you unwind the hair while it is still warm and soft the shape will soon drop.

Steam setting

The **steam set** relies on the setting of clean, dry hair, with moisture supplied by a steamer.

1   Wash and dry the hair.

2   Place the dry hair into pli.

3   Steam the hair for three minutes.

4   Place the hair under a dryer for 5–10 minutes, depending on the length of the hair.

5   Allow the hair to cool, then dress it.

This type of set produces a quick shape; the hair is shiny and easy to dress. It takes about half an hour for long hair.

Heat moulding techniques

Heat can be applied to hair in a number of ways when styling by using:

- A blowdryer
- Tongs
- Straighteners
- Crimpers
- Hot brush or combs

They are used to give the hair curl, to straighten the hair or to provide waves and crimped effects.

Like other methods, heated styling equipment depends on the heat softening the hair. The new moulded shape in the hair must be allowed to cool before it will hold its shape – if you comb through it while it is still warm you will lose or soften the shape. Hair moulded in this way returns to its natural state if combed with hot water.

Tip

If the hair is left to dry naturally it takes the shape of natural growth patterns (see page 121), which need to be fully considered.

L'Oreal. Errol Douglas at Neville Daniel

Successful curling

Learning to curl, like other practical techniques, requires patience and practice. You need to experiment, preferably on practice blocks. Try combing, sectioning, subdividing smaller hair sections, handling different hair textures, and practising the sequence of movements required to form the curl.

When you are fairly competent, transfer your skills to live models. In a way, this is like starting again. Dealing with the model, and coping with different hair textures, hair lengths and style requirements, creates further opportunities for you to explore techniques of curling.

Common faults

- Wet hair stretches more than dry hair. If the hair is too dry the curl spring will be reduced.
- Hot hair is soft. If you start to dress it before it has cooled, spring and shape will be lost.
- To form a movement you need to make several similar curls. If you use too few the shape becomes skimped.
- If the hair is not free of grease and other materials before setting, the shape will be loose and lank.
- If you don't dry the hair sufficiently after setting, the shape soon falls.
- The larger the curl, the looser the effects. Large rollers placed in short hair produce straight effects.
- Frizzy ends may be produced by fish-hooking or overstretching.
- Stem direction determines hair movement. If the directions are varied by too much dressing, control becomes difficult.

L'Oreal. Errol Douglas at Neville Daniel

Finger waving

Finger waving is a technique of moulding wet hair into 'S' shaped movements using the hands, the fingers and a comb. It is sometimes called water waving or water setting, as the result resembles waves in the sea. In horizontal waving the waves go from side to side; in vertical waving they go up and down.

The technique was most popular before rollers were widely available. You can see the effect in the flat, waved hair of early movie stars. Nowadays hairstyles are generally fuller, but finger waves may be used within the overall style – for example, at the lower part of the back of the head, or at the sides. They usually look better if they are at an angle. As with all styling, the use of these movements depends on the individual client's features and head shape.

Finger waving method

1   Use one finger of one hand to control the hair and to determine the position of the wave. Comb the hair into the first part of the crest, and continue along the head.

2 Place the second finger immediately below the crest formed, and comb the hair in the opposite direction.

3 Form the second crest similarly, to complete the final wave shape.

The elbow and arm should be held above the hand when it is placed on the head. Only the index finger should touch the head. This gives the required control and pressure. A comb with both widely and closely spaced teeth is the most suitable.

Finger waving: first crest

Finger waving: second crest

Finger waving: third crest

Points to remember

Ishoka

- Finger waving is most successful on medium or fine hair that is about 10 cm long. Coarse or lank hair can be difficult.
- Setting lotion, gel, mousse or emulsion will be needed to hold the waves.
- Keep your foream level with or slightly higher than the wrist, to control the hair and your hand during waving.
- Hold the comb upright and don't use too much pressure when combing, to avoid tearing the scalp.
- Keep the waves the same size and depth. About 3 cm (the tips of two fingers) between crests is usually best.
- For vertical waving, use strips about 5 cm wide.
- For short hair, make shallow rather than deep waves.
- Pinching or forcing the crests will distort the waves. Correct control and angling will produce the best waves.
- Positioning is important. Comb the hair to make it lie evenly, and return it to this position after each wave movement is complete.
- Keep the hair wet (but not dripping) during waving. If you find that it is drying out, dampen it while you work and apply more setting lotion if necessary.
- Dry the completed shape under a hood dryer, if possible. This helps to prevent the movements from being disturbed.

Ishoka

Waving all of the hair

1   Begin the waving about 75 mm from the front hairline, at the parting. The parting should ideally be placed midway above the eyebrow. Start with the larger side of the hair.

2   Place the finger at right angles to the parting, with the crest curved round to the front.

3   If there is to be no parting, begin at the hairline on one side.

Dressing the waves

The waved head of hair is not usually brushed. It should be disturbed as little as possible.

1   Place the coarse end of the comb between the two lowest crests and comb through to the ends. Support and hold the crests and hair above the combing, to prevent dragging. A slight pushing and moulding action with the hand produces full, soft wave shapes.

2   Repeat this, starting between the next higher crests.

3   Complete the dressing with the fine end of the comb.

 Activity

On a practice block set the section with the rollers so that it is over-directed. On another block set the top section with rollers on their bases. On a third block set the rollers below sections. Dry and dress all three. Note the shape and the hair direction produced in each.

 Activity

Finger wave different parts of a block or head, and dry the hair in position. Assess the wave shape formed: better waves remain in one position, poor ones drop.

Dressing technique

After all the planning and preparation, dressing is the process of adding the finishing touches to well-conditioned, cut and set hair. Setting gives movement to hair in the form of curls or waves. Dressing blends and binds these movements into an overall flowing shape, the style you set out to achieve. It produces an overall form that flows, lightening the head and face and removing dull, flat or odd shapes. The completed shape is called a dressing, **coiffure** or hair-do. It is this that the client takes away from the salon – ideally, a correct and satisfying interpretation of what was required.

Dressing uses brushing and combing techniques, and dressing aids such as hairspray to keep the hair in place. If you have planned the pli carefully and set the hair accordingly, only a minimum of dressing will be needed.

Brushing

Brushing blends the waves or curls, removes the partings left at the curl bases during rollering, and gets rid of any stiffness caused by setting aids.

1   One way of achieving the finished dressing is with a brush and your hand. The thicker the hair, the stiffer the brush bristles need to be. Choose a brush that will flow through the hair comfortably.
2   Apply the brush to the hair ends. Use firm but gentle strokes.
3   Work up the head, starting from the back of the neck.
4   Brush through the waves or curls you have set, gradually moulding the hair into shape.
5   As you brush, pat the hair with your hand to guide the hair into shape. Remember, though, that overdressing and overhandling can ruin the set.

The technique of double brushing uses two brushes, applied one after the other in a rolling action. You may prefer to use a brush and comb.

Brushes for dressing hair

Denman

Backbrushing

Backbrushing is a technique used to give more height and volume to hair. By brushing backwards from the points to the roots, you roughen the cuticle of the hair. Hairs will now tangle slightly and bind together to hold a fuller shape. The amount of hair backbrushed determines the fullness of the finished style.

Tapered hair is well suited to backbrushing: the short hairs in the sections backbrushed add bulk easily. Clubbed hair, on the other hand, does not respond to backbrushing as it is all of one length. Tapered hair, with shorter lengths distributed throughout, is more easily pushed back by brushing. Most textures of hair can be backbrushed; because it adds bulk, the technique is especially useful with fine hair.

Backbrushing method

1   Hold a section of hair out from the head. For maximum lift, hold the section straight out from the head and apply the backbrushing close to the roots.
2   Place the brush on top of the section. With a slight turning action of the brush, slide some of the hairs back towards the scalp. If you brush too strongly you will pull the entire section from your hand. After each stroke, replace the section on the head in the direction you want it to lie.

Backbrushing

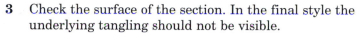

Backcombing

3 Check the surface of the section. In the final style the underlying tangling should not be visible.

4 You may need to backbrush only a small amount of hair – it depends how much volume you want to add.

5 Offer your client guidance about how to achieve the same effect at home, and about how to remove backdressing without tearing or breaking the hair.

Backcombing

The technique of **backcombing** is similar to that of backbrushing. Here a comb rather than a brush is used to turn shorter hairs in a section, giving support and volume to dressed hair. Back combing is applied deeper in the hair, right down at the roots, so this technique can add more volume than can backbrushing.

Backcombing method

1 Hold a section of hair out from the head. Use different angles with different sections.

2 Place the fine end of the dressing comb underneath the section, near the roots. Don't push it too far in. Gently turn it, and push it back towards the head.

3 Repeat this movement of the comb along the length of the section, moving away from the roots and towards the points.

4 Push the backcombed section out of your way, and comb another section. Continue until you have achieved the desired height or fullness.

5 Finish the dressing by positioning the hair with your fingers. Smooth the hair with the wide end of the comb.

Tip

Backcombing is applied to the *underside* of a hair section. Don't let the comb penetrate too deeply (towards the surface of the section), or the final dressing will drag the backcombing out and lose the effect.

 Activity

Practise differing amounts of backcombing. Notice how backcombing produces firmer and higher effects than backbrushing.

Tip

Angle your hands so that the palms don't touch the head, and don't pat the hair too much – you could easily undo the effect of the earlier dressing.

Teasing

After brushing the hair and backcombing it if necessary, you may need to place small areas of hair individually. This is called **teasing**.

It is important at this stage not to disturb the rest of the dressing. Use your fingertips and a pin, the end of a tailcomb, or a wide-toothed Afro comb to lift the hair carefully into position, to finish the balance, or to cover an exposed area.

Simple dressing

Hair does not always need backcombing. If the hair has been suitably cut and blow-styled it may already have sufficient shape and bulk. After setting, tonging or hot brushing, for example, this kind of dressing may be quite adequate:

1   Brush the hair firmly, starting at the nape. Gradually work up the head until you reach the front.

2   As you brush, move freely – first *against* the direction of the set, then in the intended direction.

3   Having blended the set in this way, distribute the hair using a comb or brush. Follow the movements of the hair. Lightly stroke the hair with your hand as you position it. Gently push the hair from the head to achieve any extra height.

Overdressing

One of the commonest faults in dressing is overdressing – doing too much. You need to plan the whole dressing from the outset, and watch what you are doing so that you recognise when you have done enough. Don't fiddle with the hair: look for the overall shape, balance and movements.

Mirrors

Ishoka

As you work, keep looking in the mirror to check what you are doing. If you spend too long concentrating on one area you will lose track of the overall shape. Step back from time to time and look at the shapes and movements you are producing. This will save time-wasting alterations later.

At the end, hold a hand mirror at an angle so that your client can see the finished effect from behind and from the side.

 Activity

Practise the following:
- combing hair stems in different directions
- placing stems in different directions
- rolling your wrist as you curl the hair
- using your fingertips to hold the hair and the curls.

 Tip

Before securing long hair, give it a slight twist. This will help to keep it in place.

Long hair dressings

Long hair needs particular consideration, but is not difficult to manage. If it is in good condition and has been well cut it will hang naturally. Flowing styles can be finished with a hand dryer and a brush.

Charlie Taylor

Stephen Reay

Long hair dressed
symmetrically

Long hair dressed
asymmetrically

Health & Safety

Whatever you use to secure
the hair, make sure it
doesn't damage the hair or
scalp.

Because long hair is heavy, it is important to centralise the weight.
This will help it to stay in place. You can secure it in position using
pins, grips, rubber bands, combs or ribbons.

When the bulk of the hair is in place, you may dress lengths by
plaiting (see page 110). If you do use plaits, angle them carefully so
that you keep the weight well distributed. Take care not to disturb
the *base* of the secured hair – you need this to remain firm.

Long hair can be dressed **symmetrically**, with matching hair
arrangements on either side, or **asymmetrically**, with unmatched
but balanced arrangements.

The following are popular long hair dressings:

- a pleat, French roll or vertical roll
- a horizontal roll
- plaiting.

Pleating

A **pleat**, or **French roll**, is a vertical fold of hair, commonly worn
on the back of the head. It is most suitable for long hair, but can be
achieved even with shorter lengths. The pleat is one way of dressing
long hair to make it appear to be shorter.

A pleat or vertical roll – method

The steps for attaining a successful pleat are as follows:

1   Brush and smooth the hair into the position required, either to
the left or to the right.

2   Secure the crown hair out of the way, if necessary. Otherwise,
include it in the pleat. The side hair can be included, or it can be
dressed separately.

Luster

Pleat roll

3   Keep the head upright so that the pleat does not loosen. Backdress the hair to give added fullness.

4   Place one hand on the sweeping hair, at the angle you require the pleat to lie. Secure the hair firmly in position with grips, making sure that you overlap them.

5   Now grasp the hair and tidy it, but without loosening the gripped base. Turn it up and round to cover the grips.

6   You can now slowly slide your hand towards the crown and pin the folded hair into position.

7   With the pleat secured firmly in place, dress the top front or crown hair into place, depending on the look you require. No pins or grips should be visible in the finished dressing.

Pleat/vertical roll:

1 Smoothing hair into position

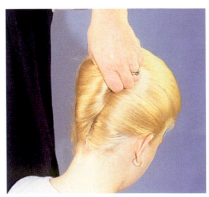
2 Backdressing

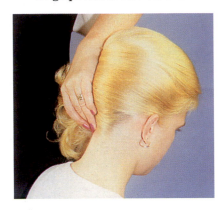
3 Securing with grips

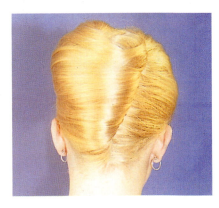
4 Positioning pleat

5 Pinning folded hair

6 The completed roll

Tip

During consultation with the client you may find it helpful to manipulate the hair at a styling unit. By moving and changing the hair into different positions, you and your client will be able to see what possible final shapes look like. When styling longer hair, this will save valuable dressing-out time while achieving the agreed final appearance.

The horizontal roll – method

The steps for attaining a successful horizontal roll are as follows:

1   Take the hair into your hands and carefully position the hair bulk where required.

2   Sweep the hair in the direction it is to lie. Securely fix the base using overlapping grips or pins.

3   Fold the hair, in the opposite direction to that of the base. Hide any fixing pins or grips by pushing them in or teasing hair over them.

4   Secure the fold in position. (A base of cottonwool, or net-covered pads of various shapes, may be used to lift and round out the roll: this must be placed on the base before the roll is secured.)

5   For greater variety, smaller sections should be taken: a series of rolls can be placed artistically to achieve a pleasing effect.

6   The side hair may be unswept into small or large rolls, covered partially by the top or crown hair. The lower back should be positioned first, and the side and top hair built upon it.

7   The hair may be interlaced to give added support to the dressing. In this process, a strip of hair is taken from one side and crossed and interlocked with another strip taken from the opposite side.

Horizontal roll:

1 Positioning hair

2 Securing hair

3 Folding hair

4 Securing hair

5 Positioning sides

6 The completed roll

Le Noir Salon for Designer Touch

Plaiting

Plaiting, or braiding, is achieved by intertwining sections of hair. It can be an attractive way of dressing long hair. A variety of sizes and shapes is possible. The three-stem plait is the one most commonly used, but others may be used. Plaited or unplaited hair offers a wide range of dressings. Basket-weave shapes have become popular recently. You can interlace coloured materials, if you wish or add additional hair to:

- increase volume or add colour to the style
- add length to short hair
- protect hair that has been damaged.

The Richardson Group

Cornrowing – continuous plaits running along the scalp, also called **scalp plaits** or ethnic plaits.

Dreadlocks – long thin plaits.

Hair extensions – synthetic hair plaited and added to the natural hair lengths, by heating, to imitate dreadlocks.

Hair threading – the process of wrapping plaited, or unplaited, hair with coloured threads.

Hair twists – oiled or gelled hair twisted together to form tufts.

Hair wrapping – coloured ribbon wrapping the hair, or plaiting with ribbons or wrapping with an extended strip of hair.

Hair weaving – the interlacing of strands of hair, over and under one another, to produce a variety of basketweave effects.

There is an almost infinite range of plaiting, braiding, twisting and weaving effects, as you can see among the ethnic groups of the world, particularly those of Africa. Many dressings of international origin are being used in British and European fashions.

 Activity

Look out for examples of plaiting/pleating/basket weaving in your trade and fashion journals. Sketch and keep publication/copy/date to credit the source of the information.

Chris Moody

French plait – method

1   Comb the front and top hair together at the crown. Divide it into three equal stems.

2   Starting from the left or right, cross an outside stem over the centre stem. Repeat this action, crossing the opposite stem over the centre stem.

French plait:

1 Sectioning the hair

3   With the little finger, take in a further section of hair, about half the thickness of the initial stems. Add it to an outside stem.

4   Cross this thickened stem over the centre one. Repeat this, too, from the other outside stem.

5   Continue in this way, adding hair to each of the outside stems before crossing them over the centre stem.

6   When there is no more hair to be added, continue to plait to the hair ends. Secure the plaits.

2 Plaiting the sections in with the main stem

3 Continuing to plait

4 The completed plait

Tracey Gallagher of the Saks Team

Added hair

Ornamentation

Ornaments can be used to enhance and complete hair dressings. Combs, ribbons, jewels, grips and slides can all be used, as can flowers, feathers, glitterdust, coloured sprays, beads and sequins.

Added hairpieces – also known as **postiche** – can be an attractive means of ornamentation. Apart from covering injuries or scars, bald patches and other defects, they can be decorative and interesting. The means of securing hairpieces vary: most are attached by combs, grips or pins. For a complete change of dressing, styled wigs can be used. To see the range of postiche available, refer to wigmaking textbooks or manufacturers' brochures.

Added colour is a most popular means of increasing shape and line throughout a dressing. You may like to refer to Chapter 9, Colouring hair.

Hair ornamentation

Dressing and finishing aids

Health & Safety

Some aerosol sprays contain CFCs (chlorofluorocarbons). These are the propellants that force the spray out of the can. It is now known that CFCs damage the ozone layer in the upper atmosphere. Sunlight contains ultraviolet (UV) light which can be harmful to the skin: the ozone layer protects us by absorbing most of this UV light.

CFCs are gradually being replaced by less harmful chemicals. Make sure that the hairsprays you use do not contain CFCs.

Dressing and finishing aids

Hairsprays

Hairsprays contain a variety of chemicals with different functions. These may be dissolved in water or in alcohol. Some sprays contain polyvinyl pyrrolidone, or PVP, which helps to reduce the absorption of water from the atmosphere. Others include **plasticisers**, which make the hair more flexible, **cetrimide**, which helps in conditioning the hair and minimising static electricity, or **silicones** which add sheen to the hair. Finally, they may contain colouring, perfume and often preservatives.

To achieve a fine spray and an even distribution, hold the can upright, about 30 cm from the hair. (If you hold it closer you will wet the hair and loosen the set: sticky beads will form, and the hair will hang in strands. If you spray from too far away, most of it will miss the hair.) For a firm hold, spray into the roots. For a lighter hold, sweep your hand across the hair. You can always add a little more, but you can't remove it if you've applied too much.

Other dressing aids

As you comb or brush hair, especially when it has just been dried, the friction produces **static electricity**. The hairs each carry a very small *positive* charge, causing them to fly away from each other. The brush or comb carries a very small *negative* charge, which attracts the positively charged hair. You can reduce the amount of static electricity by lightly touching the hair with your hand, which earths it. There are also dressing aids which may help; these include control creams, oils, gels and mousses.

These aids may be used for other reasons, too: to add gloss, to hold the hair, or to make combing smoother. **Emollients** or **moisturisers**, such as lanolin and olive oil, reduce water loss; **humectants**, such as glycerine, absorb moisture.

Dressing aids come in various forms, including aerosols. Some are applied to wet hair and others to dry hair. Always check the manufacturers' instructions before using them.

Ishoka

Health & Safety

Store hairsprays away from heat. They may explode if overheated.

Never use them near naked flames. They are flammable.

Never crush or burn used cans. Even when apparently empty, cans are still pressurised and can explode.

When spraying, protect your client's face and clothes. Chemicals may harm or irritate the eyes, especially if your client wears contact lenses.

Never try to unblock the spray with a pin or the end of a tailcomb – the can might explode.

To clean the spray head and prevent blockage, use alcohol or spirit. Check the manufacturer's instructions.

Assignments – Setting and dressing hair

A practical activity

Collect together photographs, sketches and magazine clippings about setting, styling and dressing hair. Include styles for long, medium, short, thick, fine and coarse hair. Plastic jackets or pockets can be useful particularly if you intend to present them to your clients. A section on ornamentation would give added interest. Make sure you cover the following information:

- a list of the different types of pincurl
- the effects of the different forms of pincurl
- methods of rollering, including the effects of differing roller sizes
- methods of finger waving, and the effects of growth patterns
- the questions you need to put to your clients
- how you determine direction for your hair styles
- how setting differs from blow-styling
- the important factors in setting hair
- an outline of the possible links with cutting and styling

- the problems that might arise in setting, and how you might resolve them.

For you to find out

Investigate the range of setting and dressing techniques. Use your practice blocks and models to determine the effects of them. Consider how, where and when each technique might be used. Try to capture the differences by sketching or photography. Include the following information and retain for your folder.

1   Examine different types of pincurl. Note the formation of the bases, how direction is determined, and how lift and volume might be achieved.

2   Examine the different types of roller and the techniques for their use. Note how lift or flatness is achieved.

3   Examine how finger waving is achieved. Note the natural hair pattern growth and its effect on wave direction.

4   Consider how setting differs from blow-styling, and the different effects achieved by each.

A case study

A client asks you to change from blow-styling to setting their hair. How would you deal with this request? Work through the following sequence, and record your answers for your folder:

1   What factors need to be considered? List them and discuss them with your client.

2   How do you determine whether setting is going to be satisfactory?

3   How do you present the techniques involved in setting, and what determines which need to be used?

4   How do you demonstrate the care required for the set style? Explore how the client will be able to manage it at home.

5   How do you present the range of setting and finishing products, and recommend the most suitable?

6   How do you deal with long, medium and short hair? What are the differences?

7   How do you secure long hair?

8   What dressing products are available? How do you present these to your client?

9   Outline the problems that you might encounter, and how you might resolve them.

Preparing for Assessment

In preparing for assessment on setting and dressing hair the following checklist may be helpful. Check that you have covered, and understand these items:

- determining clients' requirements
- considering the important influencing factors
- agreeing with the client which setting and dressing techniques to apply
- understanding the differences between the different setting techniques and the effects to produce or reduce curl
- applying setting techniques
- understanding such terms as 'hard pressing' and 'soft pressing'
- understanding the effects produced on the hair structure

- introducing a range of suitable products to your clients
- recognising the links with cutting and styling
- appreciating different types of hair dressings
- dealing with different hair lengths
- handling different hair textures, conditions and shapes
- recognising and dealing with problems that might arise
- applying relevant safety factors and precautions
- completing setting and dressing within acceptable time limits.

When you feel that you are ready, talk to your trainer and arrange a suitable time for your assessment.

By reading this chapter, carrying out the above activities, assignments and the case study, and by meeting the requirements in preparing for assessment you will have worked towards the key skill requirements in Communication Level 1 (C 1.1) (C 1.2) (C 1.3) and Level 2 (C 2.1) (C 2.2) (C 2.3).

If you have used a computer to complete your assignments or activities you will have worked towards the key skill requirements in Information Technology Level 1 (IT 1.2).

Cutting and styling hair

6

Java for Hair

Learning objectives

The following are some of the topics covered in this chapter:

- **hair styling – design and choice**
- **important factors influencing style**
- **style suitability**
- **aesthetic appreciation**
- **cutting tools and equipment**
- **cutting techniques**
- **cutting procedures**

Introduction

Professional and competent hair cutting is the basis of good hairdressing. As a stylist you must be able to create styles by using different cutting techniques and adapting those techniques to suit individual client requirements and hair types. Cutting hair is the main base for styling hair. Designing a cut style needs care, precision, artistic appreciation, technique combination and control. It includes the elements of balance, line and movement. It is reflected in all hairdressing services – setting, blow-styling, dressing and more. Good cutting design leads to hair arrangements which become suitable, pleasing and acceptable styles.

This chapter needs to be studied together with Chapter 4, Drying hair, and Chapter 5, Setting and dressing hair.

Cutting and styling hair – principles

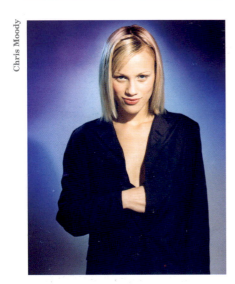

Chris Moody

Hair styling is the creating or designing of attractive hair shapes or arrangements. It involves competent cutting, setting, blow-drying and dressing.

A hairstyle is an expression of form and shape. It is achieved by arranging the hair into suitable, balanced lines, which complement the shape of the head and the facial features.

The aim of the style is to enhance your client's appearance. This helps to boost their confidence and make them feel good. There are styles for work, play, special occasions, business meetings, parties and so on. The hairstyle should be considered a part of the complete **ensemble**, including the clothes, make-up and accessories.

The client

- Make sure you have protected your client's clothes adequately.
- Before attempting a new style, talk it over with your client to be sure that you are in agreement.
- Discuss what is required and make sure that you consider all your client's needs, including their general lifestyle.
- Examine the hair type, texture, length, colour, quality and quantity – all can influence the hairstyle. Look at how the hair has been cut previously, and decide whether there is enough hair for a change of style.
- Analyse the client's requirements and requests. Beware of requests for named styles: the name a client uses for a certain style may mean something completely different to you! Make sure you interpret your client's wishes correctly.
- Assess the limitations. Do not make the mistake of being persuaded to cut hair into a style you are sure would not suit your client.

Lawrence Anthony

- With your client, select the style. Many clients are swayed in their choice of style by pictures of attractive young models in magazines. If you think the style favoured by the client is unsuitable, tactfully suggest an alternative. Not giving the client exactly what they have requested should not be the result of your whim, bias or incompetence, nor a wish on your part to dominate the situation. Your professional initiative is required.
- Advise the client how long cutting will take – anything from 15 minutes for a trim to one hour for a complete restyle.
- Agree with the client how much hair should be taken off.
- Help your client by advising them how to manage the hairstyle at home successfully.
- Reassure the client afterwards – the resulting style, if new, may need getting used to. If your client is not immediately pleased with the result, don't be disappointed but keep your comments positive.

Choosing a hairstyle

The hairstyle you choose with your client must be designed to take into account a number of influencing factors:

Barrie Stephen, Hair Envision

- the shape of the face and head
- the features of the face, head and body
- the dress and occasion for the style
- the quality and quantity of the hair
- the weight, shape and distribution of the hair
- the age of the client
- the way the hair grows, its position, proportion and form in relation to other styling requirements.

The shape of the face and head

This is the base on which the hairstyle will rest. The proportions, balance and distribution of hair should relate to the underlying structure and features. Use features such as the eyes, nose and chin as a guide to the finished style.

If you look at the outline of your client's face, you will see that its outline is quite individual – round, oval, oblong, heart-shaped, square, and so on. An oval shape is considered ideal, as most hairstyles fit it.

Tip

Creative interpretation of your client's wishes may be necessary, but always consult your client first.

Tip

To view the face shape, brush/comb the hair back from the face and hairline.

- The apparent length of square and oblong faces may be increased by sleek, flat styles, or reduced by full sides.
- A large, round face looks even rounder when the hair is full and foaming around it; it looks longer when dressed high at the front and less full at the sides.
- Hard-looking shapes – resulting, for example, from prominent jaw bones – appear harder still when hair is dressed back, but softer with forward hair movements.

Face and head shapes

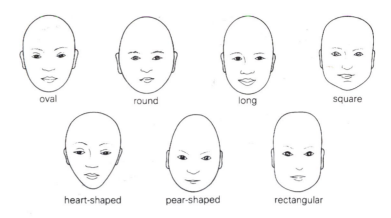

oval   round   long   square

heart-shaped   pear-shaped   rectangular

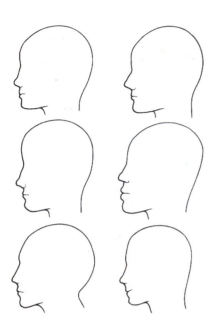

Profiles

Tip

A common fault when trying to disguise a defect is to make it more obvious by using too much hair to hide it.

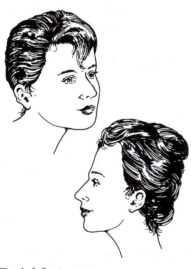

Facial features

- The roundness or flatness of the head shape and the profile – the side view of the chin, mouth, nose and forehead – affect the look of the style.
- The neck – its length, fullness and width – directly affects the fall of the back and nape hair.

Features of the face, head and body

- Note the size, shape and characteristics of your client. The way the head and body are held is important – you can see this best when you first receive the client.
- A prominent or large nose may be diminished by dressing the front hair at an angle, or avoiding a central parting.
- Square jawlines may be softened by fuller side dressings; protruding ears are best covered.
- A double chin is exposed if hair is taken away. A longer, fuller dressing may be helpful.
- Wrinkles round the eyes are made more obvious by straight, hard-line dressings. They may be diminished by softly angling the hair away from the eyes.
- Low, high, wide or narrow foreheads may be disguised by angling the hair and varying fringe positions.
- A large, fussy style on a big person can look unsightly. Yet a small, head-hugging style may be completely out of proportion.
- High-dressed styles accentuate height. Flat styles make short people look shorter.
- The shape of facial features – their lines and the shadows they cast – should be used to counterbalance the hair bulk, and enhance or soften overall features.
- Spectacles and hearing aids will influence your choice of style. Keep hair off the face and away from spectacle frames. Bring hair over the ears to disguise hearing aids.

Dress and occasion

The dress and occasion for which the style is to be worn will help you decide on a suitable hairstyle.

Vidal Sassoon

Wella

Charles Worthington

Tip

The more the unwanted features are highlighted, the less suitable the style will be. The most suitable style is one that is individually designed.

Tip

Set a good example yourself by wearing a suitable hairstyle that reflects current fashion.

- A style suitable for a special occasion may differ from one worn at work: a beautiful evening gown requires an elegant hairstyle, normal working clothes may require one that is smart and unexaggerated.
- Many clients require styles that are practical and easy to manage. Practicality is less essential for special events, but remember that the hair has to be returned to normal afterwards.
- Particular jobs require particular hairstyles. For example, nurses and canteen workers need to wear their hair off the face and shoulders, and many people wear hats as part of their uniform. Do not choose a hairstyle that makes this difficult.
- Usually, lower necklines require longer hairstyles. Higher necklines allow higher dressings. There are exceptions: dancers and ice skaters will not want loose, flowing styles that will impede movement or vision.
- Models require specific and often elaborate hairstyles for demonstrations or photography.

The quality and quantity of hair

- Hair that is in poor condition and poorly textured never looks attractive and will not style well. Shining, healthy hair is essential for good styling.
- Thin, scanty hair is difficult to manage and requires attention. Styles which make it appear thicker and fuller are usually successful.
- Very fine, thin hair is soon affected by damp and loses its shape. Use setting aids, hair thickeners and practical styles.

Cheynes Training for
Paul Mitchell Luxury Haircare

Greys for L'Oreal

Mahogany

- Dry, thick hair requires sleek, smooth, styles to contain it. This hair type soon fluffs and loses its shape. A control dressing (a cream, gel or spray) may help.

- Very tight curly hair requires careful and frequent combing. It looks shorter than it really is. As it is combed the true length becomes apparent.

- With wavy hair, you need to avoid cutting across the wave crests, which could make the hair unmanageable. Try to remove hair below the crests and carefully blend the ends.

- Straight hair, particularly if it is fine-textured, can be difficult to cut. Cutting marks or lines can easily form if sectioning and cutting angles are not accurate. The sections you take should always be small.

The age of the client

Men and women of different ages may require different styles.

Ishoka

- Children require simple hairstyles that don't require much dressing at home. Shorter styles often suit younger children best.

- Young men and women can wear most styles. Striking, often odd, effects are used by this group. Straight or curled, long or short, hard or soft effects may be used to advantage. A younger client may want a style that is unique and individual, or something 'trendy'. Teenage fashion tends to exclude styles worn by older men and women. The more extreme glamorous styles are generally requested by young women.

- Young career women and men generally go for fashionable styles which they wear as part of their everyday dress. Such hairstyles need to be practical and easy to manage as well as fashionable.

- Older women require greater consideration for suitable styling. Facial features – lines, wrinkles and double chins – need to be 'styled out' (made less obvious).

- Young businessmen may require the smart, well-shaped, perhaps less extreme styles than those favoured by teenage boys.

- More mature men usually require flattering or traditional, practical shapes, generally less fussy and easier to manage than most women's hairstyles.

Hair position, proportion and form

- The outline formed by hair in relation to the shape of the face contributes to the overall effect.
- Dressing the hair varies this outline. It is important that you maintain balance between hair and face to achieve a suitable distribution and shape.
- Consider hair growth directions or distributions – strong movements and natural partings, hair streams, hair whorls, cowlicks, widow's peaks, and double crowns. Make allowances for these when cutting and dressing, and particularly when designing the style.
- Hair growth patterns need to be checked before and after shampooing. The way the hair falls or moves is best seen when the hair is wet as it gives a clearer indication of the degree and strength of the pattern. Hair styling can disguise the natural position and form of the hair.
- A hairstyle that follows the natural fall and growth is more likely to retain its shape for longer between salon visits.
- Cutting a nape whorl too short produces difficulties – the hair may stick out in all directions.

Styling requirements

You will often come across the terms suitability, balance or imbalance and weight distribution, soft and hard effects, and originality. You should understand what these terms mean, so that you can choose different hairstyles with confidence.

Suitability

Cheynes

Suitability refers to the effect of the hair shape on the face, and on the features of the head and body. A hairstyle is usually suitable when it 'looks right'. This is achieved when the moulded hair shape fits the other shapes of the head. A line of the face may be accentuated when the hair lines are continuous with it. It may be softened when they are angled away.

A young, fashionable style dressed on an older woman may be unattractive. This is because the lines of the face, eyes and forehead are accentuated by the harder lines of younger styles.

Most fashion styles are designed for younger women and must be adapted if they are to meet the needs of older women.

A hairstyle with balance

Hair direction and flow

Chris Moody

A hairstyle with movement

soft line
(classical Greek)

hard line
(Egyptian)

Hard and soft effects

Balance

Balance is the effect produced by the amount, fullness and weight distribution of hair throughout the style. Imbalance is lack of proportion. Symmetrical, even balance is achieved when the hair is similarly placed on both sides of the head. Asymmetrical, uneven balance is achieved by, for example, dressing long hair on one side of the head and countering the weight with one earring on the other. Here the lines and proportions created by the dressing produce the balanced look. A good hairstyle should be balanced from all angles of view.

The line of the style

Style line is the direction, or directions, in which the hair is positioned. It should flow throughout the shape. If the line suddenly ends, the style becomes unbalanced and the wrong effect is produced.

The line of the style is affected by the way it fits in – or fails to fit in – with the features and contours of the face. It should carry the eye of the viewer along the directions in which the hair is placed. Many style lines produce **illusionary effects** by accentuating or diminishing different facial features.

Partings

Partings have a strong effect. A long, straight, central parting appears to make the nose more prominent. A short, angled parting diminishes a prominent nose. Round, fat faces appear larger with central partings and smaller with side partings.

Movement

Movement is the name given to varying directions of style line; the more varied the line, the more movement there will be. Curly or wavy hair displays movement. The style line should move from one point of the head to another in a fluid fashion reaching to the ends of the hair. Styles with movement are usually complimentary to older women.

Hard and soft effects

Hard and soft effects depend on balanced lines and movements. Hair dressed without divisions, without sudden line variation and without any abrupt finish to the movement looks natural and soft. Careful colouring enhances soft effects – careless colouring produces hard, unwanted effects. Lack of movement and irregular, unbalanced shapes together produce hardness. Rhythmical movement and balancing are softening.

Originality

Creating completely new style lines requires a great deal of thought and work. You can adapt styles and fashions to create interesting and sometimes original variations. Displays, demonstrations and

Vidal Sassoon

competitions offer more opportunities for original hair styling. Whatever hairstyle you choose, it should be designed for the individual client.

Types of hairstyle

You need to be able to cut and dress hair in a range of styles to meet the requirements of different clients. The following are some of those in general use:

Day styles should be attractive, uncluttered and easy to manage, without extreme ornamentation, colour or elaboration.

Evening styles are generally more elaborate, not necessarily practical, and suitable for special occasions.
They are usually augmented with colour or ornament.

High fashion (haute coiffure) refers to the latest style trends. At first they may appear to be extreme; they become more acceptable when better understood. This type of styling requires originality, good techniques and experience.

Fashion styling (usually adapted from high fashion) is favoured by the smart and trendy. There seems to be an endless round or range

Children's hairstyles

Regis

Regis

Guy Kremer

Guy Kremer

of fashions stimulated by events, advertising, dress designs and other sources of inspiration.

Children's styles should be natural and suitable, never artificial – in general, the simpler the better.

Men's styles are based on principles similar to those that apply to women. They should be natural, balanced and suited to the client's face and features.

Equipment and safety

You have considered the artistic part of hairstyling – choosing a style to suit your individual client. Now you need to consider the practical part – the tools used for cutting and how to use them safely, and the terms and techniques used in cutting into style.

Cutting tools

Tools should always be clean, sharp and well balanced. They should fit the hand and feel comfortable in use.

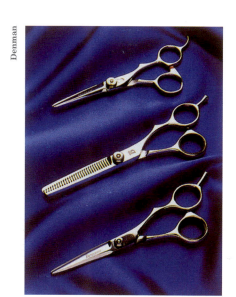

Scissors

- **Scissors** with straight or curved, and long or short blades may be used. They should never be too heavy, nor too long, to control. Since scissors need regular resharpening, you will need at least two pairs, preferably of the same type. Choose the scissor size that best suits the size of your hand – this will help you to cut neatly, quickly and efficiently.

  The best way to hold a pair of scissors is with the thumb through one handle and the third finger through the other. This ensures ease of use, good control and little effort. It also minimises stress on your hands, arms, back and body.

- A **razor** – the open, 'cut-throat' type – consists of an edged steel blade protected by the handle. A solid or hollow ground blade may be used for cutting hair. Modern counterparts are called **hair shapers**. The modern razor-like hair shaper has a replaceable blade and a protecting handle. There are other types and shapes.

Scissors: their parts and how to hold them

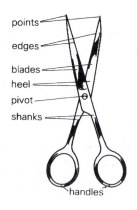

points
edges
blades
heel
pivot
shanks

handles

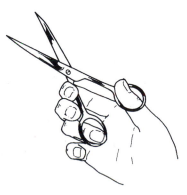

With the handle open, the thumb and index finger hold the back of the guarded blade, between the pivot and the tang. The two middle fingers rest on the tang, on either side of the handle. The guard restricts some razoring movements; this may be overcome by using shorter strokes.

Hair shapers

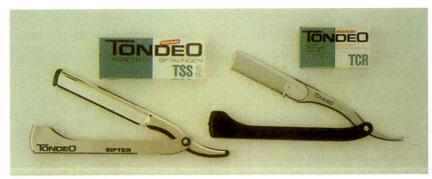

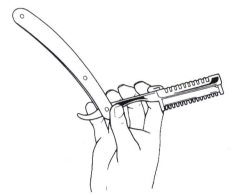

How to hold a hair shaper

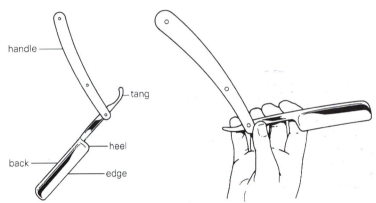

A razor and how to hold it

☀ **Activity**

Visit a hairdressing wholesaler. Note the different types of cutting tools and their prices. You will see that there is a great variety of scissor lengths and weights. It is important that scissors and other tools are comfortable to use. Ask a senior stylist or your trainer to advise you on the best tools to purchase.

- **Thinning scissors** have one or both blades serrated. The size of the serrations determines the quantity of hair that is removed at each cut: the more often they are closed on the hair section, the more hair is removed. They may be held in the same way as cutting scissors, but are used in an opening and closing fashion. They cannot be used in a slithering action.

- **Clippers** – both hand and electric (the latter are now more popular) – consist of two blades, with sharp-edged teeth. The blades are positioned in such a way that one blade remains static and the other moves across it. Hand clippers are

Clippers

!

Health & Safety

The disposable blade or razor is now recommended for general use

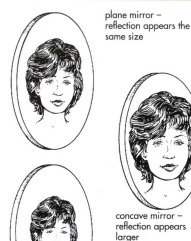

plane mirror – reflection appears the same size

concave mirror – reflection appears larger

convex mirror – reflection appears smaller

Mirror reflections

Goldwell

A cutting collar

operated by pushing the handles together; electric clippers are operated by a motor. The distance between the blade points and the spacing of the teeth determines how closely the hair can be cut.

- **Combs** suitable for use while cutting are thin and pliable, with both fine and coarse teeth. Fine teeth allow the hair to be controlled and closely cut. Coarse teeth allow for repeated combing and positioning of the hair. The comb should be comfortable in use and easily positioned.

  Hold the comb so that both ends are supported, to prevent breaking. When cutting over the comb, one end should be held between the index finger and thumb, with the finger on the teeth edge and the thumb on the back of the comb. As the comb is turned, so the finger and thumb grasp the back of the comb.

- **Mirrors** are important while cutting so that the shape can be seen clearly from different angles. The client, too, will want to see the final result: hand mirrors can be used for this. Three different types of hand mirror are available:
  - *plane* mirrors, which give a normal view
  - *concave* mirrors, which magnify
  - *convex* mirrors, which give a smaller, distant image.

  Plane mirrors are commonly used in the salon.

!

Health & Safety

Do not use clippers if the top, movable blade protrudes beyond the bottom, static blade – you might cut or damage the skin.

- **Cutting collars** are useful pieces of equipment to protect the client from hair clippings. They are placed over the shoulders, around the neck, and remain firmly in position. They do away with towels which can constantly slip and disrupt cutting procedures.

Cleaning cutting tools

- Never use dirty or broken tools. Germs breed in the many corners and may be transferred from one client to another.

- Clean all tools before disinfecting or sterilising. Remove all loose hairs. Use spirit or alcohol to remove any grease.

- Special disinfectant oils may be used to lubricate moving parts.

- Some disinfectants corrode metal and blunt edges. Check the manufacturers' advice before using any disinfectant.

- If corrosion or rusting occurs, light rubbing with emery paper helps to restore the metal surface. Badly marked tools may be corrected by professional servicing.

- Scissors and razors are easier to clean than clippers. Hand clippers can be dismantled. It is not advisable to take electric clippers apart, though some clipper heads are removable for cleaning.

- All repairs should be carried out by the manufacturers, or by qualified electricians.

- All clean and sterile tools should be stored in a dry disinfectant cabinet, or at least covered. See Chapter 12.

Precautions when cutting hair

Examine the hair and scalp thoroughly – signs of disease, infestation or infection indicate that you should not proceed with cutting.

Do not place sharp tools in overall pockets – this is unhygienic and dangerous. You might cut your hands, or stab yourself when bending.

Make sure that the edges of all sharp tools are covered when they are not in use.

Allowing loose, cut hair to gather on the floor is unsightly, dangerous and unhygienic. It is easy to slip on loose hair.

Take care not to cut yourself when replacing shaper blades.

Do not use clippers or combs with broken teeth – they can pull, drag or tear the scalp.

Use only tools that are sharp, to prevent splitting or breaking hair. Beware of clients moving suddenly, particularly children.

Watch out for a sneeze – you might stab your client!

Clean tools after use and store them in a safe place.

First aid

If skin is cut, take the following action:

1   Bathe the area with cold running water.

2   If it is a minor cut, cover with a plaster.

3   If it is severe, apply direct pressure to stem the blood flow and seek immediate help from a qualified first aider. If bleeding does not stop, seek medical help as soon as possible. If necessary, treat your client for shock.

4   Avoid contact with blood – use plastic gloves – to prevent cross-infection.

5   Wash and disinfect any bloodstained surfaces.

6   Write all accidents into the accident book.

 Activity

In case of accidents at work, or someone being taken ill, it is important to know what to do. With a trained first aider in your salon, you are prepared for any emergency. Think about taking a first aid course yourself.

Cutting and styling technique

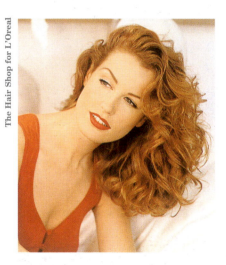

The Hair Shop for L'Oreal

Cutting hair to fit the shape of the head is one of the most important hairdressing processes. It forms the basis of all hair shapes and styles. When a client washes her own hair, the cut shape is what remains. The cut affects the way that the hair lies on the head and influences all other hairdressing processes. A well-shaped head of hair should be pleasing to look at and easy to manage.

Terms and techniques

When different people use particular terms they don't always mean the same thing. Below is a list of useful terms, with explanations of what they mean in this book.

Tapering

Tapering or **taper cutting** means reducing hair so that it tapers easily to a point and unwanted weight is removed. It may at the same time be used to shorten the hair.

Scissor tapering – used on dry hair – is done with a slithering, backwards-and-forwards movement along the hair section. The hair is cut in the heel of the blades from the third of the section that includes the points.

Razor tapering – used on wet hair – achieves a taper effect. The razor is placed, at a slight angle, on or under the hair section. The hair is cut in a series of slicing actions. The length may be reduced at the same time. Cutting should be restricted to the third of the section that includes the points.

Cutting: scissor tapering
(always on dry hair)

Cutting: razor tapering (always
on wet hair)

Cutting: point tapering

Point tapering achieves a taper effect by using the scissors points to remove hair from the point ends of the hair section.

Feathering is another name given to tapering. It also describes the overall effect of dressed, tapered hair.

Backcombing taper achieves its effect by first backcombing a section of hair. The points ends remaining in the hand are then tapered with a sliding, slithering action of the scissors or razor. The amount of backcombing determines the degree of taper.

Clubbing

Club-cutting or **clubbing** is a method of cutting hair sections bluntly, straight across. It reduces all the cut hairs to the same length. It may be used on wet or dry hair. If too large a section is clubbed the resulting line of the hair ends will be irregular. You need to cut small sections of hair at a time.

Scissor clubbing – of wet or dry hair – is the most common. Small slicing actions ensure a clean cut.

 Activity

Taper one hair sample and club cut another. Then curl them both, and dry them. Note the difference in the amount of curl shape achieved.

Thinning

Thinning reduces the length of some of the hairs in a section without shortening the hair overall. The hair's bulk is reduced. Hair is cut at the middle third of the section – if cuts are made too close to the scalp, thinning will cause short stubble to stick out.

Cutting: clubbing
over finger (above)
over comb (below)

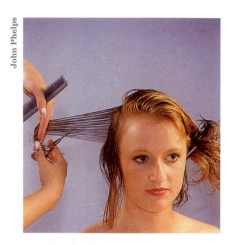

John Phelps

Cutting: thinning

Scissor thinning is achieved with scissors used in a long tapering action. It can also be achieved by deep backcombing and tapering, or by point cutting at the middle third of the section.

Thinning scissors have serrated blades. When closed on to a section they thin it automatically. Cuts should be made at the middle third of the section and towards the points.

Razor thinning reduces thick bulky hair. Make long slicing cuts from mid-lengths to the hair points. Use little pressure or you will cut through the section.

Modern hair shapers with removable blades are used in short, sharp movements to thin hair. The blade is angled slightly and cut from mid-section to points.

Root thinning, with scissors or a razor, is achieved by cutting small hair sections level with the scalp. It is a drastic method, rarely used on the average head: it is used in some fashion and competition styles.

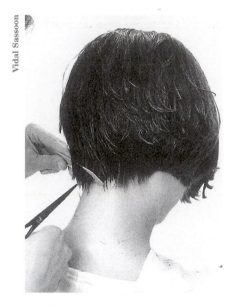

Vidal Sassoon

Cutting: texturising

Activity

Using hair samples that are naturally curly, note the effects of clubbing, tapering and thinning on the curl strength.

Producing varied lengths

Texturising, **castle serrations**, slicing, chipping and chopping are terms used to describe methods of varying lengths of hair within a section. They also describe the look of the cut hair, which gives the effect of some hairs being lifted and supported by others.

Castle serrations are produced with special serrated scissors which drastically reduce parts of the hair section. The amount of hair to be removed is determined by the style effects required.

Wet and dry cutting

Wet and **dry cutting** refers to methods of scissor or razor cutting. *Scissors* may be used on wet or dry hair. Scissor tapering should not be used on wet hair as the action of the blades is restricted. *Modern shapers* are commonly used to taper or thin wet hair; they are never used on dry hair as they drag and tear it, cause the client pain, and blunt the cutting edges. *Clippers* and *thinning scissors* are best used on dry hair.

Graduation

Graduation is the process of creating a difference in length between the upper and lower layers of a section of hair. It refers to the slope produced, from longer to shorter hair, by the ends of the hair.

If a section of hair is held out at right angles to the head, and cut at right angles to the section, the hair will lie evenly on the head. The angle of the cut and the contours of the head together make the ends lie neatly over each other, producing a graduated curve (**uniform layering**). This may best be achieved by clubbing.

A graduated cut can be produced by clubbing the hair, to make it short in the neck graduating to long at the crown, or longer at the nape and shorter at the crown.

Reverse graduation refers to a graduated line being shortest at the lowest layers and longest at the higher layers. This is used where the hair is required to turn under, as in some long or short bob styles.

Cutting women's hair

Classic graduation – step by step

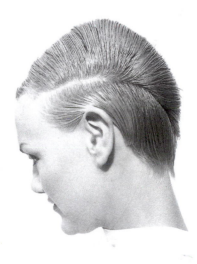

1 After shampooing and conditioning, a natural side parting is established in the hair.

2 A curved back section is then taken, from the low point of the recession area, down into the nape.

3 The hair in front of the ear is combed down to its natural fall and elevated to two fingers' depth of graduation. The line is worked horizontally back to the centre of the ear.

4 Following the curve of the parting, the hair behind the ear is combed forward and out, and the line worked down into the nape.

5 The next section is taken from the middle of the recession area at the front, curving down, to the other side of the nape at the back.

6 Starting at the front, the hair is combed down to its natural fall and elevated to exactly the same level as the guideline underneath.

7 and 8 Curving the line down into the nape, all of this section is pulled out and down to the same level of graduation as the section underneath. The line is continued across to a point on the other side of the nape.

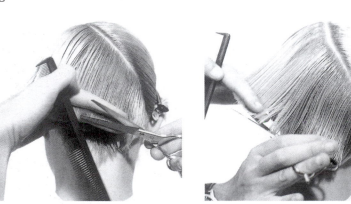

9 and 10 Sections are continued up the head, and each section is pulled to the stationary graduation guideline.

11 The last section on this side of the natural parting is then worked down and followed through into the back.

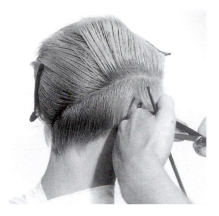

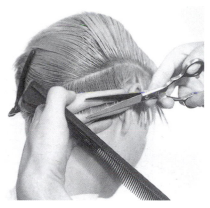

12 Starting on the other side of
   the head, a balanced parting
   is taken from the low point
   of the recession area,
   curving down into the nape.

13 This section is worked back
   at the same level of
   graduation as the first side.

14 and 15 Sections are worked up on this side, until reaching the
          natural parting, and each section is pulled down to
          exactly the same point of graduation, curving from the
          front down into the nape.

16 and 17 The back area is then cross-checked for balance by
          pulling all of the hair out to the graduation level and
          curving any excess areas of weight.

Cutting: layering

Freehand cutting

Layering

Layering is the term given to the process of cutting sections of hair to similar lengths. It produces a uniform, unbroken shape. A uniform layer can be produced by holding hair sections out at right angles to the head and cutting across them at right angles.

Layering is also used to describe thicker and more distinct layers, cut directly into the hair shape. These layers are *not* uniform: there is a sharp difference in section length.

Freehand cutting

This is the process of taking small sections of hair, gently pushing them and allowing the natural movement to take the hair section, and then cutting the section without stretching the hair out of its natural line. The hair must be free from any forced directional pull. Pushing (or lifting) the weight of the lengths of hair allows them to move in their own natural manner.

This is a useful technique for dealing with hair growth patterns, such as a calf lick.

Controlling the shape

Angles must be considered when you are applying any method of cutting. Two in particular are important:

- the angle at which the hair section is held out from the head
- the angle at which the cut is made across the hair section.

By varying these two angles you can produce a wide variety of effects.

Cutting lines or perimeter lines are the lines described by the hair-ends when they are held directly out from the head or combed flat to the scalp. They encircle the contours of the head and must be followed carefully throughout any cutting procedure. The curves of these lines determine the shape of the cut style. The main ones to consider are:

- the head contours from top to bottom
- the head contours from side to side across the back
- the outer circumference of the hair lines (nape, sides and front, for example), which also act as cutting guides.

Guides for cutting are specially prepared sections of hair. Each is cut so that both the length and the cutting line are visible. The guide can be followed throughout the cutting process to produce even and precise results. Cutting haphazardly, without guides, produces peculiar and usually unwanted effects.

To prepare guide sections you should carefully note the features of the head – the position of the eyes, ears, nose, hairline points and so on. Further guides may be prepared in the neck, at the sides and at the front, to be followed throughout the cutting process.

Tip

Always use part of the previously cut hair as a guide to cutting and shaping the next part.

Tip

It is important to consider the amount of hair that will be left on the head after cutting. The closer the cut is made to the head, the more hair is removed.

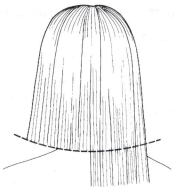

Cutting: guides

Cutting: guide sections

John Carne

Cutting: angles

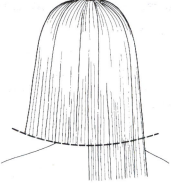

Cutting: lines

Cutting practice

To a certain extent, you can learn and practise tool movements and positions, combing hair at different angles, control of hands, hair and so on before you start cutting. Use practice hairpieces (slip-ons) which slip over a block. These allow your first cutting attempts to be monitored by your supervisor. You will soon be able to practise on live heads.

Cutting for the first time can be successful if you use a simple pattern and take a slow, methodical approach. You will only achieve speed in cutting after lots of practice. Never cut fast at the expense of a good hairstyle.

Cutting the lines and angles

Comb the hair and hold neat sections of it away from the head. The position in which you hold and cut the hair determines the positions the cut sections take when combed back on to the head.

The angles and lines of cutting depend on the different lengths required by the style. The first cutting line – the outer perimeter line – may be determined in the nape, as well as determining length. The second cutting line – the inner perimeter line – depends on the different lengths required throughout the style.

General style cutting

Although the methods of cutting you use may vary, the end results should not. Whether cutting horizontally, vertically or diagonally, or any combination of these, the hair should fit the head. There should be no visible steps, broken curves or lines, unless these effects are actually required. The finished cut should not need to rely on blow-drying, setting or dressing for its shape – you should use these techniques only to enhance and position the cut hair.

Tip

A section of hair held out at right angles (90°) to the back of the head and cut at right angles (90°) to the section, produces a 45° angle of graduation – that is, the gradient between the top and bottom of the hair section when positioned back on the head.

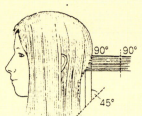

hair held at a 90° angle,
cut at a 90° angle,
gives a 45° angle of graduation

A section of hair held at 90° and cut at a 45° angle produces a steeper graduation.

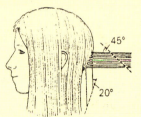

hair held at a 90° angle,
cut at a 45° angle,
gives a 20° angle of graduation

A section of hair held at 90° and cut at a 145° angle produces a level length, in which all the ends of the hair fall level, without graduation.

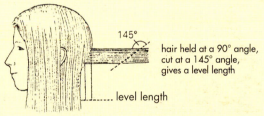

hair held at a 90° angle,
cut at a 145° angle,
gives a level length

level length

Cutting perimeter lines

Tip

It is important to follow the contours of the head, and the cutting lines must match the outline, the shape and the lengths required.

- A good approach to cutting is to choose a suitable starting point, providing yourself with a clear, visible guide for continuous cutting lines. This will help you to cut the hair easily. Be sure that all guide sections – particularly the first – are accurate so that following sections fit correctly. Make sure you are positioned in line with the cutting guide line so that the angle of the cut does not change during the cutting process, as this will create differing angles and an unbalanced cut. Consider carefully which techniques to use – tapering, clubbing, cutting the hair wet or dry, using scissors or a razor, and so forth.

- Make sure throughout that the client's head is held in a suitable position, so that you achieve the required shape.

- When sectioning hair, take sections that are small enough to hold comfortably. If the sections are too big, you will not be able to control your cutting and the result will be inaccurate. Keep checking your progress throughout the cut to make sure it is balanced.

● At the end, show the hairstyle to your client. Hold the hand mirror behind her at an angle, so that she can see the back and sides of her head reflected in the large mirror in front of her.

Activity

Using hair samples, practise the various haircutting techniques. Sketch the effects or shapes produced with each of the hair samples. Note the effect on the samples when trying to curl or wind them.

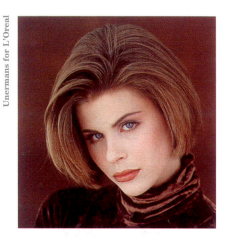

Unermans for L'Oreal

Bob cut

One-length shapes

In a one-length shape, or **bob cut**, the top layers of the hair fall into a line level with the underlying layers. With the weight of the hair on the outside, the ends can be made to turn under. The term **level length** is commonly used.

Classic bob – step by step

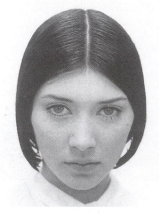

1 After shampooing, leave-in conditioner is applied evenly throughout the hair. A centre parting is taken from the forehead back to the crown.

2 This centre parting is continued down the back from the crown to the nape, and two slightly diagonal forward sections are taken from the centre out to the bottom of each ear.

3 The hair is combed down to its natural fall, with the head forward and, starting in the middle, the length is determined by combing flat on to the skin.

4 and 5 This line is then continued out to both sides, forming a slight arc. The balance on both sides is then checked before continuing.

 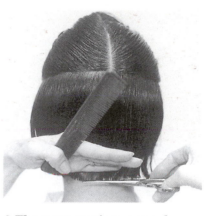

6 The next two sections are continued up the head, from the centre out to the middle of each ear.

7 Combing the hair down to its natural fall, the baseline is followed, working in the middle and then out to each side.

8 The next sections are taken from the top of the occipital bone at the back, out to the hairline at the front on both sides.

9 Moving the head into a natural upright position, the hair is combed down to its natural fall. Using no tension, the guideline is followed, starting in the middle at the back.

10 The line is then continued around the side to behind ear level.

11 When working with the hair over the ear it is very important not to use tension but allow for the protrusion of the ear and the fact that it may jump the hair up when it is dry.

12 Continue line through to the front without using tension. Exactly the same line is cut on the other side of the head.

13 Both sides are then checked for balance by pulling equal sections on to specific points on the face.

14 The next sections work up the head incorporating both the back and side areas.

15 Starting in the middle at the back, the hair is combed down to its natural fall and, without tension, the baseline is followed.

16 Allowing for the protrusion of the ear, the line is worked forward to the front. Exactly the same line is worked on the other side of the head.

17 One inch deep sections are continued up the side of the head on both sides.

18 and 19 Each section is combed down, without tension, and the baseline followed.

20 The last sections are combed down on either side of the centre parting. The balance on both sides is cross-checked again.

Hair by Toni & Guy.
Products used:
TIGI Essentials Leave-in conditioner,
TIGI spray mousse,
TIGI Essentials spray shine

Layering the hair

Most cutting techniques, except for those aimed at a one-length look, produce a layered effect to some degree. You can produce different layered looks by cutting the hair to different lengths – below or above shoulder length – or with or without partings or fringes.

Square layers – step by step

The square layer cut creates internal texture and shape on a mid-length baseline by working layering up to a square guideline.

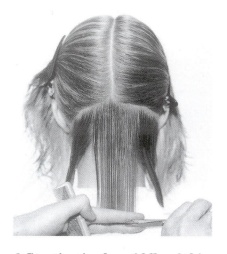

1 After shampooing, leave-in conditioner is applied evenly throughout the hair. A centre parting is used, from the forehead down to the nape, and two slightly diagonal sections are taken from the centre out to the bottom of each ear.

2 Starting in the middle of this section, the hair is combed down cleanly and held between the fingers. The length is determined, just below shoulder level.

3 The baseline is then worked squarely across to the side.

4 To complete the baseline, the other side is worked back into the centre. The balance is checked before continuing.

5 The next two sections are taken slightly diagonally from the centre out to the middle of each ear. Starting in the middle, the hair is combed down and the baseline underneath followed.

6 The baseline is followed out to the left-hand side.

7 This section is completed by working into the middle from the right side. One inch deep sections are continued up the back of the head until all of the hair has been cut into the baseline.

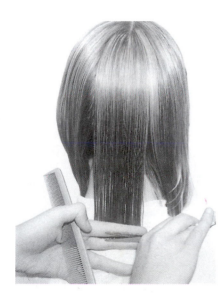

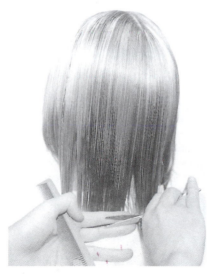

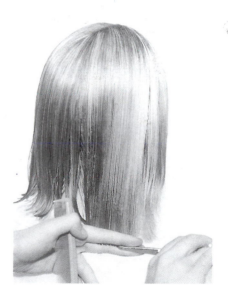

8, 9 and 10 As all the hair is combed down for the last section, the same technique is followed by starting in the middle and working out to each side. The balance is finally checked on both sides.

11 Showing the centre parting in the front.

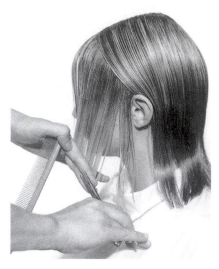

12 Using the forward graduation technique in the front, a diagonal section is taken on both sides from the centre down to the top of the ears. A guideline is determined from the baseline.

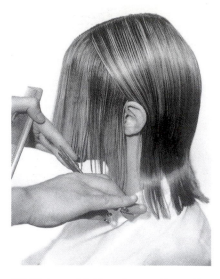

13 This guideline is continued up to the lip level and worked exactly the same on the other side.

14 Both sides are checked for balance.

15 An inch wide section is then taken from the forehead down to the nape. This is called a *profile line*.

16 Starting at the front, the graduation line that was cut to lip level is used as a guideline for layering length. The profile line is worked squarely back to the crown.

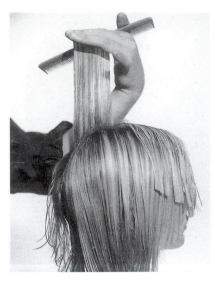

17 Continuing from the crown to the occipital bone area, the hair is over-directed up to the crown to maintain squareness and length.

18 A radial section is now taken across the top of the head from ear to ear.

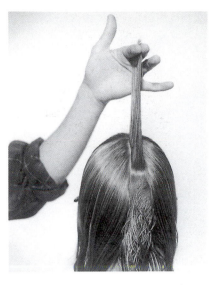

19 Starting with the central guide, pie-shaped sections are worked around the back using the crown as a pivot.

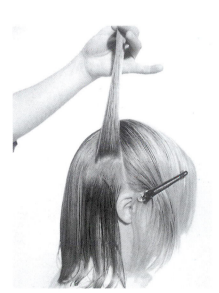

20 and 21 Each section is pulled up to the crown point and worked squarely across. These sections are worked around to the radial parting on both sides.

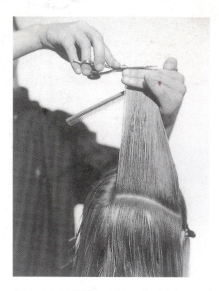

22 and 23 The entire back area is now cross-checked by using horizontal sections and pulling everything up to the square layering point.

24 A slight diagonal block section is now taken at the curve of the head, from the centre, down to the back. This section is pulled up to the square layering angle and blended, from the centre guideline into the back.

25 The next section is taken, moving forward, pulling the hair up at 90° and blending from the centre, across the sides and into the back.

26 The last section at the front, incorporating the hairline, is pulled up and slightly back to the square layering guideline. Exactly the same sectioning pattern is now used on the other side of the head.

27 Both sides are now cross-checked together to ensure balance through the sides. This is done visually, by pulling all of the hair up to the square layering guideline.

Hair by Tom & Guy.
Essential wash

Wet Essentials leave-in conditioner
THO1 Essentials spray gel

Short round layers – step by step

The short round layering technique creates texture through the internal area of the cut, and softness around the perimeter.

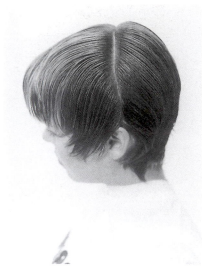

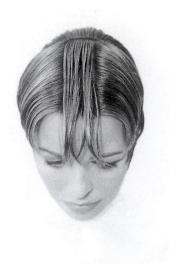

1 After shampooing and conditioning, mousse is applied evenly through the hair with the hands. The hair is separated into two by using a radial parting across the head from ear to ear.

2 A one inch section is then separated in the front from the forehead, back to the radial section. This will create the front part of the profile line.

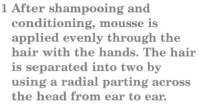

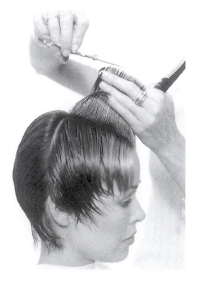

3 Starting in the crown area, this section is pulled up at 90° from the head and the layering length determined.

4 This section is continued to the front hairline.

5 A central, vertical section is now taken from the crown, down to the nape. This will create the back part of the profile line.

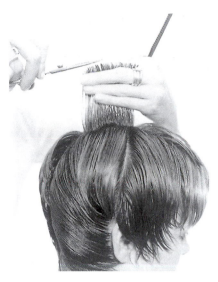

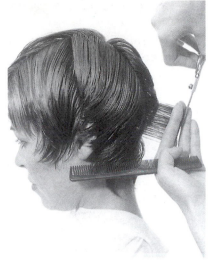

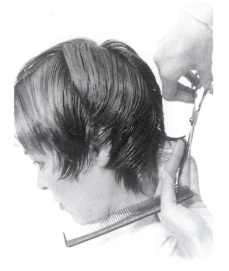

6 Using a guide from the front part of the profile line, the crown section is lifted up at 90° and curved with the shape of the head.

7 Continuing down this central section, all of the hair is cut to the same length.

8 This line is curved down into the nape area.

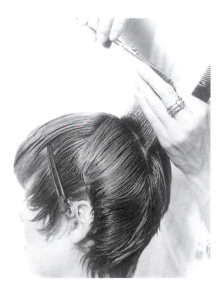

9 The next section is separated, using the crown as a pivot, with a pie-shaped section.

10 Using the guideline in the crown, the hair in this section is pulled out at 90° from the head and curved down.

11 This section is continued down into the nape.

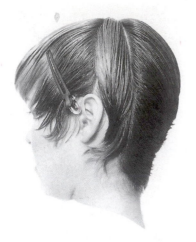

12 Pie-shaped sections are continued around the back of the head, using the crown as a pivot, until the last section on this side is taken behind the radial section. Each section is pulled out at 90° and worked down into the hairline. Exactly the same sectioning pattern is used on the other side at the back. The layers are cross-checked by using horizontal sections across the back.

13 A centre parting is taken from the crown to the forehead.

14 and 15 Continuing using the crown as a pivot, the next section is taken as a pie shape in front of the ear. Starting with the crown guideline, the hair is pulled out at 90° and curved with the shape of the head.

16 This section is continued down to the hairline at the side.

17 Pie-shaped sections are continued around this side of the head until the last section by the centre parting is reached.

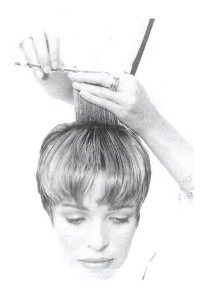

18 This section is pulled up to
   90° and worked forward.
   Exactly the same sectioning
   pattern is used to layer the
   other side at the front.

19 and 20 Both sides are cross-checked together by working
   forward from the crown with horizontal sections.

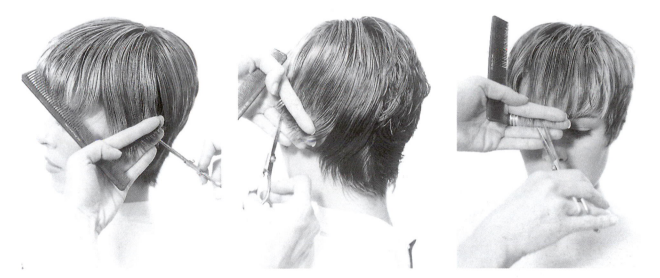

21, 22 and 23 The perimeter of the cut is now personalised by point-cutting up into the hair around
   the ears and in the front. This eliminates excess weight and length but maintains
   softness and personalises the cut for the individual.

Hair by Toni & Guy.
Products used:
TIGI Mousse, TIGI Extra Strong mousse,
TIGI hair glaze

Layered bob – step by step

The layered bob is a commercial, versatile look that maintains weight through the perimeter at the back, with softness and texture around the face.

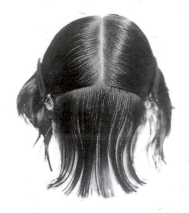

1 After shampooing and conditioning, spray gel is applied evenly through the hair. A central, vertical section is taken from the forehead, down to the nape and two slightly diagonal sections are taken from the centre out to the middle of each ear.

2 The hair is combed down to its natural fall and, starting in the middle of this section, the length is determined by holding the section at one finger's depth of graduation and point-cutting up into the hair.

3 and 4 The baseline is worked squarely across the back by first working out from the middle to the hairline on the left and then working back from the right-hand side to the middle.

5 and 6 Diagonal sections are continued up the back area, with each section combed down to its natural fall.

7 Starting in the middle, each section is held between the fingers and point-cut to follow the baseline.

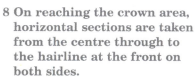

8 On reaching the crown area, horizontal sections are taken from the centre through to the hairline at the front on both sides.

9 and 10 Combing the hair down to its natural fall, the baseline is curved up at the sides to lip level. The balance on both sides is checked before continuing.

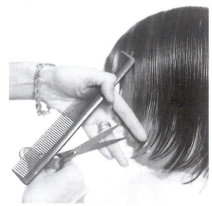

11, 12 and 13 Horizontal sections are continued up the side of the head until reaching the centre parting at the top, when all the hair is combed down to its natural fall. The curved baseline is followed by point-cutting.

14 A central vertical section is now taken from the crown, down to the nape.

15 and 16 Starting at the crown, the hair is pulled out to 90° and layers worked down, curving with the shape of the head.

17 Using the crown as a pivot, a one inch wedge-shaped section is now taken on the left of the central section.

18 and 19 Using a guideline from the crown, the hair is pulled out at 90° and curved down into the base.

20 and 21 Wedge-shaped sections are continued around the back to the ear and each section is curved down into the base.

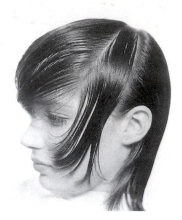

22 and 23 Continuing in front of the ear, the next section is over-directed back to the last layering guideline in order to maintain weight and length through the perimeter at the front.

24 The next section is taken from the crown to the recession area.

25 and 26 This section is again over-directed back to the layering guide behind the ear.

27 The rest of the hair, on the side of the centre parting, is now pulled back and layered.

28 To personalise the fringe area and work to the natural hairline growth, the fringe is point-cut by lifting out to a graduation level and working a slightly asymmetrical line.

Hair by Toni & Guy.
Products used:
TIGI Envirofixx,
TIGI Original hair glaze

Natural inversion – step by step

The natural inversion cut introduces a long layering technique that maintains length and weight through the perimeter of the hair while releasing and texturising the internal shape.

2 and 3 The baseline is created by determining the length in the middle and working squarely out to both sides.

1 After shampooing and conditioning, protein spray is applied evenly throughout the hair. The baseline at the back is achieved in exactly the same manner as for the one-length cutting technique. Starting in the nape, the hair is combed down, section by section until all of the back area is included.

4 A central one inch section is then taken from the forehead down to the nape.

5 Starting at the front, the existing fringe is ignored and the layering length determined by pulling up to 90° and gradually increasing in length to just in front of the crown.

6 and 7 The crown area is over-extended up to maintain length and weight in the baseline at the back.

8 The next section is taken diagonally back from in front of the crown, down into the nape.

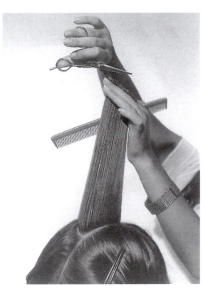

9 This section is over-directed into the central layering guideline.

10 and 11 Continuing the diagonal sections forward, each section is pulled up into the central layering guideline.

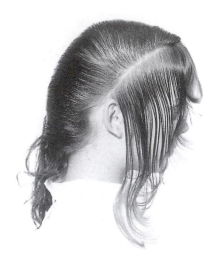

12 Working forward, the next
section is taken diagonally
to the top of the ear.

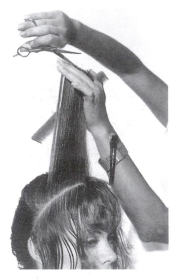

13, 14 and 15 Starting at the top, each part of this section is pulled up and into the centre, working
down and into the back area.

16 and 17 The rest of the hair on this side is then pulled up and
into the centre, following the guideline.

18 and 19 Exactly the same sectioning pattern is then used on the other side of the head, working with diagonal sections and pulling everything into the central guideline.

Tip

People don't always mean the same thing by 'an inch' (2.5 cm). Make sure that client and stylist agree about what they mean.

20 and 21 The fringe area is then separated using a triangular-shaped section from the centre out to the recession areas on both sides. Starting in the centre, the length is determined using the bridge of the nose as a guide and point-cutting up into the ends of the hair. This line is worked squarely across to the sides.

22 and 23 The perimeter at the sides is now checked by using a diagonal section on each side to the top of the ears. The line is defined by working up from the baseline to lip level.

Hair by Toni & Guy.
Products used:
TIGI Protein spray,
TIGI extra strong mousse

Cutting men's hair

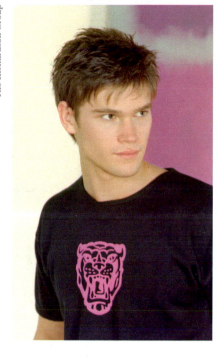

The Richardson Group

Introduction

Short layered looks, with different necklines, are worn by most men and many women. To achieve such a look, precise movements and accurate cutting angles are required. With the shorter styles the hair is too short to hide mistakes, so great care is necessary. Dressing is minimal and the styles rely on sharp definition and perfection of detail.

There are subtle differences between women's and men's styles. This is largely dictated by the differences in hair distribution, neckline patterns, facial hair and other characteristics. Pretty, fussy styles are not required by most men, while the decidedly shorter men's styles are generally not required by women (although fashion may dictate otherwise). Masculine and feminine looks are areas of study which, for those of you who intend to become expert, cannot be ignored. Moreover, client consultation may reveal special considerations which need to be applied to your cutting.

Preparation

Prepare your client so that he will be comfortable and well protected throughout the cutting process (see page 116). Cutting short layered styles will involve a lot of small, sharp, spiky hairs which need to be kept constantly cleared. Be careful that you do not expose yourself to flying hairs: position yourself so that your face is not in line.

Decide, with the help of your client, what needs to be done and which techniques you are going to use, and in particular whether you will cut the hair wet or dry.

Ralph Kleeli

Examination of hair and scalp

While you are making your initial examination of your client's hair and scalp, note the texture of the hair. If it is coarse and tightly

Vidal Sassoon

Ralph Kleeli

Ralph Kleeli

curled, you will need stronger combs to stretch the hair out from the head before cutting, and firmer movements will need to be applied. The density of the hair is important: if it is abundant, styles with varied hair length are possible. Sparse hair, particularly if it is fine, requires a great deal of attention and expertise. If finely textured hair has to cover sparse areas of the head, it will have to be longer than hair of coarser texture. The amount, type and distribution pattern of hair are all important too. Younger men may have distinctly higher forehead hairlines than women of similar age. Thinning crowns and decreasing density of hair marks many male patterns, though these are not usually seen in women until much later in life. Take this into consideration when designing and cutting hairstyles specifically for men and women. Hair growth, at a rate of about 12 mm each month, is more noticeable with shorter layered styles. To keep them tidy, regular trimming is essential.

 Activity

Arrange a visit to a local art and design studio. Make careful notes of anything you see that will help you in styling hair.

Interpretation of your client's wishes

 Tip

The principles of hairstyle design apply equally to men's and women's styling.

 Tip

Remember that heavy fringes used with the intention of hiding bald areas can do the opposite and make them more obvious. Careful angling and placing of the hair in line with the style is usually more effective.

Understanding the wishes and requirements of your clients is important. Creatively interpreting their needs and wants is a major part of hairstyle design. Clients of different age groups, careers, lifestyles and social positions require separate consideration. Factors such as practicality, suitability and the client's ability to cope with his hair are matters which you must not overlook. The final designs will be influenced by other considerations too – the amount of hair, its distribution, its texture and so forth. Unless all these are taken into account mistakes, and eventually a dissatisfied client, can be expected. By carefully and creatively interpreting your client's requirements from the beginning, you will be able to achieve professional results.

Short layered hairstyles can range from skin-cropped heads with 'coconut' crown shapes and forms to full, soft uncut looks which are perhaps more acceptable to a greater proportion of your clients. A whole range of styling effects can be produced, from the once-traditional short back and sides to longer, natural, more sculptured layered shapes. Named styles are fashionable from time to time. Some of these names, such as the various crew cuts, the 'DA' or duck-tailed shapes, have passed into the general vocabulary. Always make sure exactly what your client means if he names a style: it may be completely different from your idea of that style! Discuss with your client in detail what shape he wants, and apply it as agreed.

Activity

With your colleagues, take turns at acting as a stylist, or a client, and go through the consultation process for a new cut hairstyle. Notice how different stylists adopt different approaches.

Outlines

Many short, layered cuts are graduated at the sides and nape (clipper contoured). The necklines, the front hairlines and the sides are emphasised and require careful attention.

Natural necklines in men are usually less well defined than in women and need to be outlined. Women generally have softer, natural napelines which do not usually need defining. The more natural the napeline, the softer and less severe will be the look. The deeper are the cuts made into the hairline, the harsher and starker the look becomes.

The napeline can be of a variety of shapes – V-shaped, tapered, round, square and so forth. These can be achieved by shaping with the electric clippers, or shaving the outlines. Traditionally shaving was carried out with open-bladed razors; now electric shavers or safety razors can be used. Often outlining is done with the points of the scissors. Softer, graduated lines are to be preferred to blocky, blunt effects. The precise outline must be determined by the style required.

The shaping of front hair into a **fringe** (see page 173) can produce various acceptable effects on the chosen style. In many men, the front hairline recedes to some extent, however, due to male pattern baldness. This affects the choice and range of fringe shape. Think carefully about this before cutting the hair.

In men, the side hairlines, **sideburns** or **sideboards** bridge the hairstyle and beard shape. These need to fit, and care must be taken in shaping them. Lining the hair above the ears and along the sides of the nape is usually carried out with the scissor points or with inverted clippers. (In women there is little if any hair below the cheek bone at the side of the face. Recent styles have required shaping what little hair there is into points, and other forms.)

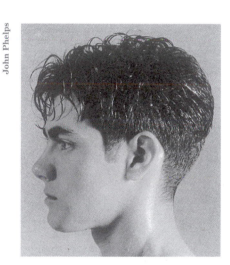

John Phelps

Tip

Necklines will be
- V shaped.
- U Round.
- ⊔ Square.

Activity

When you compile your men's style book, include notes on style design. Use pictures (rough sketches, detailed drawings or photographs), as appropriate. You may wish to use your book when consulting with clients, so consider the format carefully.

Ralph Kleeli

Cutting with or without partings

Partings in a hairstyle can be used to produce a variety of effects. Central partings divide the hair mass and can help to make a heavy head of hair look more tame. If the hair is distributed evenly and symmetrically, it becomes more manageable. Side partings can be used to divert attention from a prominent point, such as a large nose or unlevel ears; they can carry the eye of the viewer away from the unwanted look. Changing hair fashions affect the way in which partings are used, and many styles or dressing have no partings at all. Before attempting to cut, experiment by combing the hair to lie in different directions. Part the hair in several ways, diagonally, short or long, straight or angled. Longer lengths of hair or fuller effects may be required at the sides.

Ears

The ears, which in some people are not placed evenly, may be large or small, or irregular in shape. They may protrude from the head too noticeably and need to be considered, particularly when changing to a shorter hairstyle.

At this point you should also note whether your client uses spectacles or a hearing aid, and take these into your deliberations.

Between you and your client you will be able to agree exactly what look is required, and you will then have a basis on which to decide how the work is to be carried out.

Hair type

If your client's hair is very curly, do remember that it will coil back after stretching and cutting. Wavy hair, if cut too close to the wave crest, can be awkward to dress since it will tend to spring out from the head. Very fine straight hair will easily show cutting marks or unwanted lines if the sections are not divided and sectioned accurately, or if too large sections are taken. Tapering and thinning will encourage any tendency for the hair to curl at the ends, while clubbing will decrease that tendency. Feathering and texturising can produce extra lift and bounce.

Suitability and satisfaction

As you will by now understand, the main aim of every hairdressing service is that the client feels satisfied with the results when he or she leaves the salon. In men's cutting and styling, the central aim is to fashion shapes that are suitable to the individual client: that is, that he will find them acceptable and pleasing.

Tip

Competent handling of tools achieves the most precise results.

The client will be helped to feel safe, comfortable and satisfied if you are thoughtful and considerate in every aspect of client care. Indeed, that must be built into your activities in the salon.

Wet and dry cutting

If the hair is dirty, then for hygienic reasons it must be washed before you cut it. Wet hair may be preferred for blow-shaping and finishing, but on wet hair some scissor tapering movements have to be restricted. Clean, dry hair should not be cut with a razor because of the discomfort to your client and the tearing and dragging of the hair.

If you wish to dry-cut, then wash and dry the hair first. Explain this to your client so that he can express his wishes and needs.

Remember, wet hair stretches by anything from a third to half its length. Allow for this if you cut stretched hair, so that when it reverts back to the original length it is not too short.

More cutting techniques

John Phelps

Clubbing over fingers

As well as the techniques featured on pages 128–131. you may find the following particularly helpful when you are dealing with short layered styles.

Club-cutting or clubbing is more often required for shorter styles. Clubbing can be done 'over the comb'; continuous clubbing over the comb with scissors is often used for short graduations, such as that at the nape or the lower sides, or **shingling**. With an 'over the fingers' technique the hair is combed out, transferred to the fingers, and then cut straight across. Angles are determined by the amount of graduation required and the size of the section taken.

In another technique that may be helpful and effective, you lift a small section of hair with the scissors, transfer it to the comb, and then cut across.

Thinning techniques, using special thinning scissors with serrated blades, may be required but you must take great care with short hair. The hair could become spiky, particularly when it begins to grow again.

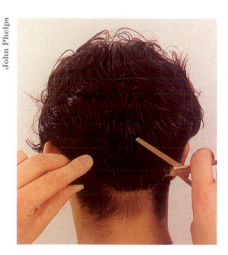

John Phelps

Thinning hair with serrated scissors

John Phelps

Point thinning with serrated scissors

John Phelps

Root thinning with serrated scissors

Clippers *(above)*
Clipper clubbing *(left)*

Razoring

Razoring, on wet hair, may be easier than scissor tapering. Take short, gentle strokes with the razor, to ensure evenness.

Clippering over comb or fingers is ideal for clubbing level lengths on short styles. It can also be used on its own; it is an invaluable technique for graduation. Clippers are made in a range of sizes for different purposes, and are numbered accordingly (see table).

Clipper Size	Length of cut hair
0000*	Very close to skin, like shaving
000*	0.3 mm (close cutting)
00	0.4 mm
0*	0.8 mm
0A	1.2 mm
1*	3.3 mm
1A	4.0 mm
1½	4.8 mm
2†	6.4 mm
3†	7.9 mm

*Most commonly used
†Mainly for beards and short crops

Activity

Each manufacturer may have its own sizing system for clippers, so make sure that you are aware of the maker's system before you buy. Make notes, and keep them in your folder.

Cutting techniques: a summary

Club-cutting or clubbing:

- over the fingers with scissors or clippers
- over the comb with scissors or clippers
- with razor between fingers and head.

Tapering:

- with scissors, backcombing first or slithering along section
- with razor, lightly under sections
- with clippers, with light stroking movements
- with thinning scissors towards hair points.

Thinning:

- with scissors
- with clippers
- with razor
- with thinning scissors.

Graduation:

- with clippers, varying the blade sizes to produce the slope (see page 131), between short and long hair
- with scissors over comb, lifting sections
- with scissors over fingers
- with scissors, lifting sections, transferring to comb and clubbing.

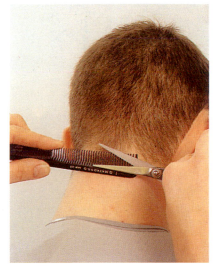
Graduation: scissors over comb

Activity

Check with the salon's wholesaler and equipment manufacturer to see what cutting tools are available. Try to get illustrations of the current models. There are frequent changes in types and models and this enables you to keep up to date. Make notes on the various tools and the differences between them.

Layering

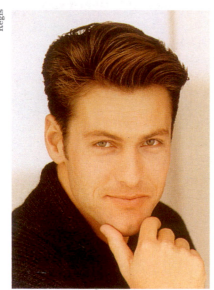

Regis

In layer cutting or **layering**, sections of hair are cut at varying angles from the head. The aim is to achieve an unbroken series of tiny, imperceptible lines or layers. The higher the sections are taken and cut, the greater is the amount of layering produced. Conversely, the lower the sections are held and cut, the less is the layering produced.

Layering is a method of shaping and controlling a head of hair. If you cut the layers that follow the underlying contours of the head and face, you can achieve attractive and satisfying results: of course, as usual, you have to take into consideration the limitations of the hair, growth patterns, head and face shape, wearing of spectacles or hearing aids and so on. Make allowance too for any varying face shapes, such as bumps and hollows, that need to be disguised or hidden by the overlying hairstyle.

Procedure

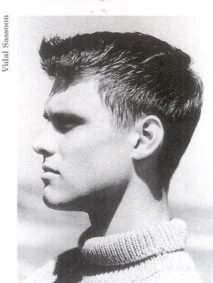

Vidal Sassoon

- Prepare your client for cutting and styling.
- Fully discuss your client's requirements with him.
- Examine his hair and note its length, quantity and texture, his face and head shape, and any abnormal or unusual features.
- Determine what needs to be done, with the agreement of your client.
- Decide which cutting techniques are likely to achieve the desired results.
- Make sure you have all tools and equipment to hand.
- Position your client's head carefully so that you can carry out your chosen techniques efficiently.
- Where to start the cut is an individual choice. The best position is one at which you can make the following cuts continuously, without hindrance.

Cutting method

- Accurate graduation achieves fine layering. This is partly determined by how much hair there is to cut. Longer lengths can be sectioned with the comb and taken between the fingers. Shorter lengths are best tackled by club-cutting with clippers, lifting sections with the comb and scissor-cutting, lifting with scissors and cutting over the comb, and so on.
- With short layered styles, clippers must be used to tidy the neckline, graduating from the natural line out from the head. How far up the head and how short this cut needs to be is determined by the style and shape agreed with your client. If longer lengths are required higher in the back hair, then the clippers need to graduate away from the head sharply.

Tip

The sequence is: comb the section, transfer to the fingers of the other hand, cut the hair, resection; move across the back of the head, cutting as you go.

- If you are just removing a few hairs clipper size 0000 may be used.
- If you are cutting deeply into the hair bulk, clipper size 1 may be more suitable.
- Graduate with scissors over comb into the napeline.
- This is the point at which to shape a man's sideburns, if required (and the lower side hair for a woman).
- If the hair is long enough comb a small section out from the head with the right hand, and transfer it to the fingers of the left. Cut the hair protruding beyond the finger straight across. If the hair is too short to section in this way, lift sections with the scissors and cut over the comb.
- Repeat this movement from the starting point. Continue taking small sections of hair out from the head, gradually moving over the side towards the lower back hair.

Cutting method:

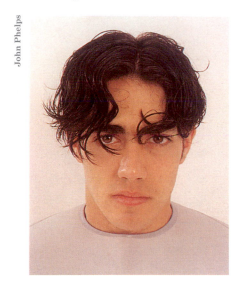

1 Before – front

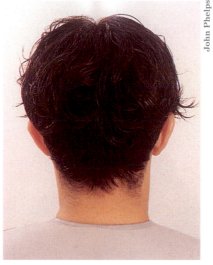

2 Before – back

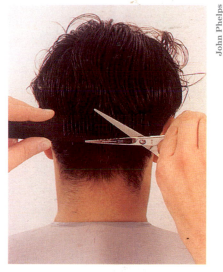

3 Clubbing: scissors over comb

4 Clubbing: over fingers

5 Clipper clubbing

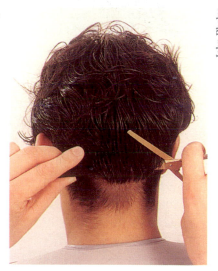

6 Thinning

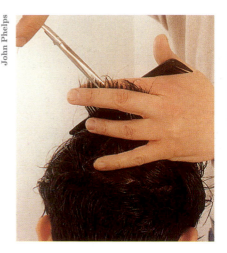

7 Texturising

8 Razoring

9 Fringe shaping

10 Outlining

11 Completed cut: front/side

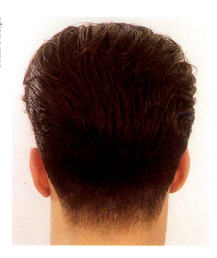

12 Completed cut: back

- Slightly overlap the sections so that the previously cut hair acts as a guide for cutting the next section.
- Continue to the centre back; then start at the other side and work towards the centre back again.
- When both sides and lower back hair have been cut, move up the head following the contours and begin to cut the upper sides and upper back towards the centre.
- Again move to the opposite side and repeat the process to the centre back.
- Repeat these movements as necessary until all the hair has been shaped.

Activity

There are many different methods of cutting short layered hairstyles. Make notes of all the procedures that you meet in the salon, training centres, shows and demonstrations. Include notes on the techniques applied, the sequence of methods, and the style produced. Use sketches or photographs where possible of layered hair styles.

Fringes

The front hair can be included in this procedure or it can be first combed into a fringe shape, either left to right or right to left, straight forward, blunted, feathered, pointed, rounded, tapered or layered.

A fringe shape should not be left looking too heavy and 'wiggy'. It should not be reduced so much that it looks so fine that the hairline can be seen through it. You have to strike a balance that looks just right. Make sure that you do not make areas of strong growth too short, or the hair will lift at the front and cause problems. Shape the fringe going with, rather than against, the natural movement flow. Don't overtaper or overthin, don't club-cut too short, and don't forget to refer constantly to the features of the head and face.

Method variations

Methods of cutting vary. You can start at any part of the head. You can use any of the cutting techniques you find most comfortable. You can work in whichever way you feel will achieve the results required. All good methods of cutting have the following in common: continuous sections are taken throughout the process, smaller rather than larger sections of hair are taken, and movements must (of course) ensure a single technique or a combination of techniques can be used.

If after clubbing the hair is still too bulky, it can be given its final shape by razoring. When razoring, make sure that you do not cut the top sections too heavily. This would produce too many short ends which might spike out.

Fashion looks

High-fashion styles represent the very latest trends in hair styling. These styles are intended to be worn by the model only, or at most a few others. Without adaptation, they are generally unsuitable for most people. At first sight they may appear to be extreme, and are often disliked, but they become more readily accepted as the fashion becomes understood, worn and seen. You need originality, good technique and experience to carry them out well.

Fashion styles are adapted high-fashion lines. They are created to suit different types of head or hair, or for different clients. These are favoured by the smart, well-dressed client and by people who like to look trendy. The new, different fashion styles and shapes – sometimes a return to older ideas – reflect the constant demand for novelty, ideas stimulated by an endless variety of events, moods and habits, and above all the wish to be different. As fashion styles become current and familiar, new ones appear to replace them.

Before starting to cut a client's hair to achieve a particular fashion look, you must closely examine and analyse their head and hair. Carefully assess the techniques you could use to produce the effects they want. Various questions need answering before you begin; these might include the following:

- How long is the client's hair now?
- Is the hair long enough for the required shape?
- How short will the hair be after cutting?

Fashion looks

Vidal Sassoon

Tip

Cutting techniques should be adapted and combined as required.

Tips

Increase volume by texturising.

Increase body or weight by club cutting.

Decrease volume by thinning.

Increase curl tendency by tapering.

Increase texture by razoring or pointing.

Bobs Hair Company/Rawson Partnership

- Does the client agree to this?
- Has the hair texture sufficient body for lifted, full or sweeping movements?
- What does the client mean by phrases like 'cut it long', 'a full forward fringe', 'short at the side' or 'make it thicker'?
- What effects are realistically achievable? Are they practical? Will they last?
- Will the effects requested be suitable? Can simple sketches help? When should you, as stylist, take the initiative?

Fashion style cutting

This involves cutting hair to a particular shape. It requires a blending of effects, methods and techniques. For you to achieve unique creations you should prepare your patterns of work, and carefully follow them exactly. Base them on the elements of styling as well as cutting.

Different parts of the head require different effects and techniques. The fringe hair may be 'skinny' and little reduction of length and body needed. The back hair may be thick and bushy and may well need to be tamed or shaped. You can only feel confident with a technique when you have practised it thoroughly. Then you can go on to attempt and perfect others: advanced fashion styles are rarely based on a single technique. Fashion styling is attained by progressing from the basic principles to more intricate aspects. Once you have grasped the essentials of cutting – cutting guidelines, understanding angles, holding sections – and can work accurately, then you can progress to the combination of techniques and effects that fashion requires.

Necklines

These may be shaped in various ways. They may be cut curved, straight or pointed, or graduated high or low. Low graduation produces soft effects. When cutting above the natural hairline, be careful to avoid harsh effects. Where hair is cut shortest, particularly at the nape, make sure that hair growth patterns do not distort the effects required.

Carl Shaw

Trimming

This is a term used for the removal of small amounts of hair. It is usually done to retain the original cut style. To reproduce the original shape, use techniques, cutting lines and angles similar to those used for the original cut.

Restyling

To **restyle** is to design a completely new hair shape. You need to check that the hair is long enough for the style requested. Some styles require certain lengths, and it may take time for the hair to grow before these can be achieved. If your client is particularly keen to have a certain style, you may need to work on it gradually over several months – for instance, to allow earlier layering to grow out.

Assignments – Cutting and styling hair

Closely watching your senior colleagues and trainer working is an invaluable means of learning. At first, cutting hair can be slow and difficult. With practice this soon changes.

To gather together information on cutting and styling you will need to visit hairdressing demonstrations, exhibitions and competitions. Using photography and video recording is ideal. Practising first cuts, or experimenting with the various techniques, can be carried out on practice blocks, slip-ons and models. You need to record as much as you can. Include the following:

1   Carefully list the movements and techniques that you see and outline the effects produced. Try to capture the section positions taken, angles of cut, direction of cutting lines and so forth.

2   Practise cutting as soon as possible after seeing or recording a movement. Remember that your cutting actions will be slow to start with and that will affect your results.

3   Outline the plan of the cut and list the important factors to consider.

4   How do the different growth patterns affect your cutting? Describe these and try to illustrate them.

5   Try to describe the different cutting procedures and refer particularly to the different parts of the head – the fringe, sides, nape, top and back. Say how these parts are blended together.

For you to find out

Investigate the sources of haircutting information. In addition to demonstrations, competitions and seminars, wholesalers and manufacturers of cutting tools are extremely helpful. Video tapes of a wide range of methods and techniques are available. The information you collect should include these items:

● how to choose suitable cutting tools
● the effects produced by the different tools
● how metal cutting tools are maintained and cleaned
● how to select the right tool for the effect required
● the difference between wet and dry cutting, and the tools used for each
● how tools should be used safely
● which razors are considered to be most hygienic.

A case study

A new client has come to you for a hair cut. The hair is fine, shoulder-length, and in poor condition. Outline how you would deal with this client. Work through the following sequence:

1   List the questions and points you wish to make.

2   What styles may be suitable for your client, and why?

3   Discuss face shapes, hair growth patterns, and other important factors.

4   Is a fringe to be cut? Should the hair at the sides sweep back or forward? What type of neckline is required?

5   Which cutting technique or combination of techniques should be applied?

6   Should partings be used?

7   List the problems that you might meet. How could you overcome them?

8   Do you need to demonstrate how to maintain the new style?

9   What action would you take if the client did not like the new style?

10   What aftercare advice do you need to give your client?

Preparing for Assessment

In preparing for assessment on cutting men and women's hair the following checklist may be helpful. Check that you have covered and now fully understand these items:

- discussing and agreeing with clients' requests
- consulting and advising clients
- determining a suitable hairstyle to cut
- assessing the hair quality, quantity, density, texture, condition and growth patterns
- selecting the right tools, techniques and combination of techniques
- competently cutting graduated layered styles
- competently cutting basic layered styles
- finishing with appropriate dressings if required
- advising on the aftercare and maintenance required
- recommending suitable hair care products or cosmetics
- making a 'before-and-after', perhaps pictorial, record of work carried out
- achieving client satisfaction
- dealing with the problems that may arise

When you feel that you are ready for assessment, talk to your trainer and arrange a suitable time.

By reading this chapter, carrying out the above activities, assignments and the case study, and by meeting the requirements in preparing for assessment you will have worked towards the key skill requirements in Communication Level 1 (C 1.1) (C 1.2) (C 1.3) and Level 2 (C 2.1) (C 2.2).

If you have used a computer to complete your assignments or activities you will have worked towards the key skill requirements in Information Technology Level 1 (IT 1.2).

Perming and neutralising hair

7

Lino Carbosiero at Daniel Galvin for L'Oreal

Learning objectives

The following are some of the topics covered in this chapter:

- perming principles
- perming – how it works
- preparation and planning
- examination and consultation
- tests to be taken
- sectioning and sub-sectioning
- techniques for winding the hair
- processing and neutralising the hair.

Introduction

Perming is the name commonly used to describe the process of permanently waving or curling hair. There are various perming systems and procedures. Throughout history, people have experimented with their hair in attempts to make themselves more beautiful. Changing straight hair to curly, or curly hair to straight, have alternated in popularity for centuries. More recently there have been rapid developments in technique, and newer perming systems are regularly introduced. In the past there have been systems using heat, tepid and cold processes. Some have used electrical attachments and 'cooked' clients' hair for hours at a time. Your grandmother or your great-grandmother could probably tell you some strange tales of what she went through in her search for beauty!

In this chapter we will look at the methods that are currently being used in salons.

Perming – the principles

Cross-section of hair

Perming, also known as permanent waving or curling, is a technique for making straight hair curly. Some methods use warmth, but the most popular techniques, called cold perming (or **CPW**), do not. Unlike the curls produced by setting and blow-styling, the curls produced by perming really are permanent: the hair does not straighten out later when it absorbs water from the atmosphere. Hair grows, however, and new hair takes its natural form. So the waves and curls produced by perming gradually get further and further from the scalp as the hair grows. To keep the style, sooner or later the hair will need to be permed again.

Because perming really does make a permanent change to the hair, you cannot easily correct mistakes (as you can with blow-styling, for example). The process also involves various chemicals. It is therefore important that you make sure you understand what you are doing.

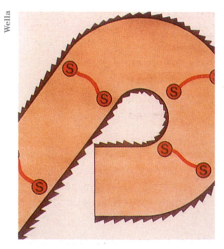

Disulphide bridges

How perming works

Before going ahead with this section, re-read 'The chemical properties of hair' in Chapter 1 (page 7).

Changing the keratin

Of the cross-links between the polypeptide chains of hair keratin, the strongest are the **disulphide bridges** – these give hair its strength. Each disulphide bridge is a chemical bond linking two sulphur atoms, one in each of two polypeptide chains lying alongside each other. Each sulphur atom forms part of an amino acid unit called **cysteine**; the pair of linked units is called **cystine**.

During cold perming some of these bridges are chemically broken, converting each cystine into two cysteine units. The breaking of the

Wella

Reduction: breaking existing disuiphide bridges

bridges makes the hair softer and more pliable, allowing it to be moved into a new position of wave or curl.

Only about 20 per cent of the disulphide bridges need to be broken during a perm. If too many are broken, the hair will be damaged. You need to keep a check on the progress of the perm, and stop it at the right time. You do this by rinsing away the perm lotion and **neutralising**/normalising the hair. During neutralising, pairs of cysteine units join up again to form new cystine groups. The new cross-links thus formed hold the permed hair firmly into its new shape.

Changing the bonds

The hair is first wound on to some kind of **former**, such as a curler or rod. Then you apply perm lotion to the hair, which makes it swell. The lotion flows under the cuticle and into the cortex. Here it reacts with the keratin, breaking some of the cross-links within and between the polypeptide chains. This softens the hair, allowing it to take up the shape of the former. You then rinse away the perm lotion, neutralise the hair, and allow it to harden in its new, curlier shape.

This process is often described in chemical terms. The first part – softening the hair by breaking some of the cross-links – is a process of **reduction**. The disulphide bridges are split by the addition of hydrogen from the perm lotion. (The chemical in the perm lotion that supplies the hydrogen is called a **reducing agent**.) The keratin is now stretched: it is beta-keratin.

The last part of the process – hardening the hair by making new cross-links – is an **oxidation** reaction. New disulphide bridges form, and the hydrogen that was added is lost again. The hydrogen reacts with the oxygen in the neutraliser, forming water. (The chemical in the neutraliser that supplies the oxygen is called an **oxidising agent** or **oxidant**.) The keratin is now in a new, unstretched form: it is alpha-keratin again.

Reducing agents

Most alkaline perms contain ammonium thioglycollate, this is the most common reducing agent used in perm lotions. Its purpose is to break down some of the cystine linkages in the hair. However some alkaline perms are 'non-thio' and these tend to be gentler in their action on the hair.

Alkaline perms vary in strength and can have a pH range of 8.2 to 9.6. When an alkaline perm is applied to the hair the cuticle swells and opens, allowing the perm solution to enter the hair shaft.

In the 1970s acid-balanced perms were introduced. Their main ingredient was glycerol monothioglycolate, which gave the perm lotion a pH of around 4.5 to 7.9. These types of perms were kinder to the hair than alkaline-based perms and usually used on delicate hair types, for example hair that had previously been chemically treated or very fine hair.

However some ingredients for acid-balanced perms were found not to be 'friendly' to the skin and could cause irritation. Most

Charlie Taylor

Wella

> **Tip**
>
> Reducing agents e.g. ammonium hydroxide, ascorbic and oxidising agents e.g. hydrogen peroxide and sodium bromate are common ingredients of some perms.

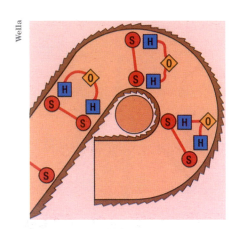

Oxidation: forming new disulphide bridges

manufacturers' have replaced acid perms with a perm that has a low alkaline content of around pH 7.1 and are often called pH-balanced or mild alkaline perms.

Acid/pH-balanced perms produce a softer curl formation than alkaline perms. To produce a similar curl result to that of an alkaline perm a smaller rod size may need to be used. Because these perms do not contain a high alkaline content, they do not swell the hair shaft to the same extent as an alkaline perm, are slower to penetrate the hair and may take longer to process. Heat is often used to speed up processing.

Alkaline perms

- Do not need heat

- Are used on resistant/ difficult to perm hair

- Give a strong curl

- Process quicker than acid perms

- Are long lasting.

Acid/pH-balanced perms

- May need heat to help process

- Are used on delicate hair

- Are kinder to the formation hair structure

- Give a soft curl formation.

Oxidising agents

Hydrogen peroxide is the best-known oxidant. Others include sodium perborate, sodium percarbonate, sodium bromate and potassium bromate.

Preparing and planning the perm

The client

For the client a perm is a major step – they will have to live with the result for several months. Clients may not be familiar with the range of perms available: they will need you to explain what is involved in each and to help them decide which is the most suitable.

- There are several cold perms designed to curl straight hair. See the brochures produced by manufacturers.

- Acid-balanced, pH-balanced or mild alkaline perms are popular because their effects are gentle. Strongly alkaline perms can be too harsh: new forms are being developed.

- Not all perms contain ammonium thioglycollate: 'non-thio' perms tend to be gentler in their action.

Health & Safety

Always bear in mind how your perm will affect the client's hair structure.

Discuss your client's requirements. Find out what they expect from a perm, and determine whether this is the best solution.

Permed hair

Tip

Always read the client's record card to refer to previous services done on the hair.

- Consider the style and cut, together with your client's age and lifestyle.
- Examine the hair and scalp closely. If there are signs of inflammation, disease, or cut or grazed skin, do *not* carry out a perm. If there is excessive grease or a coating of chemicals or hairspray, you will need to wash these out first (see Chapter 3). Previously treated hair will need special consideration (discussed later in this chapter).
- Analyse the hair texture. Carry out the necessary tests to select the correct perm lotion. See Chapter 1 and the section on tests on pages 183–184.
- Always read manufacturers' instructions carefully.
- Determine the types of curl needed to achieve the chosen style.
- If this is a regular client, refer to their record card for details of previous work done on their hair.
- Advise your client of the time and costs involved. Summarise what has been decided, to be sure there is no misunderstanding.
- Minimise combing and brushing, to avoid scratching the scalp before the perm.
- Ensure that a client record card is prepared.

 Activity

List all the factors that could influence your choice of perm.

 Activity

List the different types of perming products, with notes on the main differences between them.

By completing this activity you will have worked towards the key skill Communication Level 1 (C 1.3).

By using a computer to extract information on products you can work towards the key skill Information Technology Level 1 (IT 1.1) (IT 1.2).

 Activity

Bleach some samples of hair to varying degrees of lightness. Rinse, clear, and dry them. Then wind and perm them all, using the same size of curlers, the same length of time (5 or 10 minutes), and the same perm lotions. Compare the results.

Activity

On your practice block or collected hair samples (all of the same texture), use an alkaline perm on one part and an acid perm on another. Follow the directions for the use of each. Wind carefully; and apply the neutralisers properly. Compare the results.

Use pH papers to test each of your perm lotions. Which are acid and which alkaline?

Activity

In your work folder, list all the signs and symptoms of the hair and: scalp diseases, states or defects that indicate that you should not carry out a perm.

By completing this activity you will have worked towards the key skill Communication Level 1 (C 1.3).

Examination

It is important to make sure you choose the most suitable perm lotion, the correct processing time and the right type of curl for the chosen style. Consider the following factors.

Hair texture – for hair of medium texture, use perm lotion of normal strength. Fine hair curls more easily and requires weaker lotion; coarse hair is harder to wave and requires stronger lotion.

Hair porosity – the porosity of the hair determines how quickly the perm lotion is absorbed. Porous hair in poor condition is likely to process more quickly than would hair with a resistant, smooth cuticle (see Chapter 1).

Previous treatment history – 'virgin' hair – hair that has not previously been treated with chemicals – is likely to be more resistant to perming than hair that has been treated. It will require a stronger lotion and possibly a longer processing time.

Length and density of hair – long, heavy hair requires more perming than short hair because the hair's weight will pull on the curls. Short, fine hair may become too tightly curled or over-processed if given the normal processing time.

Style – does the style you have chosen require firm curls or soft, loose waves? Do you simply wish to add body and bounce?

Size of rod, curler or other former – larger rods produce larger curls or waves; smaller rods produce tighter curls. Longer hair generally requires larger rods. If you use very small rods in fine, easy-to-perm hair, the hair may frizz; if you use rods that are too large you may not add enough curl. To check, make a test curl before you start (see below).

Incompatibility – perm lotions and other chemicals used on the hair may react with chemicals that have already been used – for example, in home-use products. Hair that looks dull may have been treated with such chemicals. Ask your client what products they use at home, and test for incompatibility (see the chart in Chapter 1).

Tests

Cleanliness – check that the hair is clean. Dirt or grease will block the action of the perm, and the results may be straight rather than curly.

Elasticity – stretch a hair between your fingers. If it breaks easily the cortex may be damaged, and perming could be harmful.

Porosity – rub the hair between your fingertips to feel how rough or smooth it is. Rougher hair is likely to be more porous and will therefore process more quickly.

Incompatibility – protect your hands by wearing gloves. Place a small cutting of hair in a mixture of hydrogen peroxide and ammonium hydroxide. The mixture is made up of twenty parts hydrogen peroxide with one part ammonium hydroxide. (The ammonium hydroxide is used to speed up any reaction that may take place. Hydrogen peroxide can be used on its own but will take a lot longer to react.) Watch for signs of bubbling, heating or discolouration: these indicate that the hair already contains incompatible chemicals. The hair should not be permed, nor should it be tinted or bleached. Perming treatment might discolour or break the hair, and might burn the skin.

Incompatibility reactions

Tip

Always document the tests that have been carried out, plus the questions you have asked and the client's response on the client's records. Record the results of all tests. If test results are positive (i.e. incompatible), do not carry out the perm service.

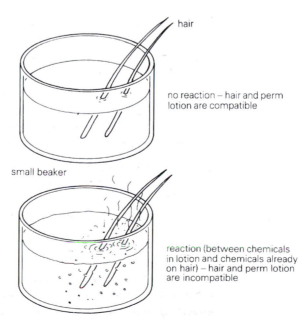

hair

no reaction – hair and perm lotion are compatible

small beaker

reaction (between chemicals in lotion and chemicals already on hair) – hair and perm lotion are incompatible

Health & Safety

Before processing, check the salon temperature, because of its influence on the course of the perm.

Test curl – wind, process and neutralise one or more small sections of hair. The results will be a guide to the optimum rod size, the processing time and the strength of lotion to be used. Remember, though, that the hair will not all be of the same porosity.

Processing – unwind – and then rewind – rods during processing, to see how the curl is developing. If the salon is very hot or cold this will affect the progress of the perm: heat will accelerate it, cold will slow it down. When you have achieved the 'S' shape you want, stop the perm by rinsing and then neutralising/normalising the hair.

Perming technique

Permed hair

Perming is a straightforward procedure – the more organised you are, the simpler and more successful it will be. Once you have consulted with your client and made the necessary tests, you are ready to start.

Preparation

1 Protect your client as necessary with a gown and towels.
2 Shampoo the hair to remove grease or dirt which would otherwise block the action of the perm lotion.
3 Towel-dry the hair. (Excess water would dilute the lotion, but if the hair is too dry the perm lotion won't spread thoroughly through the hair.)
4 Some perm lotions contain chemicals to treat porosity. If you are going to use a pre-perm lotion to help even out porosity apply it now. Make sure you have read the instructions carefully. Too much pre-perm lotion may block the action of the perm itself.
5 Prepare your trolley. You will need:
   - rods, curlers or formers of the chosen sizes
   - end papers, for use while winding
   - a tailcomb and clips, for sectioning and dividing
   - cottonwool strips, to protect your client
   - gloves, to protect your hands
   - perm lotion and a suitable neutraliser, normaliser (read the instructions carefully)
   - a water spray, to keep the hair damp
   - a plastic cap and a timer for the processing stage.
6 Check that your client's skin and clothing are adequately protected.

Tip

By estimating the number of perm rods you will need and the ratio of the different sizes, you will have worked towards key skill application of number Level 1.

Health & Safety

Be sure you wear protective gloves before using any chemicals/perm lotions.

Sectioning/sequence of winding

The first operation is to divide the hair into **sections**. This makes the hair tidier and easier to control. Done properly, sectioning

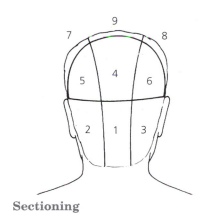

Sectioning

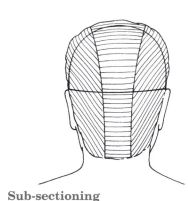

Sub-sectioning

Winding: taking a hair section

Tip

To gain control of hair ends, practise winding without using papers. These aids help to make winding quicker, but you still need good technique.

makes the rest of the process simpler and quicker. If it's not done well, though, you will have to re-section the hair during the perm, and this may spoil the overall result.

Cold perm sectioning

1   Following shampooing and towel-drying, comb the hair to remove any tangles.
2   Make sure you have the tools you will need, including a curler, to check the section size.
3   Now divide the hair into nine sections, as follows. Use clips to secure the hair as you work.

- Divide the hair from ear to ear, to give front hair and back hair.
- Divide the back hair into lower, nape hair and upper, top back hair.
- Divide the front hair, approximately above mid-eyebrow, to give a middle and two sides.
- Divide the top section along the same lines, to give a middle and two sides.
- Divide the nape section likewise, to give a middle and two sides.

Once the hair has been divided into the nine sections and firmly secured with clips you can start to wind in the perm rods. The diagram on sectioning shows the nine sections. The numbering refers to the order in which the sections are wound. You start winding in the nape area first because the hair tends to be the most resistant and the hair line at the front tends to react quicker to chemicals. Each section is sub-sectioned to the same size of the perm rod being wound in, so that the rod sits on its own base.

Winding

Winding is the process of placing sectioned hair on to rods, curlers or formers. There are various winding techniques, designed to produce different effects, but the method is basically the same in each case. In modern cold perming systems you need to wind the hair firmly and evenly, but without stretching the hair or leaving it in tension.

First practise winding wet hair on a block. It should be dampened with water rather than perm lotion, as this gives you more time. When you can wind a block in 40–60 minutes, move on to a live model. When you can do this in 20–30 minutes, you can try 'live perming' with perm lotion.

Winding – method

1   Divide off a section of hair, of a length and thickness to match the curler being used. (See the diagram on sub-sectioning above.
2   Comb the hair firmly, directly away from the head. Keep the hair together, so that it doesn't slip.

Winding the section on to the curler

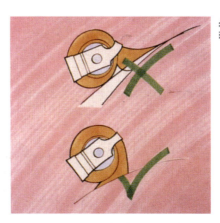

Winding: securing the curler

3 Place the hair points at the centre of the curler. Make sure the hair isn't bunched at one side and loose at the other.

4 Hold the hair directly away from the head. If you let the hair slope downwards, the curler won't sit centrally on the base section: hair will overlap, and the curler will rest on the skin.

5 Before winding, make sure the curler is at an angle suited to the part of the head against which it will rest when wound.

6 Hold the hair points with the finger and thumb of one hand. The thumb should be uppermost.

7 Direct the hair points round and under the curler. Turn your wrist to achieve this. The aim is to lock the points under the curler and against the main body of hair – if they don't lock, they may become buckled or fish-hooked. Don't turn the thumb too far round or the hair will be pushed away from the curler and won't lock the points.

8 After making the first turn of the curler, pass it to the other hand to make the next turn. The hands need to be in complete control: uncontrolled movement, or rocking from side to side, may cause the ends to slip, the hair to bunch, or the firmness to slacken.

9 After two or three turns the points will be securely locked. Wind the curler down to the head. Keep the curler level – if it wobbles from side to side, the hair may slip off or the result may look uneven.

10 At the end, the curler should be in the centre of the section. If it isn't, unwind it and start again.

11 Secure the curler. Don't let the rubber fastener press into the hair – it might damage it.

Winding: depth of section

Spiral winding

Winding: width of section

Winding techniques

There are various winding techniques, used to produce varied effects. The following are the most commonly used.

Spiral winding – the hair is wound from roots to points, around a variety of sticks, shapers, hair moulders or curlers of one shape or another. Triangular and square shapers have been used. The effects

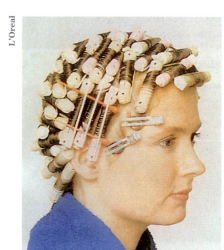

Directional winding

Staggered or brick winding

produced are mainly in the lengths of the hair, the root ends being less affected. This is probably the oldest form of winding. It is most effective, and most practical, with long hair.

Croquignole winding – this starts at the hair points and works down to the roots. This technique has been commonly used for years in cold perming. It is best used where the hair curl needs to be strongest at the points. (The term 'croquignole' comes from the old wigmaking trade.)

Directional winding – the hair is wound in the direction in which it is to be finally worn. This technique is suitable for enhancing well-cut shapes. The hair can be wound in any direction required, and the technique is ideal for shorter hairstyles.

Staggered winding or **brick winding** – the wound curlers are placed in a pattern resembling brickwork. By staggering the partings of the curlers, you avoid obvious gaps in the hair. It is suitable for short hairstyles.

Weave winding – the normal-size section is divided into two and then the hair is woven. A large curler is used to wind the upper sub-section, and a smaller one is used for the lower sub-section. This produces two different curl sizes, giving volume without tight curls. Alternatively, one sub-section is wound and the other left unwound. With short hair this produces spiky effects.

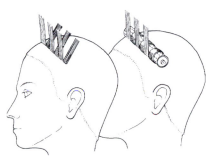

Weave winding

Double winding – this technique consists of winding a section of hair halfway down on a large curler, then placing a smaller curler underneath and winding both curlers down to the head. This produces a varied curl effect.

Double winding

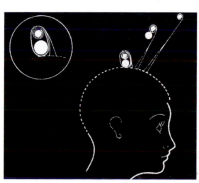

Piggyback winding – this is winding using a small and a large curler. The normal-size section is wound from the middle on to a large curler, down to the head. The ends are then wound from the points on to a smaller curler, which is placed on top of the large curler. This produces softly waved roots and curly points. Alternatively this technique can be used to produce root movement only by not winding the point ends.

Piggyback winding

Stack winding – this is used where fullness of long hair is required, with little curl movement on top – it is ideal for bobbed hair lengths. The sections are wound close to the head in the lower parts; the upper sections are part wound only, at the points. This allows the curlers to stack one upon another.

Stack winding

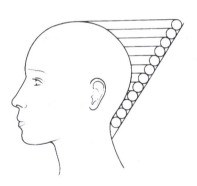

To appreciate the effects of different techniques of winding you need to experiment with them. Many professionals are continually trying out new approaches, sometimes with exciting results.

 Activity

Using blocks, practise the different winding techniques. Process them as well, so that you are familiar with their effects before live perming.

Winding aids

- The **tailcomb** is useful for directing small pieces of hair on to the curler. Don't let the tail pass around the curler, as this causes unevenness and hair may slip out of the wound section.
- **End papers** or **wraps** are specially made winding aids and they are the most frequently used. They ensure control of

the hair when it is wound. Fold them neatly over the hair points (never bundle them). The wrap overlaps the hair points and prevents fish-hooking. For smaller or shorter sections of hair, half an end wrap is sufficient – a full one would cause unevenness. Other types of tissue may absorb the perm lotion and interfere with processing, and these are best avoided.

- **Crêpe hair** is useful for holding the hair points when winding: it allows enough grip and prevents the ends from slipping. As with end papers, only a little should be used. Too much makes the hair bunch together.

- Many kinds of curler are suitable for cold perm winding. Plastic, wood, bone and china are amongst the materials used. Different colours are used to indicate size. The greater the diameter, or the fatter the curler, the bigger the wave or curl produced. The smallest curlers are used for short nape hair, or for producing tight curls. Most curlers are of smaller diameter at the centre: this enables the thinner hair points to fill the concave part evenly and neatly as the hair is wound. This is particularly useful with tapered hair. Clubbed hair should be evenly spread across the centre of the curler.

 Activity

Try out different curlers, rods and winding shapes. Note the varied effects they produce.

Practise the different curler positions for perming. Try these out on blocks or models to appreciate the differences.

 Activity

On a practice block of sample hair cuttings, experiment with the effects produced by different faulty windings. This will help you to recognise and to avoid these effects.

Processing and development

Perm lotion may be applied before winding, (**pre-damping**) or when winding is complete (**post-damping**). Pre-damping is often used on long hair to ensure the solution penetrates evenly through the hair length. When pre-damping, you have to work quickly to avoid over-processing the hair. Your work should be complete within 35 minutes. Follow the manufacturer's instructions on the type of application to use. Post-damping is perhaps more convenient: you can wind the hair without wearing gloves, and the time taken in winding doesn't affect the overall processing time.

Health & Safety

Cold perm lotions and neutralisers are potentially hazardous substances. Use them with care. Always follow the manufacturer's instructions for their use, and check with your salon's COSHH list of potential hazards (see page 296) for correct usage. Refer to the HMWA leaflet Health and Safety in the Salon and the Health and Safety Executive's Completing COSHH Assessments.

Tip

Perm lotion and neutraliser may be similarly packed. Double check to avoid mistakes.

Goldwell

Perming products

Tip

Choose a winding technique according to the effects you require.

Health & Safety

Always check electrical equipment is operating properly before using it on your client

Applying the perm lotion

Most perm lotions come in an applicator bottle, ready to use. Others may need to be applied from a bowl, using cottonwool, a sponge or a brush. Read the instructions carefully before applying.

- Underlying hair is usually more resistant to perming. Apply lotion to these areas first. e.g. of the nape of the neck (see the diagram on sectioning on page 185).
- Keep lotion away from the scalp. Apply it to the hair section, about 12 mm from the roots.
- If post-damping apply a small amount of the perm lotion to each rod; do not over saturate as the lotion will flood onto the scalp and will drip on to the client. This could cause either irritation or burning on the scalp or skin.
- It is better to apply the lotion again once the first application has started to absorb into the hair.
- Don't overload the applicator, and apply the lotion gently. You will be less likely then to splash your client.
- If you do splash the skin, quickly rinse the lotion away with water.

Processing time

Processing begins as soon as the perm lotion is in contact with the hair. The time needed for processing is critical. **Processing time** is affected by the hair texture and condition, the salon temperature and whether heat is applied, the size and number of curlers used, and the type of winding used.

Hair texture and condition – fine hair processes more quickly than coarse hair, and dry hair than greasy hair. Hair that has been processed previously will perm faster than virgin hair.

Temperature – a warm salon cuts down processing time; in a cold salon it will take longer. Even a draught will affect the time required. Usually the heat from the head itself is enough to activate cold perming systems. Wrap your client's head with plastic tissue or a cap to keep in the heat. Don't wrap the hair in towels: these would absorb the lotion and slow down the processing.

Some perm lotions require additional heat, from computerised accelerators roller balls or dryers (see Chapter 3). Don't apply heat unless the manufacturer's instructions tell you to – you might damage both the hair and the scalp. And don't apply heat unless the hair is wrapped; the heat could evaporate the lotion, or speed up the processing too much.

Curlers – processing will be quicker with a lot of small sections on small curlers than with large sections on large curlers. (The large sections will also give looser results.)

Winding – the type of winding used, and the tension applied, also affect processing time. A firmer winding processes faster than a slack winding – indeed, if the winding is too slack it will not process at all. Hair wound too tightly may break close to the scalp. The optimum is a firm winding without tension.

Tip

During processing, don't leave your client while you do something else. You might lose track of time or forget to check the curls. Besides, your client might become anxious.

Health & Safety

Don't pack curlers with dry cotton wool. This would absorb the perm lotion, it would also put it in direct contact with the skin, causing irritation.

Mop up any surplus lotion on the skin, then use a barrier cream across the hairline. Don't let barrier cream get on the hair, however, as this would block the lotion from penetrating into the hair.

Testing curls during processing

As processing time is so critical, you need to use a timer. You also need to check the perm at intervals to see how it's progressing. If you used the pre-damping technique, check the first and last curlers that you wound. If you applied the lotion after winding, check curlers from the front, sides, crown and nape.

- Unwind the hair from a curler. Is the 'S' shape produced correct for the size of curler used?
- If the curl is too loose, rewind the hair and allow more processing time. (But if the test curl is too loose because the curler was too large, extra processing time will damage the hair and won't make the curl tighter.)
- If the curl is correct, stop the processing by rinsing.

Permed hair

Health & Safety

Take care not to splash your client's face while rinsing. Even dilute perm lotion can irritate the skin. If perm lotion enters the client's eye, flush out immediately with cold running water. Ensure the water drains downwards away from the face. Seek help from a qualified first aider.

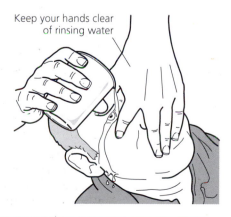

Keep your hands clear of rinsing water

Neutralising – introduction

Kathleen Bray for Clynol. Photo: Ian Hooten

Permed hair

Whether or not a perm is satisfactory to the client depends in part, of course, on correct processing of the hair, but also on correct neutralising of the perm lotion after the correct period of time.

In this section we will look at:

- principles of neutralising
- how neutralising works
- choosing a neutraliser
- neutralising techniques
- what to do after perming.

Neutralising – the principles

Tip

Read labels and check contents of boxes – before use.

Wella

Neutralising

Neutralising is the process of returning hair to its normal condition after perming. The word is a little misleading: chemically speaking, a 'neutral' condition is neither acidic nor alkaline (pH 7.0). In fact, healthy hair is slightly acidic (pH 4.5–5.5).

How neutralising works

As described earlier, perm lotion acts on the keratin in the hair. The strongest bonds between the polypeptides are the disulphide bridges. Perm lotion breaks some of these, allowing the keratin to take up a new shape. This is how new curls can form.

What neutralising does is to make new disulphide bridges. If you didn't neutralise the hair would be weak and likely to break, and the new curls would soon fall out. Neutralising is an oxidation process – a process that uses oxidising agents such as hydrogen peroxide, sodium bromate and sodium perborate.

Choosing a neutraliser

Manufacturers of perm lotions usually produce matching neutralisers. These are designed to work together. If possible, always use the neutraliser that matches the perm lotion you've used.

A neutraliser may be supplied as an emulsion cream, a foam or a liquid. Always follow the manufacturer's instructions. Some can be applied directly from the container, others are applied with a sponge or a brush.

Activity

Try perm processing with one type of perm lotion on two or more hair samples or practice blocks. Use a different neutraliser for each. Note the different effects, if any.

Neutralising technique

Neutralising follows directly on from perming. Imagine that you have shampooed, dried and wound the hair. The hair is now perming, and you are timing the perm carefully and making tests to check whether it is complete. You will also be reassuring the client that they have not been forgotten! As soon as the perm is finished, you need to be ready to stop the process immediately.

Preparation

1   Gather together the materials you will need.
2   Make sure there is a washbasin free, preferably one where the client can put their head back to use it. (This makes it easier for you to keep chemicals away from the eyes.)

First rinsing

1   As soon as the perm is complete, move your client immediately to the washbasin. Make sure they are comfortable. Offer them hand towels or tissues in case any liquid trickles over the face.
2   Carefully remove the cap or other head covering. The hair is soft and weak at this stage, so don't put unnecessary tension on it. Leave the curlers in place.
3   Run the water. You need an even supply of warm water. The water must be neither hot nor cold as this will be uncomfortable for the client. Hot water will also irritate the scalp and could burn. Check the pressure and temperature against the back of your hand. Remember that your client's head may be sensitive after the perming process.
4   Rinse the hair thoroughly with the warm water. This may take about five minutes or longer if the hair is long. It is this rinsing that stops the perm process – until you rinse away the lotion, the hair will still be processing. Direct the water away from the eyes and the face. Make sure you rinse *all* the hair, including the nape curlers. If a curler slips out, gently wind the hair back on to it immediately.

Tip

Always check that you're using the right chemical. Because they are designed to match, the container for the neutraliser may look similar to the container for the perm lotion.

Tip

Perm detectors can be used (they are like litmus paper and change colour if perm lotion is still in the hair). They are used after rinsing to ensure the perm lotion has been removed before applying the neutraliser.

Tip

Make sure nape hair is evenly rinsed.

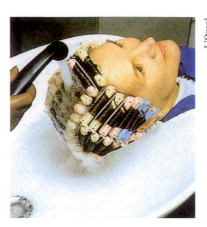

Neutralising: first rinse

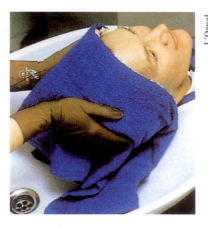

Neutralising: towel-drying the hair

Applying neutraliser

1   Raise your client to a comfortable sitting position.

2   Blot the hair thoroughly, using a towel or tissues. It may help if you pack the curlers with cottonwool.

3   When no surplus water remains, apply the neutraliser. Follow the manufacturer's instructions. These may tell you to pour the neutraliser through the hair, or apply it with a brush or sponge, or use the spiked applicator bottle. Some foam neutralisers need to be pushed briskly into the hair. Make sure that neutraliser comes into contact with all of the hair.

4   When all the hair has been covered, time the process according to the instructions. The usual time is 5–10 minutes. You may wrap the hair in a towel or leave it open to the air – follow the instructions.

5   Gently and carefully remove the curlers. Don't pull or stretch the hair. It may still be soft, especially towards the ends, and you don't want to disturb the curl formation.

6   Apply the neutraliser to the hair again, covering all the hair. Arrange the hair so that the neutraliser does not run over the face. Leave for the time recommended, perhaps another 5–10 minutes.

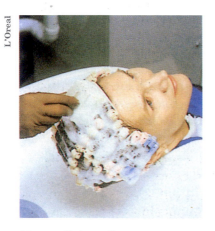

Neutralising: first application

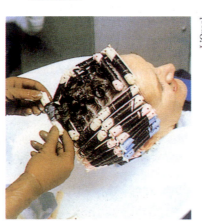

Removing curlers

Second application of neutraliser

Tip

After using the curlers, remove the end wraps. Rinse, dry and powder the curlers. This prevents the rubbers from becoming soft. Separate the curlers into different sizes and colours, ready for the next time they are used.

Second rinsing

1 Run the water, again checking temperature and pressure.
2 Rinse the hair thoroughly to remove the neutraliser.
3 You can now treat the hair with an after-perm aid or conditioner. Use the one recommended by the manufacturer of the perm and neutraliser, to be sure that the chemicals are compatible.

Perm aids or conditioner and balanced conditioners (antioxidants) help neutralise the effect of the chemical process by helping to restore the pH balance of the hair to pH 4.4–5.5 and smooth down the hair cuticle.

When applying a conditioner apply to the palms of the hands first and gently work the conditioner through the hair. Do not massage the scalp or pull the hair as it may soften the newly formed curl.

 Activity

Wind several curlers and perm process them. Neutralise in the normal way. When unwinding, make a point of stretching some of them. Compare the result with others that were more carefully undone. Note the differences when the hair is dry.

 Activity

Collect together several hair samples. Wind and process each with perm lotion. Follow the manufacturer's instructions. Apply neutraliser to each sample. Process the neutraliser, allowing 5, 10, 15 and 20 minutes and longer. Compare the results. Record the effects produced by the different neutralising times.

At the end of the neutralising process, you will have returned the hair to a normal, stable state.

- The reduction and oxidation processes will have been completed.
- The hair will now be slightly weaker – fewer bonds will have formed than were broken by the perm.
- Record any hair or perm faults on the client's record card. Correct faults as appropriate.
- Under-neutralising – not leaving neutraliser on for long enough – results in a slack curl or waves.
- Over-oxidising – leaving the neutraliser on too long or using oxidants that are too strong – results in weak hair and poor curl.

L'Oreal

Hair ready to be styled

The hair should be ready for shaping, blow-drying or setting.

After the perm

Mahogany

- Check the results of perming.
    - Has the scalp been irritated by the perm lotion?
    - Is the hair in good condition?
    - Is the curl even?

- Dry the hair into style.
    - Depending on the effect you want, you may now use finger drying, hood drying or blow-drying.
    - Treat the hair gently. If you handle it too firmly the perm may relax again.

- Advise the client on how to manage the perm at home.
    - The hair should not be shampooed for a day or two.
    - The manufacturer of the perm lotion may have supplied information to be passed to the client.
    - Discuss general hair care with your client.

- Clean all tools thoroughly so that they are ready for the next client.

- Complete the client's record card. Note details of the type of perm, the strength of the lotion, the processing time, the curler sizes and the winding technique. Record any problems you have had. This information will be useful if the hair is permed again.

Perming faults and what to do about them

Fault	Action now	Possible cause	Action in future
The perm is slow to process	Increase warmth but do not dry out; check the winding tension and the number of curlers	Winding was too loose	Wind more firmly or use smaller curlers
		The curlers were large, or too few were used	Use smaller curlers, and more of them
		The wrong lotion was used	Double-check labels on bottles
		The sections were too large	Take smaller sections
		The salon is too cold	The temperature should be comfortable
		Lotion was absorbed from the hair	Don't leave cotton wool on the hair
		Too little lotion was used	Don't skimp the lotion or miss sections

Fault	Action now	Possible cause	Action in future
The scalp is tender, sore or broken	Seek advice from a qualified first aider	The curlers were too tight	Don't apply too much tension when winding
		The wound curlers rested on the skin	Curlers should rest on the hair
		Lotion was spilt on the scalp	Keep lotion away from the scalp
		There was cotton wool padding soaked with perm lotion between the curlers	Renew the cotton wool as necessary, or don't use it
		The hair was pulled tightly	Don't overstretch it
		The perm was over-processed	Time perms accurately
There are straight ends or pieces	Re-perm, if the hair condition permits*	The curlers or sections were too large	Take sections no longer or wider than the curler used
		Sections were overlooked	Check that all hair has been wound
		Too few curlers were used	Put curlers closer together
		The winding was too loose	Be a little firmer next time
		Lotion was applied unevenly	Take care to apply it evenly
There are fish-hooks	Remove by trimming the ends	The hair points were not cleanly wound	Comb the hair cleanly
		The hair points were bent or buckled	Place hair sections evenly on to the curlers
		The hair was wrapped unevenly in the end papers	Curl from the hair points
		Winding aids were used incorrectly	Take more care; practise winding
Hair is broken	Nothing can be done about the broken hair; after discussion with your senior or trainer, condition the remaining hair	The hair was wound too tightly	Wind more loosely next time
		The curlers were secured too tightly	Secure them more loosely next time
		The curler band cut into the hair base	Keep it away from the hair base
		The hair was over-processed	Follow the instructions more carefully
		Chemicals in the hair reacted with the lotion	Test for incompatibility beforehand

Perming faults and what to do about them (continued)

Fault	Action now	Possible cause	Action in future
The hair is straight	Re-perm, if the hair condition permits*	The wrong lotion was used for hair of this texture	Choose the lotion more carefully
		The hair was under-processed	Time perms accurately
		The curlers were too large for the hair length	Measure the curlers beforehand
		The neutralising was incorrectly done	Follow the instructions more carefully
		Rinsing was inadequate	Rinse more thoroughly
		Conditioners used before perming were still on the hair	Prepare the hair more carefully
		The hair was coated and resistant to the lotion	Check for substances that block the action of perm lotion: shampoo if necessary
The hair is frizzy	Cut the ends to reduce the frizziness	The lotion was too strong for hair of this texture	Assess texture correctly; select suitable lotions; read manufacturers' instructions
		The winding was too tight	Practise and experiment to avoid this
		The curlers were too small	Choose more suitable curlers
		The hair was over-processed	Time perms accurately
		The neutralising was incorrectly done	Follow the instructions more carefully
		There are fish-hooks	Avoid bending hair points when winding
The perm is weak and drops†	Re-perm, if the hair condition permits*	Lotion was applied unevenly	Apply lotion more evenly
		The neutraliser was dilute	Follow the instructions more carefully
		Neutralising was poorly done	Be more careful
		The hair was stretched while soft	Handle the hair gently
		The curlers or sections were too large	Use more curlers

Fault	Action now	Possible cause	Action in future
Some hair sections are straight	Re-perm, if the hair condition permits*	The curler angle was wrong	Wind correctly
		The curlers were placed incorrectly	Wind correctly
		The curlers were too large	Use smaller curlers
		Sectioning or winding was done carelessly	Practise before perming again
The hair is discoloured	Tone the hair to correct this	Metal in the tools or containers reacted with the lotion	Test for incompatibility beforehand
		Chemicals coating the hair reacted with the lotion	Check for substances that block the action of perm lotion; shampoo if necessary

*Don't re-perm the hair unless its condition is suitable. For example, you should not re-perm if the hair is over-processed. Conditioning treatments, cutting and careful setting and styling may help. Discuss the problem with your senior or trainer.

†Before attempting to correct this fault, make sure that the hair is not over-processed. Dampen the hair to see how much perm there is.

Assignments – Cold permanent waving

A practical activity

Collect together a range of hair samples, or use a suitable practice block. Try out different perming processes and techniques, such as handling the hair, sectioning and sub-sectioning, winding, using different formers and curlers, processing, developing and so on. Make a careful record of your results and retain it for your folder. Include the following:

1 Outline the processes of cold permanent waving.
2 Note how the different hair textures react.
3 Note the effects of different winding techniques.
4 Describe, and sketch, what happens to the hair structure during perming.
5 Describe the reduction process.
6 How does body/salon temperature affect perm processing?

7 List the precautions to be taken during perming.
8 List the problems that might arise during a perm, and how you would resolve them.

Make careful notes, and keep them in your folder.

For you to find out

Investigate the theory and practice of perming. Use your reference books and examine the history of perming. Take note of the development of the perming processes. Compare modern processes, and effects, with some of the earlier ones. Keep a record, crediting your sources. Answer the following questions:

1 What are acid perms and alkaline perms? What are tepid perms and hot perms? How do they differ from cold perms?

Assignments – Cold permanent waving (cont.)

2 How do these differ from early hot perms?

3 What are the advantages and disadvantages of older perms?

4 What are the advantages and disadvantages of modern perms?

5 Why do you test for perm results?

6 What do you do if an incompatibility test proves negative? If it proves positive?

7 What do you do if a perm results in frizz, discolouration or straight pieces?

8 How do you determine the most suitable perm to use?

9 List the precautions that you should take when giving a perm.

10 What are the problems that might arise during perming, and how might you deal with them?

A case study

A client requests a cold perm. Their hair is fine, greasy and below shoulder length. Previous results at other salons have been unsatisfactory. How do you deal with this? Simulate the event, make careful and precise notes and retain them for your folder. Work through the following sequence:

1 Describe the client examination and discussion.

2 List the questions that you would ask. Include those that refer to past problems.

3 How would you select a suitable perm process? What are the chemical processes involved?

4 What tests might you make?

5 What determines the most suitable perm curler/former size?

6 How do you select suitable section sizes?

7 How do you know the correct tension to apply?

8 How do you know when the perm has 'taken'?

9 How should your client manage the new perm? What advice will you give?

10 What are the problems that might arise when perming? How do you deal with these?

11 List the precautions you should take.

12 You need to ensure that all information is carefully recorded. Describe how you would do this.

13 What fashion style have you decided to give your client? State why.

Assignments – Neutralising

A practical activity

Using several hair samples – hair that has been through the cold permanent waving process and is ready to be neutralised – try out different ways of neutralising. Note the different effects produced, and record them for your folder. Carry out this assignment systematically using the following procedures:

1 Without rinsing the hair sample, apply the neutraliser and time as the instructions direct. Note the effects produced when the hair is still wet and again when it has been dried.

2 Using another permed hair sample, rinse the hair but do not apply any neutraliser. Note the effects when it is wet and when it is dry.

Assignments – Neutralising (cont.)

3 On a third permed hair sample, omit both rinse and neutraliser. Note the effects both wet and dry.

4 To a fourth sample, apply rinses and neutraliser as directed by the perm manufacturer. Note the effects wet and dry.

5 Retain these four samples and compare the results when the hair has dried out. Then check again after 12, 24 and 48 hours.

6 List and try out different types of neutraliser, with varying times of application. Compare the results.

7 Repeat these experiments using hair of different textures.

Make sure that you have a correctly permed and neutralised sample with which to compare your results.

For you to find out

Investigate the chemical processes of applying neutraliser to a variety of perms, from both a theoretical and a practical point of view. Use your textbooks, the manufacturers' instructions and your practical experience. Retain your record for your folder, crediting your sources of information. Answer the following questions.

1 Outline the chemical process of cold permanent waving neutralising. Use diagrams where possible.

2 What are the effects of neutralising hair of different textures?

3 What are the effects of temperature on neutralising?

4 What would you do if you spilt the last batch of neutraliser?

5 Why should the hair be moved gently after neutralising?

6 What processes can you apply after completing the neutralising process? Describe what these do to the chemical structure and state of the hair.

A case study

A client has returned to complain of services received at your salon. Describe the following:

- the action or actions you would take
- how you would record what the client has told you
- the questions you would need to ask
- what you would do if you could not deal with the problem yourself
- what you could do to calm an angry or upset client.

Preparing for Assessment

In preparing for your assessment on cold permanent waving and neutralising the following checklist may prove to be helpful. Check that you have covered and now fully understand these items:

- determining the client's requirements and needs
- explanation of the perming processes
- gaining the client's approval and agreement to proceed
- selecting suitable perm processes, with your client, for the results required
- assessing the type and condition of the hair, its length, and when it was permed last
- preparing the client for processing

Preparing for Assessment (cont.)

- sectioning the hair appropriately
- determining curler sizes and type of winding to use
- using the correct techniques for the required style effects
- determining when the perm process should stop
- the reasons for using the correct neutraliser (and the need for checking instructions) and the different chemicals used
- the reasons for rinsing the hair thoroughly and removing excess moisture
- applying the neutraliser evenly, timing accurately, and removing as directed

- understanding the effects of neutraliser on the hair structure
- understanding neutralising as part of the perm process
- being aware of problems that may occur, and knowing how to deal with them and when to refer to senior staff
- understanding the health and safety requirements (see Chapter 12)
- recording information accurately and legibly
- ensuring client satisfaction
- discussing details of aftercare required.

When you feel that you are ready, talk to your trainer and arrange a suitable time for your assessment.

A case study

Your client recently had a cold permanent wave at another salon. The client did not consider the result to be satisfactory. The hair was slightly curly or wavy in parts but mostly straight otherwise. How would you deal with this situation?

Make notes of what you would say and do. List the questions you would ask, and the order in which you would ask them. Retain notes for your folder. Here are some procedures you should carry out:

1 Try to determine why the hair was not successfully treated at the other salon.

2 Find out whether the client returned there to complain, and what the outcome was.

3 State what you think might have caused the unsatisfactory results.

4 State what you think would have been successful.

5 Determine, and agree with your client, what should now be done.

6 Determine whether the hair is in a fit state for further treatment.

7 Record the results of your discussion with your client, and what you have agreed.

8 How would you record this information?

9 Add any further information you feel applies.

By reading this chapter, carrying out the above activities, assignments and case studies, and by meeting the requirements in preparing for assessment you will have worked towards the key skill requirements in Communication Level 1 (C 1.1) (C 1.2) (C 1.3) and Level 2 (C 2.1) (C 2.2) (C 2.3) and Application of Number Level 1 (N 1.2).

If you have used a computer to complete your assignments or activities you will have worked towards the key skill requirements in Information Technology Level 1 (IT 1.1) (IT 1.2).

Relaxing hair

8

Errol Douglas at Neville Daniel

Learning objectives

The following are some of the topics covered in this chapter:

- consultation, examination and preparing the client
- testing for suitability of product
- products available: their advantages and disadvantages
- important influencing factors
- methods of relaxing hair
- how relaxing works – one- and two-stage methods
- dealing with regrowth
- curly perms
- problems that might arise and how to deal with them.

Introduction

Jackie Henry at A Cut Above

Relaxing processes have always, in one form or another, been applied to hair. Throughout hairdressing development, people with very tightly curled hair have wanted less curly or smoother looks. Most early relaxing processes were physically based and temporary in their effects, but today's chemical techniques can produce effective and permanent results.

In this chapter we will look at the application of permanent methods currently used in salons to reduce or remove curl from the hair.

Relaxing hair is a process of removing curl or wave, wholly or in part. Clients with naturally very curly, kinky or frizzy hair may want it looser, softly curled or straight. Then their regrowth may need periodic treatment.

Relaxing hair – the principles

Hair by Derrick Mullings. Photo by Media Image

The chemistry of hair relaxing with a thioglycollate derivative is a two-step process, similar to cold permanent waving. The disulphide bridges in the cystine links between the keratin chains of the hair are reduced (broken) by the action of the ammonium thioglycollate in the relaxing cream/gel/lotion. This softens the hair, which can then be moulded into its new relaxed shape. This is followed by neutralisation, which is an oxidation process – reaction with oxygen. Cysteine groups pair up again to form cystines, and the disulphide bridges reform in new positions. (See the section in Chapter 7 on neutralising.)

Other chemicals, such as sodium hydroxide, can also be used. Sodium hydroxide breaks down the disulphide bonds in hair by **hydrolysis** – that is, the breakdown of a substance by, and with, water. Cystine groups are separated into cysteines, and sulphenic acid is also formed; continued processing produces lanthionine – another amino acid – and other single sulphur links. The hair softens and relaxes, tight curls are loosened, and the hair can be moulded into a more relaxed shape. When a sufficient degree of relaxation is reached the hair is shampooed with an acid-balancing neutralising shampoo, which returns to its normal acid state. No oxidising neutraliser is used.

Relaxing hair: two-stage reduction and oxidation

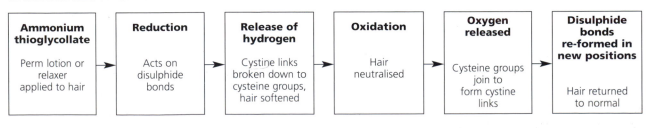

Ammonium thioglycollate	Reduction	Release of hydrogen	Oxidation	Oxygen released	Disulphide bonds re-formed in new positions
Perm lotion or relaxer applied to hair	Acts on disulphide bonds	Cystine links broken down to cysteine groups, hair softened	Hair neutralised	Cysteine groups join to form cystine links	Hair returned to normal

Tip

Once the hair has been relaxed with a sodium or non-sodium relaxer the structure of the hair is permanently changed. With only one sulphur bond the hair cannot be permed.

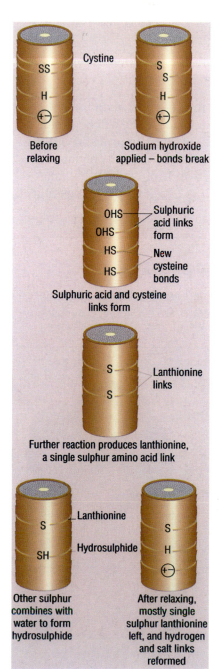

Relaxing hair: a continuous one-stage process (simplified)

This one-step chemical process differs from the relaxing and perming processes using ammonium thioglycollate reduction followed by oxidation. It is very important to vet closely the subsequent use of other chemical processes on the chemically relaxed hair because the basic nature of the hair has been changed. Fewer disulphide bridges are now present, so further reduction processes should not be used.

Preparation

In addition to the normal preparation of your client, their hair and the tools/materials required, you should double-check the following for this service:

- determine your client's needs
- determine your client's hair type (curly or wavy) and hair texture (fine, medium or coarse)
- check whether your client's hair is 'virgin' (chemically untreated) hair; if so, it may be more resistant to relaxing
- check the condition of the hair if it has previously been chemically treated e.g. coloured
- closely examine the hair and scalp for signs of poor condition, sensitivity or disease
- if contraindications are present, then refer to your seniors so a decision can be made
- agree with your client exactly what is to be done, about how long it will take, and what it will cost
- check that they are comfortable and that they remain so throughout the service.

Health & Safety

In all relaxing processes you must take great care to prevent damage to your client's hair or skin. You must ensure that the client is adequately protected throughout.

Tests

Always make tests on your client's hair to ensure that it is in a suitable state for relaxing, particularly when dryness, brittleness or breakage of the hair are evident. The following tests are recommended:

- a test cutting, to check the likely result of the intended process
- elasticity check, to determine the hair condition
- porosity check, to determine the rate of absorption
- testing a strand, to check on process development
- incompatibility test, to detect the presence of metals.

Nick Jones, Hair Design

Ishoka

Factors affecting product choice and application

Product knowledge is essential. Whatever you decide to use, you must be familiar with it. You must study the manufacturer's instructions for use before your client arrives, or before you attempt to apply the product. (This also applies to your tools and equipment.) You should only decide on the most suitable strength of chemical product after:

- the consultation with your client, and making sure you know exactly what your client requires
- checking to determine whether your client is taking any prescribed medication, and if they have any allergies
- examining the hair and scalp condition
- the results of the relevant tests are known
- checking with a salon senior or specialist (proceed only after agreement is reached)
- ensuring products are in stock, to avoid disappointing your client
- deciding whether the hair is fine, medium, coarse, thick, thin, porous or resistant (coarse hair requires the longest processing time, and fine hair the shortest; grease or heavy chemical build-up on hair can block the relaxer product; hair that has been previously bleached, permed, straightened or relaxed can be very receptive and may process very fast)
- noting any other helpful information.

You can begin the relaxation process once you have considered the following factors:

- whether the hair is in a suitable condition for processing (for instance, a rough cuticle could indicate patchy porosity, which would be likely to affect the result)
- the salon temperature – a hot salon could speed processing, a cold one could delay process time
- the hairstyle required after the hair has been relaxed; your client's head and face shape and hair growth patterns (see page 121–122); if the client's hair is to change from very curly to very straight, they may need guidance from you about managing it afterwards and about home maintenance products.

Professional

Relaxing products

Tip

New products are being launched all the time. Always check with the manufacturer's instructions, particularly for processing times suitable for the different hair textures and types (European, African, Asian and so on – see page 10).

Relaxing methods and procedures

Most of the methods of curling hair can be used to relax hair. Relaxing is the term given to describe curl and wave reduction. As with curling, relaxing hair may be temporary or permanent (see Chapter 5 for temporary methods.)

Permanently relaxing hair

The permanent methods are chemical ones. These involve the use of strong chemicals which must be used with care. The types of chemical relaxers currently available include:

- ammonium thioglycollate-based lotions, made for looser-curled hair, such as European-type hair
- specially made creams, also ammonium thioglycollate-based, intended specifically for Afro-caribbean hair
- creams or gels based on sodium hydroxide – lye – or caustic soda, made for Afro-Caribbean clients
- creams or gels based on calcium hydroxide, called non-lye products, made for tightly curled hair and a wide range of hair textures
- creams based on ammonium and sodium bisulphites, which are slower-acting and kinder to the hair, also suitable for a range of hair textures.

Important differences between these products are:

- the strengths – how much of the active chemical is present: this varies considerably and affects the process speed
- the pH – the degree of alkalinity; the higher the alkalinity the stronger the product
- the contact time (length of processing) required.

In general, do not apply any heat that would accelerate the chemical process, causing damage to the hair and irritation to the skin. Some newer products, however, specifically recommend a certain amount of applied heat.

Some products require that adequate basing – the application of protective gels or creams to the skin around the hairline and ears – is made before the relaxing process commences.

Tip

Other relaxers include calcium hydroxide, lithium hydroxide and potassium hydroxide-based products.

A relaxing method used for European-type hair

The following is an outline of a suggested application method using ammonium thioglycollate derivatives, *but this should not be used in place of the manufacturer's instructions*.

1   Section the hair into four: centrally from forehead to nape, and laterally from ear to ear (see diagram).

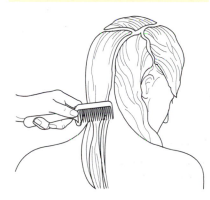

Sectioning hair

2   Apply the basing product.

3   Subdivide the nape sections into smaller ones.

4   Apply the relaxer cream, gel or lotion, avoiding the skin. Do not go closer than 12 mm from the scalp.

5   Comb the hair gently. Use a comb with widely spaced teeth. Some manufacturers advise you to wait till the hair has softened before combing.

6   Do not continually comb the hair when it is soft. Treat it gently at this stage – it can easily break. Leave the hair as straight as the client requires.

7   Processing time depends on the product and the hair. Softly curled hair relaxes quickly. Kinky hair takes longer. It is safest to monitor continuously throughout the process. Do not exceed the manufacturer's recommended time for processing.

8   When processing is complete, you may apply neutralisers. Neutralisers vary; some are based on hydrogen peroxide. Whichever product is used, it must thoroughly cover the area treated.

9   After final rinsing and conditioning with moisturisers or other products, the hair may be styled.

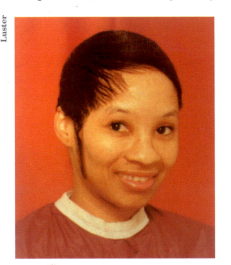

Relaxer has been applied and is allowed to process

The hair has been cut and styled for the finished effect

A relaxing method for Afro-Caribbean type hair

The following is an outline of a suggested application method for a virgin head, using a sodium or non-sodium based relaxer, but this should not be used in place of the manufacturers' instructions.

1   Apply a pre-relaxer treatment if the hair condition is dry or porous.

2   Apply a protective base to protect the skin.

3   Divide the hair into four: centrally from forehead to nape and laterally from ear to ear (see diagram on previous page).

Health & Safety

Always follow the manufacturer's instructions for the use of chemicals and products. Check with your salon's COSHH list of potential hazards (see page 296) for the correct usage.

4 Apply the relaxer to the mid-lengths and ends first. Start from the nape area or the most resistant part of the head towards the crown; leave the front hair line until last as this is usually the weakest area. Use small sub-sections of hair (see Chapter 7, Perming), smoothing and combing the hair as you work.

5 Once you have applied the relaxer to the mid-lengths and ends go back and apply to the roots.

6 Comb the hair from roots to ends and smooth the hair with your fingers until the required degree of straightness has been achieved. To check if the hair has been relaxed enough, take a strand of hair and remove the product with cotton wool. If the strand of hair stays straight and does not revert to its original curl then you can remove the relaxer.

7 Rinse the hair thoroughly, using tepid water as the scalp will be sensitive. The force of the water and gentle finger movements will remove the product from the hair. Check to make sure all traces of the relaxer have been removed from the hair and scalp.

8 Apply a neutralising shampoo to the hair. Shampoo gently and rinse thoroughly. Re-apply the neutralising shampoo at least once more to ensure that all the relaxer has been removed.

9 Post-perm treatments can be used after a relaxer, these are acidic and will help to ring the hair back to its natural pH level 4.5–5.5 and close the cuticle (see Chapter 1).

10 Gently towel dry the hair and comb through.

11 You can now apply styling products and style the hair.

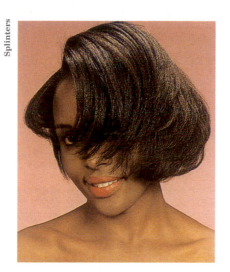

Relaxed hair

Relaxed hair

Dealing with regrowth

Since hair grows approximately 12 mm (1/2 inch) each month, within a few weeks after relaxing very curly hair will begin to show itself above the scalp. This will need to be processed if the client wishes to continue with relaxed hair. When applying a process to the regrowth – called **retouching** – you must take care to avoid the scalp; make sure it is based well where required.

New Hibiscus Salon for Black Hair & Beauty

Splinters

Health & Safety

Follow manufacturers' instructions very carefully when using chemical products. Avoid mixing products of different manufacturers, since the chemical processes may not be the same.

Applying a regrowth application

1   Apply a pre-relaxer treatment to the hair that has already been relaxed.
2   Apply a protective base to protect the skin.
3   Always use the same product type that has been used previously, either sodium or non-sodium based, as the two different types are not compatible.
4   Section the hair in the same way as a virgin application. When applying the relaxer it is best to work across two sections to keep the application even instead of applying the relaxer and completing one section first before moving onto another.
5   Use small sub-sections and starting in the nape area or most resistant area first apply the relaxer to the roots of the hair about 6 mm away from the scalp using the back of a comb. This will allow the relaxer to expand and creep up the hair to the scalp without it actually touching the scalp. Do not apply to the hair that has previously been relaxed as it will damage the hair or cause the hair to break.
6   Once you have applied the relaxer to the whole head go back to the beginning and start combing the product through the hair and smoothing it with your fingers. Make sure that you do not comb beyond the regrowth area and that you do not scrape the scalp, it is kinder on the scalp to smooth with your fingers.
7   Take a strand test to make sure the hair has been relaxed enough before rinsing and neutralising. This is done in the same way as in the virgin application described above.

Curly perms

A curly perm is a hair-straightening process designed to reduce very tight curly hair of Afro-Caribbean texture to a softer, looser curl or wave. This makes the fashioning of hair styles more practical. It may also be successfully applied to excessively tight curly hair of Caucasian and other types where curl softening is required and recommended.

The curly perm is chemically similar to perming processes where the active ingredients are based on ammonium thioglycolate (see Chapter 7). It includes the reduction and oxidation processes of cold permanent waving – although the hair is uncurled instead of being curled. The procedure includes the straightening of the hair with a curl rearranger – an ammonium thioglycollate-based cream or gel. This is available in different strengths – mild for fine hair, regular for normal hair, super for coarse hair, maximum for coarse, resistant hair – the choice depending on the condition of the hair, previous chemical treatments and the amount of curl reduction required. Once applied the hair is smoothed with the fingers and back of the comb until the hair softens and straightens, the curl rearranger is rinsed from the hair. Surplus moisture is removed by blotting and gently patting the hair with tissue or a towel.

The next stage is to apply a curl booster, either by pre-damping or post-damping. This is similar to an ammonium thioglycollate-based

Health & Safety

If allowed to remain too long in contact with the hair, all relaxers may have a depilatory action – they may remove the hair completely. Use a timer, and make sure that all processes are accurately timed.

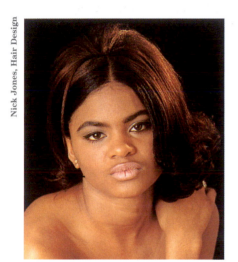

cold permanent waving lotion, usually of one strength but weaker than the curl arranger. The hair is then sectioned and wound on to rods or curlers in the same way as all other perms.

When the hair has reached its required straightness, determined by the amount of curl remaining, it is rinsed and mopped or blotted. The hair is then thoroughly neutralised. Oxidising agents, such as hydrogen peroxide or sodium perborate, are commonly used.

Other products, such as skin-protecting basing creams, prestraightening protective hair lotions, moisturisers to retain resilience and aftercare conditioners, may also be recommended. It is important to follow manufacturers' directions to achieve safe and successful treatments – this includes instructions for pre-treatment tests, application of all chemical products, amounts to use, timing of processes, use of heat (if applicable) and caring for the client's hair and skin. Do remember that products differ between manufacturers, so it is necessary to be aware of these differences by checking instruction sheets before making any application.

Regrowth treatments

It will be necessary to carry out the service again once new root hair has grown. It is better to keep to the same straightening products previously applied to the lengths of the hair for matching results. Always make a note of the materials and processes applied.

Health & Safety

Never mix different chemical relaxers when retouching.

Overlapping previously chemically treated hair must be avoided in order to avoid breakage. Protective creams are available, but must be used with great care.

Activity

Contact your salon's wholesalers and manufacturers for information about the different types of relaxing processes available. You can also research information and review how each product differs by using the following manufacturers' websites

- wella – www.wella.co.uk
- L'Oreal – www.loreal.co.uk
- Carson – www.softsheencarson.com

Collect this together and keep it in your folder, not only for your own use but also for others for whom you may soon become responsible. You can thus constantly update your knowledge of newer relaxer products which are proving to be kinder, milder and less damaging to the hair.

Relaxing faults and what to do about them

Problems	Possible cause	What to do
Hair breakage before relaxing	Poor dressing, or results of previous relaxing methods; poor condition	Do not relax hair; wait till improved; refer to your senior/trainer
Hair breakage after relaxing	Overpressing, or relaxers too strong, or poor neutralising	Condition if possible, refer to your senior/trainer
Bald areas	Traction baldness due to poor relaxing or over-processing	Do not relax hair; avoid tension, and treat gently
Sore scalp	Harsh treatment (e.g. combing) or sign of disease, or relaxers too strong or left too long	Do not relax hair; wait till improved; refer to your senior/trainer
Discolouration or pink colour	Metals present, or wrong relaxer used, or over-processing	Test and check; recondition; colour rinse; avoid using further chemicals
Hair too curly	Not relaxed enough, or wrong method chosen; or not normalising sufficiently	Condition the hair; choose the correct method, and relax again, after two weeks if the condition permits

Assignments – Relaxing hair

A practical activity

Using suitable hair switches or lengths of hair, experiment with the different hair-relaxing processes. (Alternatively, models can be arranged on which to practise these techniques.) First collect together information from product knowledge sessions, visits to hair and trade shows, wholesalers and downloading information from manufacturers websites and so forth. Make careful notes of your results, credit your sources, and include the following information:

1 List the questions that need to be put to your client.

2 Discuss your client's requirements.

3 Note any contraindications.

4 Determine what products have been used previously.

5 Examine, and discuss with your client, the condition and texture of the hair, and a suitable choice of relaxing process.

6 Apply tests as required.

7 Outline the chemical effects on the hair structure of both one-stage and two-stage processes.

8 Note the differences between the various techniques for relaxing hair.

9 List the important influencing factors.

10 Outline the precautions to be taken.

11 List the problems that could arise and how you would deal with them.

Assignments – Relaxing hair (cont.)

For you to find out

Investigate the variety of information sources dealing with relaxing hair that are available to you. Use your trade journals, textbooks, wholesalers, manufacturers, videos, internet and group training sessions for information. Collect facts and figures, credit your sources, and make precise notes to retain in your folder. Then answer the following questions:

- List the permanent methods of relaxing hair.

- Outline the effects produced.

- Why are consultations and hair tests necessary?

- What advice do you give for client aftercare?

- How often should relaxing be applied?

- What are contraindications? How do you deal with them?

- Outline one method of applying chemical relaxing.

- What is 'virgin' hair?

- How do you deal with regrowth?

- What causes hair breakage? How would you deal with this if you noticed it on your client?

- Collect copies of manufacturers' instructions. Make sure that you read them and understand how to use their products.

A case study

A client requests a hair relaxing process. How would you deal with this if the hair was

- naturally very curly?
- previously permed?
- wavy, and in poor condition?

Work through the following sequence:

1 Consult the client and determine what treatments the hair has previously undergone.

2 Determine the client's exact wishes and requirements.

3 Assess whether these are suitable and attainable.

4 List the questions that you need to ask.

5 Agree with the client what is to be done.

6 What methods would you suggest for naturally very curly hair?

7 What would you do, and what would you say to your client, if the test results indicated that treatment should not be applied?

8 When should a client be referred for a second opinion?

9 How do you ensure the products you use are suitable for your client's hair and skin?

10 Why should manufacturers' instructions be strictly followed?

11 What aftercare do you recommend to your client?

Preparing for Assessment

In preparing for assessment on relaxing hair the following checklist may be helpful. Check that you have covered and now fully understand these items:

- relaxing methods
- the effects of these processes on the hair and skin
- dealing with various hair lengths, hair and skin conditions, and previously treated hair
- choosing between one- and two-stage processes
- selecting the most suitable processes to achieve the client's satisfaction
- following manufacturers' instructions for their product use
- listing problems that could arise and dealing with them
- recording client information confidentially and legibly
- dealing with style requirements after relaxing.

When you feel that you are ready talk to your trainer and arrange a suitable time for your assessment.

By reading this chapter, carrying out the above activities, assignments and the case study, and by meeting the requirements in preparing for assessment you will have worked towards the key skill requirements in Communication Levels 1 (C 1.1) (C 1.2) (C 1.3) and 2 (C 2.1) (C 2.2) (C 2.3).

If you have used a computer to complete your assignments or activities you will have worked towards the key skill requirements in Information Technology Level 1 (IT 1.1) (IT 1.2).

Colouring hair

Carl Shaw

Learning objectives

The following are some of the topics covered in this chapter:

- the principles of colour
- types of colour
- client consultation
- preparation and procedures for carrying out colour services
- tests
- colouring techniques
- using hydrogen peroxide
- using colouring aids
- taking precautions when colouring
- colour and bleaching problems
- the principles of bleach – how bleach works
- bleaching techniques

9

Introduction

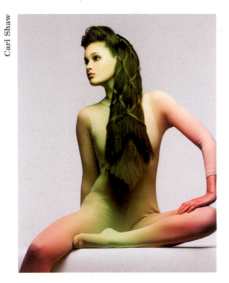

Carl Shaw

Coloured hair

The history of hair colour, together with colour used for the face, body, nails and clothes, has been a long and varied one. The social and religious reasons for the use of colour make an interesting study. Many people use colour to convey their individuality, to keep up with fashion, to enhance their appearance, or just to feel better about the way they look. All kinds of natural and artificial materials have been used. The early hair colourist was a master at creating colours from a variety of substances, sometimes with what we would now consider to be harsh, artificial and startling effects.

The application of colour to enhance appearance and hair styling has been closely tied to the developments in chemistry and cosmetic manufacturing. The range of hair cosmetics produced now is probably wider than ever before, yet is often taken for granted. Products have improved considerably over the years: their quality and effects are now of a high standard. You need to have equally high standards in their application and use.

In this chapter we will look at the application of currently used methods of colouring hair.

Colouring – the principles

Basic colouring

We are surrounded by colour. Look around the salon – at clothing, make-up, nail varnish, accessories, pictures, decor and packaging. Hair too can be colourful. Its colour can contribute to the overall style as much as its cut and finish.

It is hard to define colours – words like 'chestnut' and 'blonde' describe them but are not at all precise. This chapter introduces the International Colour Chart and examines some basic facts about colour.

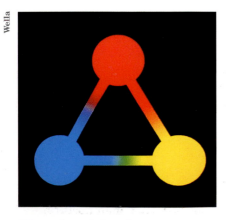

Wella

The colour triangle

Seeing colour

When you look at an object, what you are actually seeing is light reflected from it. White light is really a mixture of many colours – that is why sunlight reflected by falling rain can produce a rainbow. A white object *reflects* most of the white light that falls upon it; a black object *absorbs* most of the light falling on it. A red object reflects the red light, and absorbs everything else.

Hair colour depends chiefly on the pigments in the hair, which absorb some of the light and reflect the rest. The colour that we see is also affected by the light in which it is seen, and (to a lesser extent) by the colours of clothes worn with it.

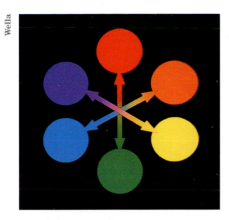

The colour circle

The colour spectrum from
visible light

DEPTHS

1/0	Blue Black
2/0	Black
3/0	Dark Brown
4/0	Medium Brown
5/0	Light Brown
6/0	Dark Blonde
7/0	Medium Blonde
8/0	Light Blonde
9/0	Very Light Blonde / Lightest Blonde
10/0	Extra Light Blonde / Pastel Blonde

Depths

TONES

/0	Natural
/1	Ash
/2	Cool Ash
/3	Honey Gold
/4	Red Gold
/5	Purple
/6	Violet
/7	Brunette
/8	Pearl Ash
/9	Soft Ash

Tones

Mixing colours

The colours of the pigments in paints arise from three **primary colours** – red, blue and yellow. Pairs of these give the **secondary colours** – purple, green and orange. The various other colours are made from different proportions of the primary and secondary colours. White and black can be added to vary the **tone** of the colour.

The primary colours in *light* are different – red, green and blue. These are the three colours used in a colour television set. The secondary colours are yellow, cyan and magenta. The many colours in 'white' light can be separated by a glass prism or by raindrops: we see the **spectrum** of colour from white light as red-orange-yellow-green-blue-indigo-violet.

Hair colour

As discussed in Chapter 1 (page 10), the natural or base colour of hair depends on melanin pigments within the cortex of the hair. Eumelanin colours the hair black or brown; pheomelanin colours it red or yellow. The colour you see therefore depends on the amounts and proportions of these pigments. If the hair contains no pigment at all, it is white or blonde. (The pale yellow in this case is due to the keratin, not to pigment.) A young child's blonde hair may get darker later as more melanin is produced.

Some people never have any pigment in their hair, a condition known as **albinism**. Such people usually have no colour in the eyes or skin either. Sometimes there is just a little colour present: this condition is called partial albinism.

With age, or following stress, pigment may no longer be produced. Hairs already on the head will be unaffected, but new ones will be white. The proportion of white hairs among the coloured ones gradually increases, and the hair appears to go 'grey' – however, there aren't any actual grey hairs. 'Greyness' is often expressed as a percentage. For example, '50% white' means that half the hairs on the head are white, and half are their original colour.

Describing hair colour

- The **depth of colour** refers to how light or dark the colour is: this depends on the intensity of the pigments within the hair.
- The **tone** is the colour that you see – the combination of pigments that gives the overall colour. Warm shades, such as gold or auburn, have more pheomelanin; cool shades, such as ash, cendre, matt or drab, have less.

Visual aids

The **International Colour Chart (ICC)** offers a way of defining hair colours systematically. Even here, though, charts may vary between manufacturers. Take note of the way each manufacturer describes the different colours.

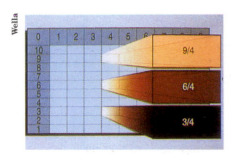

Wella

Depths and tones

Goldwell

A shade chart

! Health & Safety

Compound henna is incompatible with modern colouring and perming materials. Don't confuse it with vegetable henna.

Shades of colour are divided and numbered, with black (1) at one end of the scale and lightest blonde (10) at the other. Tones of other colours (0.01–0.9) are combined with these, producing a huge variety of colours. Charts are usually arranged with shades in rows down the side and tones in columns across the top. To use them, first identify the shade of your client's hair: that row of the chart then shows the colours you could produce with that hair. For example, if your client has light brown hair (shade 5) and you tint with an orange tone (0.4), the result should be a light warm brown (5.4). The possibilities are almost endless, as these examples indicate:

- to produce ash shades, add blue
- to produce matt shades, add green
- to produce gold shades, add yellow
- to produce warm shades, add red
- to produce purple or violet shades, add mixtures of red and blue.

Types of hair colouring products

Hair colourings, or **colourants**, may be grouped according to how long they remain on the hair:

- temporary colourings are applied as hair lotions, creams, mousses and the like
- semi-permanent colourings are applied as hair creams and rinses
- quasi-permanent colourings are applied mainly as creams
- permanent colourings are applied mainly as creams.

There are many different colouring products, developed from a variety of materials including vegetable extracts and minerals.

Vegetable colourings

These are made from the flowers, stems or barks of various plants.

Henna, or **lawsone**, is made from the powdered leaves of the Egyptian privet. It is used to add red colour to hair.

Camomile, made from the flowers of the camomile plant, has a yellow pigment. It is used to add yellow to light hair, thereby brightening the hair. It colours the surface only.

Indigo, made from the leaves of the indigo plant, gives a blue-black colour. When mixed with henna in different proportions it produces a variety of shades.

Walnut, made from the outer shell coverings, yields a yellow-brown dye. It is a surface, non-penetrating colourant.

Quassia, made from the bark of a tree, is often used with camomile to produce a useful colourant which brightens hair.

Other substances, including sage, sumach, oak bark, cudbear and logwood, have been used for their varied shades and effects.

Tip

Each type of colouring has its own set of instructions for application. Follow these carefully.

Vegetable and mineral colourings

These are mixtures of vegetable extracts and mineral substances. One of the commonest was **compound henna** – vegetable henna mixed with metallic salts. This surface colourant is no longer used in salons.

Mineral colourings

These are divided into two groups: metallic dyes and aniline derivatives.

Metallic dyes are surface-coating colourings. They are variously known as reduction, metallic, sulphide and progressive dyes. They are not commonly used in the salon, but are occasionally found in hair colour restorers.

The permanent products that we use in the salon are **aniline** derivatives. They are made from compounds found in crude oil, as are many chemicals used in cosmetics and medicines. These synthetic organic dyes, often known as 'para' dyes, include *para*-phenylenediamine and *para*-toluenediamine. These dyes penetrate the cortex of the hair as small molecules. They are then treated with an oxidising agent such as hydrogen peroxide. This makes them combine into larger molecules which remain trapped in the cortex: shampooing cannot wash them out.

You can use these aniline dyes both to lighten the melanin and to colour the hair at the same time. Colours containing para dyes may cause allergic reactions and a skin test must be carried out. (See page 222.)

Activity

Collect together your own examples of vegetable colourings.

Goldwell

Hair colouring products

Mahogany

Paterson SA

The client consultation

Your client may ask many questions about colour. What colour would be best for them? How can that colour be achieved? How long will it last? How much will it cost? How will it affect the hair? Is the hair suitable? You need to be ready with answers to such questions on all aspects of hair colouring before you start work on your client's hair.

- Discuss the client's ideas about colouring, considering the style and how colour may enhance it. Are there factors that might influence the choice of colour, such as the client's lifestyle or results of tests?
- Examine the hair for previous colouring, perming and other chemical treatments. What is its natural colour?
- Analyse the state of the hair and consider the effects of colouring treatments on it. Determine the hair's condition, porosity and elasticity.
- Refer to the client's record card, if available, for any information on past services that may influence your decision.
- Decide what sort of colouring to carry out, and agree with your client on the product you will use. Refer to a colour chart to make sure you really are agreed about the colour.
- Advise your client how long the process will take and how much it will cost.
- Carefully read the manufacturer's instructions for each product you are going to use.
- Prepare your client with a gown and other coverings. Make sure that all clothing is protected and that you follow your salon procedures
- Keep brushing and combing to a minimum – if you scratch the scalp, you will make it sensitive to the chemicals you will be using.

(See Chapter 2 Client care and consultations and Chapter 7 Perming and neutralising)

Health & Safety

Rushed work is rarely, if ever, efficient.

Health & Safety

Always refer to the manufacturer's instructions.

Choosing colour

The choice of colour depends on the following important factors:

The client's requirements – think about your client's age, lifestyle, job, fashion and dress sense, the colours they wear (both clothing and make-up), and the effects they would like to see. Younger clients may want bright colours or black. Older clients may wish to disguise the fact that their hair is going grey. In general, choose colours from a natural range that blend with the natural colour – avoid bright, harsh colours that contrast with it.

The natural hair colour – the client's base colour depends on the amounts and relative proportions of melanin, eumelanin and pheomelanin, and on the percentage of white hair present.

Tip

Colour choice must be appropriate to the client's hairstyle.

Wella

Very coarse   Coarse   Average   Fine   Very fine

Hair textures

The client's skin colour – in nature the colour of the skin tends to blend with the colour of the hair. You are altering that balance, so be careful. A deep red tint would clash with a ruddy complexion, for example; blonde, cool tints would look odd against oriental and warm, dark skins. The amount of melanin in skin increases when the skin is exposed to sunlight, so the skin darkens – this is what we see as a tan. (The production of extra melanin is the body's defence against the ultraviolet light from the sun. Too much UV light may cause skin problems, including cancer.)

The hair texture – the coarseness or fineness of the hair affects the absorption of colouring chemicals. In general, fine hair will colour more rapidly than coarse hair.

The condition and porosity of the hair – porous hair will absorb colour products quickly, and porosity depends on the general condition of the hair. Hair with a smooth cuticle absorbs less product. Uneven colour may result.

The colouring product used – tests on the hair will indicate which products may be used. This will affect the range of colours available to this particular client. For example, tests may show that it is safe to use a light, temporary colouring, but there is no point in using it on dark hair – it wouldn't show.

The shade of colour sought – this too may influence the suitability of various products. A white-haired client, for instance, may want to have a slight tone added. In this case a temporary or semi-permanent colouring might be best, in a colour such as silver, pewter, blue or violet. Lighter colourings will be preferable to heavy, darker ones; they will match the skin colour better.

L'Oreal

POROSITY

HAIR SHAFT WITH DAMAGED OR MISSING CUTICLE

UNEVEN BREAKAGE OF CUTICLE ALLOWS PRODUCTS TO BE ABSORBED UNEVENLY

RESULT MAY BE UNEVEN OR PATCHY COLOUR

L'ORÉAL

Porosity and its causes

ROOT HAIR
2-4cm normal porosity
colour good
elasticity good

MID LENGTHS
4-12cm
slightly porous

ENDS
12cm+
more porous

Wella

COLOUR

Tests

Strong chemicals are involved in hair colouring and bleaching. If misused, these could damage the hair or skin. The following are tests you should carry out – most before you start, one during processing.

Most permanent colourings contain chemicals that irritate certain skin types. This is usually stated on the label. Always test the skin 24–48 hours before applying such colourings, so that you know how the skin is likely to react. Don't assume that a product is safe just because it has been used on this client before. A skin reaction may develop even after regular use.

Skin test

A test to find out whether the client's skin reacts to chemicals in the permanent colourings you are going to use (see below). It is also known as the predisposition test, patch test or Sabouraud–Rousseau test. The method is as follows:

1   Mix a little of the colour to be used with the correct amount and strength of hydrogen peroxide.

2   Clean an area of skin about 8 mm square, behind the ear or in the arm fold. Use spirit on cottonwool to remove the grease from the skin.

3   Apply a little of the colour mixture to the skin. Allow it to dry.

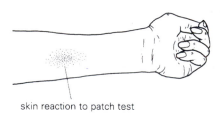

skin reaction to patch test

Skin test for an allergic reaction

Patricia Livingston

4   Cover the colour patch with collodion, which protects it.

5   Ask your client to report any discomfort or irritation that occurs in the next 24–48 hours. Arrange to see the client at the end of this time so that you can check for signs of reaction.

6   If there is a positive response – *any* skin reaction, such as inflammation, soreness, swelling, irritation or discomfort – do not use this colouring treatment. *Never* ignore the result of a skin test. If a skin test showed a reaction and you carried on anyway, there might be a much more serious reaction: this might affect the whole body, and it might for example lead to dermatitis. If there is a negative response – no reaction – you can carry out the treatment proposed.

Colour test

A test for the suitability of a chosen colour, the amount of processing that will be required, and the final colour that will result. Apply the colour or bleaching products you propose to use to a cutting of the client's hair.

Porosity test

A test to indicate how fast chemicals will be absorbed. Rub the hair between your fingertips – is the cuticle smooth or rough? The rougher the cuticle, the more porous it is, and the faster it will absorb chemicals.

Elasticity test

A test for hair strength. Pull a hair between your fingers. Does it stretch and spring back? If the hair breaks easily it may be that the cortex is damaged, in which case chemical processing might cause it to break.

Incompatibility test

A test for chemicals already on the hair. Use gloves to protect your hands. Place a sample of hair in a mixture of hydrogen peroxide and ammonium hydroxide. If the mixture bubbles, heats up or discolours, you should *not* apply a colour – to do so would cause hair loss and skin damage.

Strand test

A test during processing, to check progress (see page 231). If the colour is uneven or insufficient, further processing or more colour is required.

Preparation and procedures for colouring

- Make sure that clothes, both yours and your client's, are always fully protected by gowns and towels.

Tip

There is a large range of colouring products that are continually changing. Keep up to date by reading trade journals or exploring manufacturer's websites.

Wella – www.wella.co.uk

L'Oreal – www.loreal.co.uk

Goldwell – www.goldwell.com

Tip

Always protect the hands when colouring – use gloves.

- Confirm the client's requirements by showing them colour charts and illustrations.
- Select the appropriate colour product, tools and equipment required for the process.
- Always follow the manufacturer's recommendations, particularly when preparing and mixing products.
- Use gloves to prepare, mix, apply and remove colours.
- Isolate any hair that is not to be coloured.
- Ensure that the colour change takes into account the client's wishes, influencing factors and the results required.
- Use colouring techniques that prevent products dripping and spreading unnecessarily.
- Remove colourants effectively, by thorough rinsing on completion of the colouring process.
- Make notes of any problems you encounter. Refer them to your senior as soon as possible.
- Complete record cards by noting all details clearly and accurately including the final results achieved.

Colouring technique

Temporary hair colourings

Temporary colourings remain on the hair only until they are washed off. They do not penetrate the hair cuticle, nor do they directly affect the natural colour. They merely coat the surface of the hair. Some colourings may nevertheless be absorbed if the hair is porous and its condition poor. Temporary colourings are supplied as setting lotions and creams, coloured hairsprays and lacquers, hair colour crayons and paints, glitterdust, mascara applicators, mousses and gels. Many contain **'azo' dyes**.

There are several advantages to temporary colourings:

- the colour effect is only temporary
- a wide range of colours is available
- the colourants are easily removed, by washing
- hair condition can be improved
- subtle toning can be applied to grey, white or normal hair
- fashion effects can be used on bleached hair
- no skin test is required.

Health & Safety

Take care when using metallic colours on blonde, white or bleached hair – the hair may discolour.

Remove metallic colourings thoroughly before carrying out any oxidation process, such as bleaching.

Types of temporary colouring products

Setting lotions and creams are popular forms of colouring. The colour is usually carried in a setting agent, which gives body to the hair. No mixing or dilution is required. The colourant is applied with a sponge or brush, or directly from the container. It may be

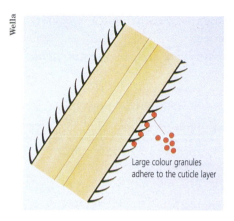

Temporary hair colouring

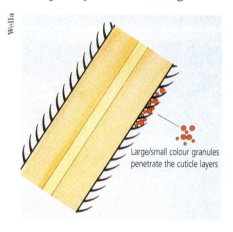

Semi-permanent hair colouring

Tip

Check that the colour in the container is the right one – it's easy to mix up the colours!

Check that the container isn't damaged. Air can oxidise the colour and make it useless.

distributed throughout the hair by light frictioning with the fingers. Towel-dry the hair before applying the lotion or cream, to prevent dilution.

Coloured hairsprays are made in liquid or powder form, and in various colours. They are used on dry, dressed hair. These are based on plastics: they coat the cuticle and are also easily removed by brushing and washing. Some contain metallic colourings; silver and bronze are popular, for example.

Hair colour crayons and paints are mainly for theatrical effects. They are particularly useful for highlighting a dressing for the stage or for television.

Glitterdust is made from shining, coloured metal dust. When sprinkled on the hair, it produces a twinkling effect. Gold and silver are commonly used. The effects are temporary and ornamental.

Hair mascaras are packaged in a similar applicator to eye mascara and applied to strands of dry dressed hair. They are a popular form of adding temporary colour to hair.

Coloured mousses and gels are popular forms of temporary colouring with advantages similar to those of coloured setting lotions. They are able to colour and condition hair, and add extra hold.

Semi-permanent colourings

Semi-permanent colourings are made in various forms and normally require no mixing, unlike some temporary rinses and permanent colourings. However, you should always check the instructions before using any commercial product.

Semi-permanent colouring is deposited in the cuticle and outer cortex. It remains in the hair longer than temporary colourings do. The colouring gradually lifts each time the hair is washed. Some last through six, seven or eight washes. Semi-permanent colourings are not intended to cover a large percentage of white hair, but they nevertheless do so to a greater extent than do temporary colourings.

The colour range is varied, but you need to choose carefully. A black rinse on white hair, for instance, will not produce a pleasing result. Timing and development are affected by salon temperature, and by the hair's texture and porosity. Heat and poor hair condition may speed absorption.

Semi-permanent colourings have several advantages:

- They are more effective and longer-lasting than temporary colourings.
- A larger colour range and choice is available.
- There is no root regrowth because unless the hair is very porous, the colour lifts by the time contrasting hair has grown.
- Natural hair colour is not affected, either directly or chemically.
- Skin tests are not usually required (but always check the instructions before you start).

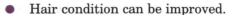

Tip

Always measure quantities of chemicals carefully and mix them thoroughly following the manufacturer's instructions.

- Hair condition can be improved.
- They add shine to the hair.
- Foaming agents within the colourants help to prevent colour dripping.

Semi-permanent colourings may be made from nitrodiamines, nitrated aminophenols and picramic acid. These are collectively known as **'nitro' dyes**. The pigment molecules penetrate the cuticle and enter the cortex, but are gradually removed by subsequent washings.

Adding semi-permanent colour to hair

Preparation

1 Check the scalp for cuts, sores, or any abnormalities that may be aggravated by chemicals in the colouring.
2 Use suitable protective coverings to protect both yourself and your client.
3 Wash the hair with a suitable shampoo, preferably one made for pre-colouring. (Some semi-permanents contain a detergent and require no pre-shampooing.)
4 Remove excess water to prevent colour dilution.
5 Comb through the hair to remove any tangles.
6 Isolate and protect parts of the hair that are not to be coloured.

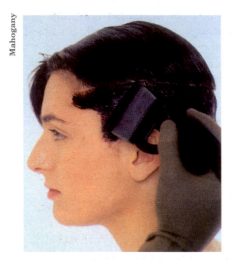

Mahogany

Application

1 Apply the colouring using a sponge, a brush, an applicator bottle, or by pouring it direct from the container, according to the manufacturer's instructions.
2 Apply it evenly, and leave the hair loose to allow free circulation of air. This helps even development. Large hair sections may be taken. (When using permanent colours small sections must be taken.)
3 Do not apply heat without first covering the hair. A plastic cap may be useful, to prevent the colouring drying out, which would adversely affect colour development.
4 Remove any skin stains with spirit or stain remover. Barrier creams help to prevent skin staining.
5 Time the process, following the manufacturer's recommendations.
6 Remove surplus colouring by thorough rinsing, but without further washing.

Quasi-permanent colourings

Quasi-permanent colours come in a wide variety of fashion shades as well as natural shades. They are popular because these types of colours are nearly permanent – they last longer than a semi-permanent colouring but not as long as the true permanent

Wella

colouring. Quasi-permanent colourings are mixed with a developer which contains a low strength of hydrogen peroxide; this helps to hold the colour within the hair. Quasi-permanent colourings usually last between 15–20 washes depending on the porosity of your client's hair. Because of this these types of colours do leave a slight regrowth and a skin test should be carried out.

Quasi-permanent colourings have several advantages:

- They are more effective and last longer than a semi-permanent colour
- They are not as harsh on the hair as a permanent colour
- Hair condition can be improved
- They add shine to the hair
- They are often used in colour correction.

Mixing quasi-permanent colours

Only mix the colour when you have prepared your client and yourself, and always wear gloves. Once mixed it should be applied straight away. Mix the colour and the developer carefully following the manufacturer's instructions, making sure you measure the amounts accurately. Quasi-permanent colours are usually applied with an applicator bottle as they have a runnier consistency to that of a permanent colour and it makes it easier to control.

Permanent colourings

A wide variety of permanent colourings is available. They are used to cover white hair and most natural colours, and to produce other natural colours as well as fashion and fantasy shades. Modern colourings are made in cream, semi-viscous and liquid forms. Most need to be mixed with hydrogen peroxide: this oxidises the hair's natural pigment and combines the small molecules of synthetic colouring into much larger molecules. This process is called **polymerisation**. Without hydrogen peroxide the synthetic colouring would rapidly be lost again.

Colouring is the process whereby the synthetic colouring penetrates the hair cuticle, and is absorbed into the cortex. There it

Health & Safety

Some permanent colourings may be diluted or mixed to produce varied quasi-permanent effects. These products do contain substances that are known to be skin irritants. Carry out skin tests first. Mixtures of this type should be made only on the manufacturer's recommendation.

Permanent hair colouring

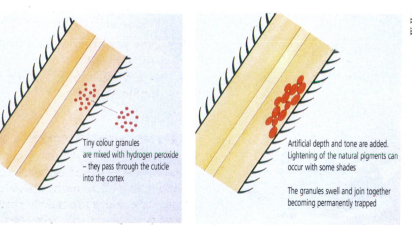

Wella

Tiny colour granules are mixed with hydrogen peroxide – they pass through the cuticle into the cortex

Artificial depth and tone are added. Lightening of the natural pigments can occur with some shades

The granules swell and join together becoming permanently trapped

Chris Moody

is oxidised and remains permanently fixed. The natural colour is bleached at the same time. Although the colours are permanent, the choice of product and the rate of hair growth affect how long the colour lasts. The condition of the hair also affects this: hair with damage to the cuticle (which can be caused by the effects of weather) will lose the colour more rapidly.

Using hydrogen peroxide (H$_2$O$_2$)

Hydrogen peroxide is one of the most commonly used oxidising agents. It can be mixed with cream or with liquid permanent colour. The mixture appears colourless at first, but darkens on exposure.

It is supplied in different strengths, described in one of two ways. The volume strength refers to the amount of oxygen that the peroxide can produce. For example, 1 litre of '30 volume' peroxide would produce 30 litres of oxygen. The percentage strength records how much of the peroxide solution is peroxide, the rest being water. For instance, in 100 g of '9 per cent' or '9%' peroxide there would be 9 g of peroxide and 91 g of water. The strength can be measured with a peroxometer.

Hydrogen peroxide – diluting to the required strength

Strength of peroxide as supplied (%)	Peroxide (parts)		Water (parts)		Strength of peroxide produced (%)
30	3	+	2	→	18
30	2	+	3	→	12
30	3	+	7	→	9
30	1	+	4	→	6
30	1	+	9	→	3
18	2	+	1	→	12
18	1	+	1	→	9
18	1	+	2	→	6
18	1	+	5	→	3
12	3	+	1	→	9
12	1	+	1	→	6
12	1	+	3	→	3
9	2	+	1	→	6
9	1	+	2	→	3
6	1	+	1	→	3
3	1	+	2	→	1

With a modern colour and hydrogen peroxide, the mixture first penetrates the cuticle. In the cortex, the natural pigment is bleached, and the colourant is oxidised. The colour becomes locked within the cortex. (Note that peroxide is needed even when you are making the hair *darker* – not to lighten the natural pigment, but to fix the new colour in the cortex.)

To lighten the natural hair colour ('colour up') two or three shades, use a higher strength of hydrogen peroxide. To take the natural colour down to a darker shade ('colour down'), use a lower strength. The percentage strength to use is determined by the manufacturers' instructions, the colour of the hair to be lightened or darkened, and the hair's porosity. (See the table of hydrogen peroxide dilutions.)

Pre-lightening is necessary when the natural colour is to be changed to a very light shade. Mixtures of hydrogen peroxide and ammonium hydroxide (or other bleaching agents) may be used. Modern colourings lighten several shades, but cannot by themselves lighten to the very pale tones.

Pre-softening is a technique used on resistant hair. Dilute hydrogen peroxide and ammonium hydroxide are applied, not to lighten the colour but to soften the cuticle. This makes it easier later for the colourant to penetrate the hair.

Health & Safety

Quasi and permanent colour products may cause a skin reaction. Carry out a skin test before applying them.

Always follow the manufacturer's instructions for the use of peroxide products. Check with your salon's COSHH list of potential hazards (see page 296) for the correct usage.

Activity

In your styling book, list the different colour products available. Collect examples from journals and magazines.

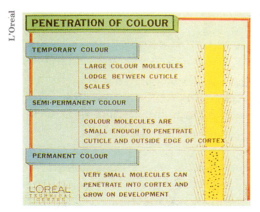

Penetration of colour

Permanent hair colouring product

Tip

Make sure that any hair not to be coloured is isolated – for example, carefully sectioned and wrapped in foil or tissue.

Hair sectioning

Adding permanent colour to hair

Preparation

Before colouring a client's hair you must make the usual preparations: consulting with the client, agreeing what is to be done, and making the necessary tests (see pages 222 and 223). Examine the hair and skin thoroughly for signs of poor condition or inflammation. When you carry out the skin test – 24–48 hours before processing – don't forget to take a cutting of the client's hair so that you can make colour tests. Unless you know exactly what products have been used on the hair previously, test for incompatibilities such as metallic dyes. The results of these tests will then be available when the client returns for the actual colour service. Gather together everything you will need:

- protective coverings, both for you and your client
- barrier cream to protect the skin around the hairline
- rubber gloves
- a measuring cylinder and hydrogen peroxide, for mixing the colour
- a dish and an applicator
- a tailcomb and clips, for sectioning
- cotton wool, to soak up excess colour
- the chosen colour(s).

Health & Safety

Colours contain strong chemicals. Unless you are using the colour as a toner after pre-bleaching, always apply colour to dry, unwashed hair. Shampoo washes away the natural oils which protect the hair and skin from the chemicals in the colour. It also stimulates the skin, bringing blood to the surface and increasing the risk of skin reactions.

Sectioning

1 Sectioning makes the hair more manageable and ensures you do not miss any hair when applying the product.

2 Section the hair from the centre of the forehead to the nape, and from ear to ear across the crown. When colouring take sub-sections about 6 mm wide, starting from the nape as this is most resistant.

3 Hair lower down the head, especially hair covered by other hair, is usually darker than that on the top. This is because of the effects of combing and brushing, which make the cuticle more porous, and because outer layers are lightened by sunlight.

Colour application

Tip

Read manufacturer's instructions carefully when measuring and mixing colour and hydrogen peroxide together. By mixing colour you are working towards key skills Application of Number Level 1.

Tip

When using electrical equipment to help colour development make sure you check the equipment is working correctly before using it on your client.

Jennifer Cheyne

Mixing a permanent colour

Don't mix the colour until you're ready to start colouring. Once mixed, it needs to be used immediately.

Mix the colour carefully, measuring amounts accurately. If the proportions are wrong, the result may not be as you intended. Add the peroxide to the colour gradually, to make sure the mixture is smooth.

Application

1. You can apply a pre-colour treatment if the hair is dry or porous. This will help even out the porosity, giving a more even colour result.

2. Place the application bowl near your client, to minimise the risk of dripping colour on them or on the floor.

3. The method of application depends on how runny the tint mixture is. Cream colours are best applied with a brush. Carefully lay the colour on to the subsection and leave it: don't scrape it off again. With practice you will judge how much to put on. Liquid or semi-liquid colours can be applied with a sponge, an applicator, a dispenser or directly from the bottle.

4. If the colour is thick, work with small sub-sections. The thinner it is, the larger the sub-sections can be, because it will penetrate more quickly. The applicator brush often gives the best control.

5. Work swiftly and methodically, from the nape upwards.

6. Distribute the colour evenly, covering each sub-section. Too little will produce varied colour; too much will be wasteful.

 Activity

Using samples of hair of one base colour, apply different shades of colour. Assess the results.

Processing: colour development

Monitor and time the processing from the point when all of the hair has been treated. Timing must be accurate. Too short a time will cause **under-processing** – the development will be incomplete and the colour won't be as you intended. Too long a time may cause **over-processing** – the shades produced may be too dark. You may be able to use accelerators to speed up the processing. Check the manufacturer's instructions.

When you think processing may be complete, carry out a **hair-strand colour test**.

1. Most colouring products just require the time recommended by the manufacturer. Check the instructions.

2. Rub a strand of hair lightly with a paper tissue or the back of a comb, to remove the surplus colour.

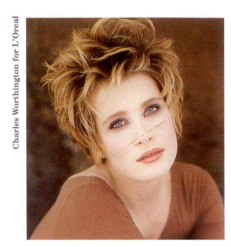

Charles Worthington for L'Oreal

Health & Safety

Always follow the manufacturer's instructions for the application of chemicals and products. Check with your salon's COSHH list of potential hazards (see page 296) for the correct usage.

Tip

When using dry heat, don't dry the hair too quickly. If the colourant is dried out too soon, it may be ineffective.

Tip

Always note the salon temperature. If the salon is warm, processing could be faster; if it is cool, processing could be slower. If the client is sitting near a heater or in a cold draught, then part of the head could be processed differently from the rest.

3   Check whether the colour remaining is evenly distributed throughout the hair's length. If it is even, remove the rest of the colour product. If it is uneven, allow processing to continue, if necessary applying more tint.

4   If any of the hair on the head is not being treated you can compare the evenness of colour in the processed hair with that in the unprocessed hair.

Colouring aids

The activation of colouring processes can be aided by the use of steamers, accelerators or rollerballs. The applied heat causes the hair to swell and the cuticle to lift. This makes it easier for the colourant to enter the cortex, and may halve the processing time.

Steamers, accelerators and rollerballs allow colour applications to be made on hair regardless of its length, even though the hair may vary in its porosity between the roots and the points. The heat distribution allows even processing throughout the hair length. Colour application must not be delayed, however, or the result may be uneven.

Removing surplus colour

Some colour can be removed by adding a little water, lightly massaging the hair, and rinsing. Others may require shampooing. You can also use an acid balancing conditioner to restore the hairs' pH to 4.4–5.5 and close the cuticle or post-colour treatments that help lock in the colour (see Chapter 3). Don't ruffle the hair at this stage or it may get tangled. If there are any skin stains, apply a little colour directly to the stain to soften it. Then rinse the skin thoroughly. Don't let the stain remain on the skin for long, as the colour will deepen.

While the hair is wet the colour will look darker. Towel-dry the hair and the true colour will be easier to assess.

Activity

Collect together four or five dark brown hair samples. Apply colour to them. Time them differently: the first for 5 minutes, the next 10 minutes, the third 15 minutes and so on. At the end of the time, rinse the hair sample. When they are all processed, compare the different colour effects produced by the different timings.

Repeat the process with mid-brown or light brown hair.

Further colouring techniques

Virgin hair

Hair that has not been coloured or otherwise chemically treated before will vary in lightness and porosity along its length. The mid-lengths are usually the most resistant to colour, and so they take

First time (virgin) application

Wella

L'Oreal

Regrowth application

the longest. The hair points are naturally lighter and more porous, because they are the most exposed to wear and weather. The roots are closest to the head, heat from which activates the colour.

For the first time colour application, use this special method:

1 Begin by applying colour to the mid-lengths (the main part of the hair).

2 Then apply colour to the hair points (the last 25 mm of the hair tips).

3 Finally, apply colour to the roots (the 12 mm nearest the scalp).

Regrowth application

Regrowth application is the process of colouring just the hair that has grown since the colour was applied last time. The colour is applied to the root ends only, not to the mid-lengths or points. It is then processed and rinsed in the usual way.

With some colour products you can add a little water and comb the colourant through the rest of the hair after processing. This dilutes the colour product and maintains an even colour throughout the hair, correcting any lifting that has occurred.

Colouring lighter or darker

With modern oxidation colours it is possible to lighten or darken the natural hair shade. As usual, you need to plan the final colour, taking into account the starting colour, the texture and condition of the hair, and so on.

To darken the hair, you will need a darker shade than that of your client's natural coloured hair and a low percentage of hydrogen peroxide. To lighten it, more peroxide will be needed to oxidise the pigment in the hair. If the client wants the hair lightened by many shades (from black to light blonde, for example), you will need to pre-bleach it. Always follow the manufacturer's instructions.

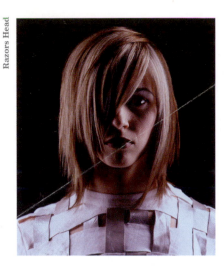

Razors Head

Resistant hair and greying hair

Some hair resists colour, usually because the cuticle isn't porous. With experience you will learn to recognise this just by feeling the hair – rough hair is more likely to be porous. Hair is likely to colour easily in certain conditions:

- if has recently been permed
- if it usually takes a perm quickly
- if it curls easily and tightly
- if it has previously been coloured
- if it has been bleached
- if it is dry.

It is likely to be resistant:

- if it takes perms slowly
- if it soon drops out of curl
- if it has a smooth surface (a tightly packed cuticle)
- if it is greasy or lank
- if it is covered with chemicals or a metallic coating.

White hair is sometimes resistant, but often it is more porous than pigmented hair. If there are white patches, colour them last of all, especially if you are using warm shades such as red.

If necessary, pre-soften the hair by applying a diluted mixture of hydrogen peroxide and ammonium hydroxide. This will cause the cuticle to lift, making the hair more porous (see page 229).

John Jenkins for L'Oreal

Highlights

Bleaching or colouring some of the hair

The following are some of the terms used to describe bleaching or colouring part or parts of the hair: slicing, tipping, blending, weaving, frosting, highlights, lowlights, polishing, brightening, shimmering and scrunching. **Highlighting** refers to shading parts of the hair with bleach or colour. **Lowlighting** refers to parts of the hair being coloured with subtle shades. These techniques can be used most effectively to enhance hair shape and style.

- It is usually more effective to lighten small pieces than large, chunky ones.
- You can use the more prominent parts of the head to highlight a shape or dressing.
- You can use toners to produce varied coloured effects. These may blend with the client's natural colour, or contrast with it.

There are various methods of part bleaching or colouring. Especially popular is the use of streaks of lightened hair. Below are two methods of part bleaching.

Regis

Lowlights

L'Oreal

Regrowth to be bleached

Bleach has been applied to the regrowth

Processing

Completed regrowth bleach

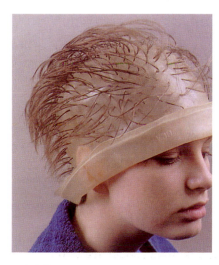

Highlighting using a cap

Highlighting

This can be done using a cap.

1 Pull sectioned strands of hair through holes in the plastic cap. (The holes must be carefully positioned.) The cap prevents the bleach running onto other parts of the hair.
2 Apply bleach, using a brush or an applicator.
3 Do not allow the hair to dry out. This would interfere with the bleaching process.
4 You may use a steamer or an accelerator if recommended by the manufacturer.

Alternatively, you can use foil:

1 Section small groups of hair strands. Weave or zigzag them so that the hair does not form clumps of lightened or coloured areas.
2 Wrap the sections in aluminium foil, making small packets. The foil retains the heat produced by the oxidants, and the required degree of lightness is reached quickly.
3 Secure the root ends of the strands tightly, to prevent the bleach from running on to them.
4 No heat is necessary. (If you *did* apply heat, the bleach might 'bubble' and run, producing unwanted yellow patches on the roots.)

Bleach wraps or packets are now made. These are specially designed to cover small sections of hair, or woven hair sections. They seal the hair securely so that the bleach does not run.

There are many other techniques for lightening and bleaching, producing a wide range of effects. Manufacturers of bleach products often suggest methods of use.

Part bleaching using a foil

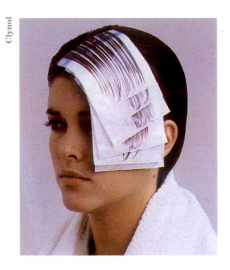

Part bleaching using wraps

Competition and fantasy colouring

This involves the application of colourants to produce a variety of special effects. The results may not be natural or suitable for normal wear: some competition colours are good examples of wearable colours, others are harsh and garish as a fashion or style requirement. Fantasy colours are more extreme, with vivid and startling colour blends.

Lighting plays an important part in colour effects and needs to be considered when planning the overall effect. Lighting has effects in the salon, as well as on competition colourings. Some of these are as follows:

- Blue light, produced by some types of fluorescent tube, tends to neutralise the warm red effect of hair colour.
- Yellow light, as from bare electric bulbs, adds warmth to hair colour and tends to neutralise blue or ash effects.
- Whiter 'daylight' lights show a truer hair colour than ordinary artificial light (tungsten bulbs).

Colours planned for special competitions can look unexpectedly different if the lighting has not been considered. In the salon the client's hair colour should be planned to fit the lighting in which the hair is to be seen. For example, the hair of a typist working most of the day under a blue fluorescent light will look greenish if it has been coloured (or left) yellow.

 Activity

You need to be clear about the different kinds of colouring – bleaching, temporary colour, semi-permanent colour, quasi-permanent colour and permanent colour. Make a list of these; then, in each case, say:

- which parts of the hair are affected
- the normal processing time
- how long the colour is expected to last
- what are the effects on the hair structure.

 Activity

Where possible, take colour photographs of successful colourings. Keep them in folders or your styling book.

Successful colouring

Precautions

Certain precautions need to be taken when using colour or colouring products:

Tip

First make your own assessment of the colouring process you will use. Then check with your supervisor. Recognise the limits of your own authority.

Remember to note down every step of the colouring process applied to your client.

Tip

When colouring curly or wavy hair, take a smaller section for control. Comb sections as smooth as possible to ensure even coverage.

Tip

When applying colour to previously chemically-treated hair e.g. relaxed or permed use pre-colour treatment to help even out porosity.

Jingles

- Always carry out a skin test 24–48 hours before colouring. (This is recommended by manufacturers.) Record results on the client's records.

- Make other tests, for hair colour and incompatibilities.

- Examine the hair and scalp for disease, inflammation or abnormalities. Avoid adverse skin reactions and the aggravation of existing problems.

- Ask your client if they are on any known medications that may affect the colour service.

- Make sure you record the information on the client's records. Seek advice from your supervisor if you are unsure whether you can proceed with the process.

- Choose colours wisely. Wrong colour applications will undermine your client's confidence.

- Check applicators before use. Clean and replace all tools and materials after use. Any remaining colouring could discolour light or blonde hair.

- Do not try to make temporary colourings do the work of permanent ones. Use products as intended by their manufacturers.

- Use reliable products, correctly stored and carefully maintained. Poor-quality products result in loss of time, effort and money – and clients.

- Measure quantities accurately. Never rely on guesswork. Avoid the use of metal containers, or hair discolouration may result.

- Avoid harsh rubbing and hair ruffling when pre-shampooing or removing colourants.

- Protect your hands and skin by using rubber or plastic gloves.

- Remove surplus water before colouring, to avoid dilution of colour.

- Keep hair colourants away from the eyes. Never use scalp hair colourants on eyebrows or eyelashes: special, non-irritant preparations are made for these. Check the numbers on the tubes or bottles with the numbers on their containers. It is easy to put a tube in the wrong box!

- Use correct dilutions of colourants and correct volume/percentage strengths of hydrogen peroxide.

- Constantly monitor and time the colour process.

- Work methodically and efficiently: this will produce confidence in the client, and good results.

- Remove stains from clothes immediately, using clean water. If allowed to remain they may become more difficult to remove.

- Ensure that all information is carefully recorded on the client's record card.

Splinters

Vidal Sassoon

Pat Wood for the Saks Art Team

Colouring hair: problems, faults and correction

Fault	Possible causes	Correction
Colour patchy or uneven	Insufficient coverage by colour	Spot-colour the light areas
	Colour poorly applied	
	Poor colour mixing	
	Sections too large	
	Overlapping (colour build-up in parts)	
	Under-processing (full colour did not develop)	
	Spirit-based setting lotion used (some colour removed)	
Colour too light	Insufficient colour in chosen shade	Choose a darker shade
	Peroxide strength too low for full colour development	Check peroxide strength
	Peroxide strength too high, causing bleaching; insufficient colour oxidised	Check peroxide strength
	Under-processing	Colour fill
	Hair in poor condition/too porous to hold colour	Recondition
Colour fades after two or three shampoos	Bleaching effects of sun	Recondition before next colour application
	Hair treated harshly (e.g. brushing, sand)	
	Hair in poor condition/too porous	
	Under-processing	Process correctly; do not repeatedly comb the colour through

Fault	Possible causes	Correction
Colour is too dark	Chosen shade too dark	Refer to a senior stylist
	Over-processing	
	Hair in poor condition/too porous	
	Hair coated with incompatible chemical	
Colour is too red neutralise	Peroxide strength too high	Apply matt or green colour to
	If pre-bleached, wrong neutralising colour chosen, or hair not bleached light enough	
	Colour development incomplete	
Hair has discoloured	Hair in poor condition/too porous	Correct green with contrasting colour (beware of producing dark brown)
	Undiluted colour repeatedly combed through hair	Correct mauve with contrasting colour, or remove with special colour reducer
	Hair coated with incompatible chemicals	
	If green, may result from blue ash on yellow base, or from metallic salt reaction	
	If mauve, may be due to presence of incompatible chemicals	
Colour coverage is good except for white hairs	Hair resistant	Pre-soften, or use lighter shade with higher strength peroxide
Hair is resistant to tint generally	Cuticle is closely packed	Pre-soften
	Under-processing	Choose colour carefully
	Chosen colour unsuitable	Time development correctly
	Materials poorly mixed or poorly applied	Check for correct mixing and application
Scalp irritation or skin reaction	Hair not washed clean, colour still present	Give no treatment, but wash hair thoroughly
	Peroxide strength too high	
	Hair badly combed, colour applied	Advise client to visit her doctor
	Client allergic to tint chemicals	Notify salon's insurance company

Bleaching – the principles

Andrew Collinge. Photo: John Swannell

Bleached hair

Tip

Make sure you follow COSHH regulations when storing, using and disposing of chemical products.

Tip

Read manufacturer's instructions when measuring and mixing bleach with hydrogen peroxide.

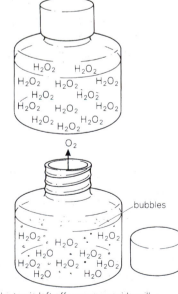

hydrogen peroxide (H_2O_2) is stabilised by sulphuric or phosphoric acid

if the top is left off, some peroxide will turn into water (H_2O) and oxygen (O_2)

Stabilised hydrogen peroxide

How bleaching works

A **bleach** is a chemical used to lighten the colour of hair. To be effective, bleach needs a ready supply of oxygen. In hairdressing the most common source of this oxygen is hydrogen peroxide, a colourless, oily liquid. In practice, peroxide is used in solution in water.

Hydrogen peroxide (H_2O_2) is an **oxidant**: it readily reacts to produce a lot of oxygen. Because it is so reactive, peroxide needs to be stabilised by other chemicals (such as sulphuric acid or phosphoric acid) and stored carefully. To allow the peroxide to work you need to counteract these stabilisers. This is done by mixing it with ammonium hydroxide or (for powder bleaches) sodium acetate or ammonium carbonate. These activate the peroxide.

When you use bleach you mix it with hydrogen peroxide diluted to the appropriate strength. The bleach now begins to work. The hair swells and the cuticle lifts, allowing the bleach to penetrate the cortex. Here oxygen released from the peroxide reacts with the natural hair pigments, making them colourless.

Eumelanin is the pigment that makes the hair black or brown. As the melanin bleaches, the **pheomelanin** becomes more noticeable. This is the pigment that makes the hair red or yellow. As bleaching proceeds, the hair becomes lighter and lighter, changing through a range of shades – from dark brown, perhaps, through a warm red, to a very pale yellow. The shades and the final colour depend on the proportions of eumelanin and pheomelanin in the hair.

At some point, the hair stops getting lighter. Some very light brown and blonde hair easily reduces to light shades without **toning** (see page 246). With darker hair, though, the final colour after bleaching may still be somewhat yellow. To make it white or platinum, you will need to neutralise any remaining yellow with a toner, usually a violet one.

Overbleaching

Bleaching is a precise process. Too much bleaching will destroy the structure of the hair. Before starting, always process a strand of hair to see how light it will become. There are several reasons why **overbleaching** may occur:

- using peroxide solution that is too strong
- processing the hair for too long
- overlapping hair sections
- combing bleach through previously bleached hair
- bleaching hair that is in poor condition and too porous.

Additionally, if you use a strong peroxide solution and a dryer, the dry heat may increase the speed at which oxygen is produced. This can cause overheating and over-processing of the hair, making it likely to break.

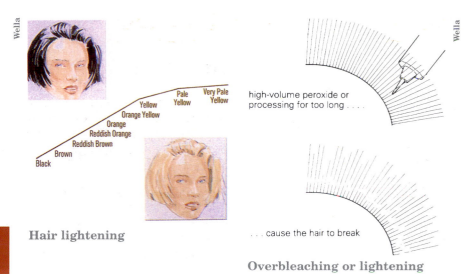

Very Pale
Yellow
Pale
Yellow
Yellow
Orange Yellow
Orange
Reddish Orange
Reddish Brown
Brown
Black

Hair lightening

high-volume peroxide or
processing for too long . . . .

. . . cause the hair to break

Overbleaching or lightening

Health & Safety

Be careful never to use too
strong a solution of peroxide.
A milder solution applied for
longer is kinder to the hair
than a stronger one applied
for a shorter time.

Health & Safety

Always follow the
manufacturer's instructions
for the application of
chemicals and products.
Check with your salon's
COSHH list of potential
hazards for the correct
usage.

**Hair bleaching/lightening
product**

Even if it doesn't actually break, overbleached hair may become
spongy, very porous and unevenly coloured. Further colouring,
toning or perming become difficult; so does hair management
generally. When wet, overbleached hair may resemble chewing gum.
The effects of blow-styling and other processes will not last. Even a
little tension will break the hair. If the hair gets into this state, you
must condition it before considering processing it chemically in any
other way. Always carry out tests e.g. elasticity and porosity (see
page 24–26). The lighter the colour hair is bleached to, the more
porous and less elastic the hair becomes. If hair is subjected to more
chemical services it would probably break.

Natural bleaching

Sun, wind, sea, sand and chlorinated water affect hair in
the same way as a peroxide bleach. Sun and wind dry and lift the
cuticle. Brushing, if sand is present, roughens the cuticle. Hair that
has previously been bleached is particularly prone to such effects.
Hair liable to be exposed to strong sunlight is best kept covered;
hair exposed to sea or **chlorinated water** should be rinsed as soon
as possible.

Choosing a bleach process

The client

When a client asks for a bleach process; discuss what they have in
mind. You can bleach the whole head, part of the head, or the hair
tips only. Or you can make highlights in the hair. Consult with your
client as you would for a colour (see page 220).

Explain to your client that bleaching, like other chemical processes,
affects the condition of the hair. Once you've bleached it your client
will need to take special care of their hair at home and return to the
salon regularly for further treatment. There will be additional costs
in maintaining the effects of bleaching.

Health & Safety

Strong peroxide solutions can easily burn skin and damage hair structure. Protect yourself and your client.

Bleached hair

Chris Moody

Bleaches

Bleaches are supplied as liquids, oils, creams, gels, emulsions, powders and pastes. Each of them needs to be mixed with an oxidant – usually hydrogen peroxide.

Liquid bleach (simple bleach) is basically ammonium hydroxide (or ammonia). 1 ml of ammonium hydroxide is mixed with 20–50 ml of hydrogen peroxide. The proportions needed depend on the shade required. If there is too much ammonium hydroxide, the bleach will redden the hair. This mixture lightens the hair by up to three shades.

Oil bleach is usually a slightly thicker liquid, containing ammonium hydroxide and sulphonated oils or a thickener. Several types are made. These too are mixed with hydrogen peroxide. They lighten by up to four shades.

Cream, emulsion and gel bleaches are thicker substances which contain alkalis (usually ammonium hydroxide), thickening agents, **boosters** or **activators** (which provide additional oxygen), conditioners and other materials. They are mixed with hydrogen peroxide or some other oxidant, and can lighten the hair from dark to light or very light blonde.

Powder and paste bleaches are made from magnesium carbonate and sodium carbonate. These too are mixed with oxidants, such as hydrogen peroxide, sodium bromate or sodium perborate. The mixture is a creamy paste – probably the thickest of bleach mixes. Ammonium hydroxide or ammonium carbonate is added. These bleaches can lighten hair from dark to very light.

Nowadays the cream or emulsion bleaches and the powder or paste bleaches are the most popular, as these offer a wide range of lightening.

Bleaching technique

Bleaching all of the hair (virgin hair)

Preparation

- Consult your client, examine their hair and scalp, analyse the condition of the hair and so on, as for colouring (page 220).
- Make a skin test 48 hours before you plan to bleach the hair, to check your client's reaction to any toner that may be used after bleaching.
- Make a test cutting to assess possible results. (You can do this when you make the skin test.)
- Make sure that your client is fully protected with appropriate gowns, towels, and so on. Make sure you follow your salon's procedures.
- If the hair is greasy or lacquered, shampoo it.
- Prepare the tools, equipment and materials so that they are at hand and ready for use.

Chris Moody

Bleach application: short and long hair

- Use a barrier cream to protect the client's hairline.
- Wear protective gloves or barrier creams to protect your hands.

☀ **Activity**

Find out how samples of light hair (of the same natural shade) can be bleached using different strengths of bleach.

Sectioning

1 Section the head of hair into four. Subdivide it into smaller sections as work progresses. Liquid bleaches penetrate easily, so large sections may be taken (about 9–12 mm). For oil bleaches sections should be smaller (about 6–9 mm); for cream and paste bleaches smaller still (about 6 mm or less). As a general guide, use larger sections for thin bleaches and smaller sections for thick bleaches. Hair quantity, too, helps to determine the best section size.

2 Clip the hair well away from the section you are working on.

3 Work methodically, to avoid missing any part of the hair.

Application

1 Mix the bleach so that it is fresh – do not leave it standing.

2 Apply the bleach mixture to the darkest areas first. These are usually around the nape.

With long hair (approximately 140 mm or more) apply bleach to the mid-lengths first. Leave about 25 mm of the hair tips, and 12–25 mm of the roots, without bleach. Allow the mid-lengths to begin to develop; then apply bleach to the hair tips. When these start developing, apply bleach to the roots. Completely cover all of the hair. This method takes account of the faster development at the roots, due to the heat of the head, and the porosity of the points.

With short hair (approximately 140 mm or less) apply bleach to the mid-lengths and the ends together. Leave about 12–25 mm of the root ends without bleach. When the mid-lengths and points start to develop, apply bleach to the roots. This method allows for the hair points not being porous.

3 Avoid overlapping previously bleached or overporous areas. Overlapping could cause overbleaching.

4 Keep on applying bleach, working up to the crown area. Complete the application by working on the sides and the top front.

5 When application is complete, check around the hairline, particularly around the ear, for full coverage.

6 Make sure that hair is not packed down. This would prevent air circulating, and slow down processing.

📎 **Tip**

Always ensure that you wear protective gloves when making applications of colour or bleaching product.

Apply bleach to some hair samples of different colours. Leave to process for varying times. When developed, rinse the hair. Compare the different degrees of lightness produced by the different times of processing.

Processing

Tip

Steamers and accelerators supply moist heat and can halve processing times. They may also be used to even out development.

1   Remember that bleach starts developing – releasing oxygen – from the moment it is applied.
2   Carefully time the bleach process. Manufacturers give approximate times, but the process is different for every client.
3   Make a hair strand colour test from time to time, to check development (see pages 231 and 232). Hair looks darker when wet and while you are removing bleach from the hair strand: it will look lighter when it dries.
4   If you let the bleach dry out, development will cease.
5   Don't apply dry heat. This would release the oxygen too fast, resulting in little bleach action.
6   As soon as the strand test indicates the level of lightness required, remove the bleach. Delay at this stage could result in overbleaching.

Bleach removal

1   Use tepid water only. Rinse the bleach from the hair. The scalp may be sensitive, so treat it gently.
2   The hair cuticle may be raised, roughened and easily tangled: take care.
3   When the hair has been thoroughly rinsed, you may apply special conditioners, antioxidants or acid balancers to return it to its natural pH of 4.5–5.5 and to close down the cuticle.
4   Comb the hair correctly – from the points – before blow-styling, setting and shaping it.

Regrowth bleaching

After two or three weeks newly grown hair will become visible. This regrowth will require bleaching if the colour is to be even.

1   Refer to the client's record for an indication of the development time.
2   Apply the bleach to the regrowth only. Do not allow it to overlap previously bleached hair.
3   Allow processing to continue until the regrowth is bleached to the same level as the rest of the hair.
4   Remove the bleach carefully.
5   Use conditioners, balancers and the like to return the hair to as near normal as possible.

Colouring back on bleached hair

You can colour bleached hair back to a 'natural' colour: it is easier to darken than to lighten. As a woman ages, her skin and hair colour fade. Resist a client's requests for the 'natural' colour of twenty years ago – the result would probably be too dark. Two or three shades lighter is more likely to be suitable.

If the hair has porous parts, **colour filling** or **pre-pigmentation** is necessary. A base colour in the hair helps other colours to fix more evenly. Red is commonly used. Aim for a warm shade. Ashen, drab and matt shades may show slightly green. Cut off porous ends to allow a normal application.

Successful bleaching

Precautions

Tip

When colouring, bleaching or toning, always check the salon temperature. You must take this into consideration when monitoring and timing processes.

- Examine the hair and scalp. If there are cuts and abrasions or signs of disease, don't carry out chemical processing.
- Test the hair for condition, porosity and tensile strength.
- Apply the bleach mixtures evenly, at the correct strength.
- Never overbleach by overlapping, or by processing too long.
- Never bleach hair coated with metallic or compound hair colourings.
- Do not allow the bleach to dry. If you do, oxidation will stop.
- If there is any yellow in the hair after bleaching, apply neutralising shades.
- On yellow hair, blue colourings or toners may produce green. Test first.
- Metallic tools and containers may be spoilt if you spill bleach on them. This in turn may cause hair discolouration. Use glass or china containers and measures.
- Never bleach hair that is in poor condition or porous. Overlapping in this case causes the hair to break.
- Never mix or apply lighteners or colourings without first checking the manufacturer's instructions.
- Thoroughly remove all traces of the bleach mixture from the hair once the correct lift has been achieved.
- Recently bleached hair needs to be treated carefully.
- After bleaching, neutralise or normalise the hair with special conditioners or acid rinses. (The oxidants in bleaches leave the hair somewhat alkaline.)
- As soon as the bleach has been removed, comb the hair. Comb from the points to the roots. Comb gently, avoiding unnecessary tension.
- To produce light shades, bleach in stages. When possible, use low peroxide strengths.

Greig Firth

Toning

Terence Renati

Health & Safety

Always make skin tests before applying toners.

John Carne for L'Oreal

Toning is the process of adding colour, usually to lightened hair. A variety of pastel shades may be used on very light bleached hair. The toner colour range includes beige, silver, rose and others. Toners give subtle effects. The lightest toners can only be used on the lightest bleached hair. If you use them on dark hair, the colour effect will be lost. Remember that colour added to colour always produces a slightly darker shade.

You can mix colours together to produce a wide range; see page 217 on colour mixing. Here are a few examples:

- red on green produces brown
- red on yellow produces orange
- blue on yellow produces green
- blue on red produces violet
- violet and orange may be used to neutralise green
- blue may be used to neutralise orange
- violet may be used to neutralise yellow.

The final colour depends both on the depth of the starting hair colour and on the shades of toners.

Toners may be temporary, semi-permanent or permanent colourings in a dilute form. There are also specially made toners for use on lightened hair. These are used like permanent colourings.

Application and processing

The mixing of toners depends on the type used. Those mixed with peroxide need low strengths only. If you use higher strengths you may cause patchy results and porous hair.

Toners are applied in the same way as permanent colourings. Some are poured on to the hair and lightly massaged. All need to be evenly applied, taking into account any porous areas.

Development and processing depends on the product used. Aniline-derivative toners require 20–45 minutes. Other toners require several applications – colour is only gradually built up in the hair.

Toning: problems, faults and corrections

Fault	Possible causes	Correction
Uneven colour	Poor application	Spot bleach areas as necessary
	Section too large	Recolour
	Incorrect mixing	Prepare a new bleach mixture, combining the ingredients slowly and thoroughly
Dark ends	Underbleached ends	Rebleach
	Toner too dark	Remove; use lightener
	Toner over-processed	Time accurately
	Remains of dark tint	Remove and tone
Too yellow	Underbleached	Bleach lighter
	Base too dark	Try stronger bleach
	Wrong toner used	Use violet
	Wrong bleach	Use a different bleach (not an oil bleach)
Too red	Underbleached	Rebleach
	Too much alkali	Use blue bleach (not an oil bleach)
	Wrong toner used	Use green, matt or olive
Dark roots or patches	Poor bleach application	Rebleach, evenly
	Toner too dark	Remove; use lightener
Roots not coloured	Underbleached	Bleach again
	Undertimed	Apply full timing
	'Drippy' toner	Apply cream (not liquid)
	Unclean or coated	Clear and re-apply
Colour fade	Over-porous	Correct the condition
	Harsh treatment	Advise on hair care
	Exposure	Keep hair covered
	Over-processed	Comb through only with diluted colour
Hair breakage	Over-processed	Correct the condition
	Incompatibles	Test
	Harsh treatment	Advise on hair care
	Sleeping in rollers	Demonstrate the effects

Toning: problems, faults and corrections (continued)

Fault	Possible causes	Correction
Discolouration	Under-processed	Correct development
	Exposure	Condition hair and cover it
	Home treatments	Test and advise
Green tones	Incompatibles	Test
	Blue on yellow	Use warm or red shades
	Too blue ash	Use violet
Too orange	Under-processed	Apply blue/ash
	Pigment lacking	Add blue pigment
Hair tangled	Overbleached	Use antioxidants
	Poor washing	Use correct movements
	Over-rubbing	Use gentle actions
	Backcombing	Reduce and demonstrate
Inflammation	Skin reaction	Seek doctor's advice
	Torn scalp	Seek doctor's advice
	Disease	Seek doctor's advice
Irritation	Skin reaction	Seek doctor's advice
	Harsh treatment	Seek doctor's advice
	Disease	Seek doctor's advice
Colour not taking	Overporous	Recondition
	Poor condition	Recondition
	Pigment lacking	Prepigment
	Product build-up	Remove excess
Colour build-up	Overporous	Recondition
	Poor condition	Recondition
Hair 'stretchy'	Over-processed	Treat carefully
	Very porous	Correct the condition
	Very poor condition	Correct the condition
Hair breaking	Over-processed	Treat carefully
	Overlapping	Correct the condition; restructure
	Combing through too much	Always dilute the colour
	Incompatibles	Test

Assignments – Colouring hair

A practical activity

Collect together all the information available on colouring hair from your varied sources, including wholesalers and manufacturer's websites. Try out on blocks or models the various techniques of hair colouring. Satisfy yourself that you are able to follow the instructions given by your trainer, and by the manufacturer. Knowledge of your test results, the effects of synthetic colour on natural colours, the colouring and bleaching, will be invaluable to you. Carefully record them for your file. Note the textures of the hair tested, the time it took, the resultant colour and any problems that arose. Then answer these questions:

1 What is colour? What is 'natural' hair and skin colour?

2 List the different terms that apply to hair colourings, and their meanings.

3 Outline the different hair colouring processes and the main differences between them.

4 List the range of available colourants, and the main differences between them.

5 Outline the chemical effects of colourants on the hair structure.

6 How do you retain information on hair colouring services?

7 List the problems that might arise and how you would deal with them.

8 List the items of information required for your assessment.

For you to find out

Investigate your sources of information regarding natural and synthetic hair colouring cosmetics. Consider too the fields of make-up, nail care and clothes design, as well as the balance between colours worn and various forms of lighting in the different situations. Then answer the following questions:

1 Why it is important to consider the colours your client wears? What do you consider to be suitable colours?

2 How do the colours of clothes interact with hair colour under different forms of lighting?

3 Collect sample colours and lay them out in different arrangements. Try to include different colour combinations of hair, clothes and accessories.

4 List the hair colours used for colour toning.

5 List the tests used for hair colouring, bleaching and toning.

6 List the possible causes, faults and problems that could arise when colouring, bleaching and toning, and how to resolve them. Describe future action that should be taken.

7 List the precautions to be taken when colouring hair.

A case study

Imagine that a client is requesting an unsuitable hair colour.

With the help of your colleagues, prepare yourself for the day when this happens to you. Simulate the possible occurrence in advance by working through the following sequence:

1 Consider your client's request. Give your reasons for thinking that it is unsuitable.

2 Offer a suitable alternative. Justify your reasons for recommending this course of action.

3 List the questions you would ask the client.

4 Describe what requires to be done, and agree with the client exactly what is to be done.

5 Describe the various colouring/bleaching/toning processes and their likely effects.

6 Explore the need for aftercare. Explain what the client is required to do and determine whether it is practicable.

7 List the important influencing factors.

8 Discuss recolouring and regrowth.

9 Outline the needs for different hair textures and conditions, and varying hair lengths.

10 Explain the various methods of part colouring/bleaching/toning.

11 Summarise the different times required for different colouring processes, and the costs to your client.

Preparing for Assessment

In preparing for assessment on colouring hair the following checklist may be helpful. Check that you have covered and now fully understand these items:

- assessing the state of your client's hair and scalp
- selecting and applying relevant hair and skin tests
- determining the previous treatments that your client's hair has received
- selecting suitable colours and colourants
- applying colourants as intended by their makers

- monitoring, processing and timing developments of processes
- effectively isolating hair not to be coloured
- effectively removing colourants
- applying suitable conditioners and antioxidants
- dealing with problems that might arise
- accurately recording all details of applied processes.

When you are ready for assessment, talk to your trainer and arrange a suitable time.

By reading this chapter, carrying out the above activities, assignments and case studies, and by meeting the requirements in preparing for assessment you will have worked towards the key skill requirements in Communication Level 1 (C 1.1) (C 1.2) (C 1.3) Level 2 (C 2.1) (C 2.2) (C 2.3) and Application of Number Level 1 (N 1.1) (N 1.2).

If you have used a computer to complete your assignments or activities you will have worked towards the key skill requirements in Information Technology Level 1 (IT 1.1) (IT 1.2).

Salon reception

10

Wella

Learning objectives

The following are some of the topics covered in this chapter:

- maintaining the reception area
- getting organised
- attending to clients
- dealing with enquiries and appointments
- handling appointments.

Introduction

Marianne Marjerus for Hairdresser's Journal

Reception area

The reception is the most important area of the salon. It is where clients are greeted, telephones are answered, appointments are made and bills are paid and usually where client records are stored, either on the computer system or in a filing system (see Chapter 2). It is a busy place. It is also the first impression a client gets of the salon and its staff. A reception area should always be clean, well organised and welcoming. It is the responsibility of the receptionist to maintain the reception area and deal with clients in a relaxed, friendly business-like manner no matter how busy they are.

This chapter deals with the role of the receptionist and the duties they will need to carry out.

Read Chapter 2, Client care and consultation, particularly the sections on communication and promoting services and products, alongside this chapter.

Maintaining the reception area

As part of your duties as the receptionist you will be responsible for making sure that the client waiting area is kept clean and tidy; that magazines are regularly updated and style books are available for clients to look at and that the client is offered refreshments. Clients who are happy in their surroundings while waiting for their appointment are less likely to become annoyed or angry if their stylist is running behind schedule. Make sure that any displays in the reception area are regularly cleaned, refilled and that retail products are checked for their condition and that price labels are clearly visible (see Chapter 2 for promoting products and related legislation). The reception desk is always active with clients arriving or wanting to pay their bill and the telephone ringing with clients wanting to make appointments.

Tip

Remember the Data Protection Act requires you to ensure that personal information is kept confidential.

It is important that the desk is well organised. Stationery such as memo pads, pens and payment documentation should be checked every morning before the salon opens to ensure you do not run out during the day. This is also true of the till – make sure that till rolls are available if needed and that you have enough change in the till and have access to different denominations of money if required. You do not want to leave the reception area during busy periods of the day. As the receptionist you are responsible for the money in the till and for making sure that no unauthorised person can obtain information that is stored at reception such as client personal details from record cards.

Remember as a receptionist you must always be ready, available and attentive. Find time to acknowledge the arrival of each client and assure them that they will soon be attended to.

Client satisfaction is the salon's main aim. Here are some important points.

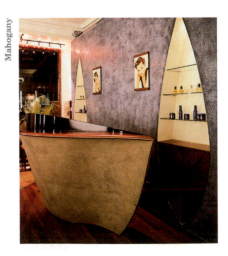

Mahogany

Reception

- Specialist hairdressing advice must be given by the hairdresser appointed to that client.

Tip

To meet the client's expectations, offer a prompt welcome, efficient service, and attention with the minimum of delay.

Tip

Find out what your salon client care policy is for offering refreshments and looking after client belongings.

- Know exactly what services and products the salon offers. A client can be put off by staff who are unsure, or cannot explain, what the salon can provide.
- Allow time for client consultation before hairdressing begins, to avoid any misunderstanding.
- However busy you are, always stay calm but unhurried. This will help you to avoid mistakes at reception.
- Create a good impression through your own appearance, by being neatly dressed and having an attractive hairstyle.
- Confirm each client's appointment, and refer them to the relevant person for action as soon as possible.
- Be helpful to anyone who arrives without an appointment.
- Refer the client to a relevant person for action if possible, or make an appointment for a future time

Getting organised

All salons use the same tabular system for organising work, although different salons use this system in differing ways. The appointment system provides them with the following:

- a daily detailed action plan
- a schedule of individual work allocations
- a clear overview of business activities
- a general indication of expected timescales
- a general indication of expected sales.

The appointment system also has direct links with:

- resource requirements (such as stock and equipment) that the stylist will need during the day
- client records which the stylist or receptionist will need to get ready
- till transactions (such as daily sheets and till rolls).

As you can see, this system is the hub of an efficiently run business. The information it contains must therefore be clear, accurate and up to date.

But maintaining the appointment system correctly will not ensure the smooth running of the salon. You will always need to be prepared for the unexpected!

Your salon may have specific contingency procedures for coping with the following unplanned situations and circumstances, but generally these simple rules apply.

Late arrivals of clients

Suppose that a client arrives 15 minutes late for their appointment and apologetically explains that they were unavoidably held up (in circumstances beyond their control). What should you do?

First and foremost, be sympathetic and understanding. Find out if their stylist still has sufficient time to provide the service. If not, find out if anyone else can attend to their needs. Find out how long they may have to wait (if at all). Will there be any extra costs to the client? Will the appointment have to be re-booked?

Arrivals of unscheduled clients

A client who arrives unexpectedly without a booked appointment should always be accommodated, provided that there is an operator available and sufficient time to carry out the service or treatment.

Over/double booking

This does occur but, it is to be hoped, not too often. Normally this situation arises accidentally when a client or a staff member has made a mistake, or through poor communications. Deliberate overbooking is only done by the over-optimistic staff member. The result is that other people will need to be drawn in to help; otherwise delays will be unavoidable.

Don't try to beat the appointment system; you may upset clients, colleagues or both. Providing a high-quality service includes making sure people know the expected time scales and duration of services and treatments, and if there will be any waiting.

Changes to booked requirements

It often happens that a client who has booked for one service will, following consultation, change their mind and require something different. Don't worry! This could be good business – a client may come in expecting a restyle cut and finish, and go out with a change of hair colour as well. In fact many salons set incentives around this type of situation; for example, staff performances and/or commissions may be based on numbers of 'client conversions'.

Staff absences

Staff absence will always stretch the salon to its limits but your salon should have contingency plans to cover this situation. Generally this will involve:

- checking client records to see if other staff members have provided the service previously
- checking availability of appointments with other staff at the same time

- rescheduling in the appropriate spaces
- if all else fails, contacting the client to rebook the appointment at a later date.

Dealing with people

The client

Every hairdressing business has to have clients. They attend the salon for what they know it has to offer. This includes not only good hairdressing, but clean, pleasant, hygienic surroundings and well-mannered staff.

Good hairdressing is achieved by patient practice and by taking time. The same applies to the skills required for dealing with people. Realising this is the key to your success.

Disagreements and bad manners have no place in successful, harmonious working salons. The client must never be aware of any staff friction there may be, nor must they ever be the subject of it. See Chapter 2 for communication skills and Chapter 11, Working effectively.

Choosing a service

In choosing or deciding exactly is to be done, the client can be helped by the receptionist in several ways.

- Discuss with the client what they want and expect. Further discussion between the hairdresser and client will determine the actual specialist hairdressing required – this is something the receptionist cannot usually do.
- Communicate with the client by listening to what they are telling you and understanding what is required. You must then interpret what is being requested and pass this information on to a competent hairdresser.
- The hairdresser will then examine the client's hair, to determine its length, condition and any other important factors that may affect the services requested.
- The hairdresser will analyse the hair type, facial features and so forth to assess whether the treatment requested is suitable, possible and safe to carry out – if not, further discussion will be needed. The hairdresser may need to take the initiative in guiding the client to a satisfactory decision.
- Make sure that the client understands and agrees to what is finally decided. This avoids any misunderstanding later on.
- Indicate how long the processes will take to complete and the cost of the service. Make sure the client knows, accepts and agrees with these.
- In conjunction with the hairdresser, decide whether tests (for example, a skin test) should be carried out. If so, try to arrange for them to be made before the appointment. This saves time and helps towards a successful result.

Tip

Never attempt to carry out any hairdressing service without the client's consent.

Tip

Never give advice you are unsure of.

Tip

Never bill the client for an amount that was not agreed to.

Requests and enquiries

These may be made by a variety of visitors – regular clients, new clients, casual clients hoping for service without an appointment, and others too. Some may have been recommended to come to the salon by friends and have knowledge of the salon; others will not.

Enquiries may be internal, from within the salon organisation, such as a stylist asking you what time their next client is due in or they may be external, from outside by a sales representative wanting to speak to the manager/owner about their products. They may be made directly – face-to-face, in person – or indirectly, by telephone, letter or via another person or existing client.

Whether enquiries are related to salon services, sales or administration generally, you need to communicate effectively, clearly and precisely in order to avoid problems and difficulties.

Making appointments

Each salon has its own system for making appointments, which should be familiar to all its staff. It involves allocating the time that is to be given to each client and the services requested. Usually you should book services that take more time, such as perming and colouring, for the early morning or early afternoon. Then you can fit around these appointments others that take less time.

The hours of the day are usually printed along the left-hand side of the appointment page, divided into fifteen-minute intervals.

Services are recorded in an abbreviated form. All those who use the appointment page must be familiar with the abbreviations. Here are some common abbreviations:

Service	Abbreviation
Cut and blow dry	C B/D
Blow dry	B/D
Shampoo and set	S/S
Cut, shampoo and set	C S/S
Permanent wave	P/W
Colouring	Col
Highlights	H/L
Lowlights	L/L
Extensions	EX
Long hair dressing	Long
Wedding/Bridal	Wed

You should bear in mind whether the hairdresser is working alone or with assistance. A hairdresser who is preparing, shampooing, arranging products, tools and materials, and carrying out other tasks by themselves requires more time for each appointment than one who has plenty of help.

Some salons allow 30 minutes for cutting, 30 minutes for blow-drying, 15 minutes for setting, and so on. Others may allow more or less time. You must know exactly how much time your salon allows

Tip

Always try to offer a client a choice of appointment times.

Tip

Use pencil to book appointments, so that an entry can be erased if it is cancelled or changed.

Tip

When making appointments ensure that you have a contact number for the client.

Time	Kate	Charlotte	Sally	Sarah	David	Tony
8.30	Jackson	Lisa			Osborn	
8.45	Wedding B/D	Wedding Put up	Beatrice	Beatrice	Wedding B/D	
9 00	Smith	Cane	Extensions	Extensions	Burtwell	Morley
9 15	CBD	P/W	Top Only	Top Only	B/D	Meche HL
9 30	Johnstone	Jacobs			Thomas	Long Hair
9 45	P/W	Col			Few Meche	
10 00	Williams	Meek D/c			Garner	
10 15	CBD	Cooper D/c			CBD	
10 30	Russell D/c	Cane			Meche	
10 45	Russell D/c	P/W CBD			CBD	Simmons
11 00	Johnstone	Jacobs			Jorden	CBD
11 15	P/W CBD	Col CBD			Semi Col	Meche HL
11 30	Davis	Webster			Godwin D/c	CBD
11 45	B/D	CBD	Gibbon	Grace	Semi Col	Jackson D/c
12 00	Lunch	Possee	CBD	CBD	CBD	Lunch
12 15		CBD	Jouhet D/c		meawell	
12 30		Waldren	Lunch	Lunch	B/D	
12 45		CBD			Cosey D/c	
1 00	Watts					Beezer
1 15	Meche HL	Lunch				HL
1 30	Lunch		Gladstone	Crane	Lunch	Jenkins
1 45			Spiral P/W	Straightener		Top P/W
2 00		Peters	(Long hair)	Corker	Cook	Jarvis
2 15	John	Semi Col		Col	CBD	CBD
2 30	CBD	Bore D/c	Payne	Straightener + Plait		Beezer
2 45	Tyler D/c	Semi Col	S/set	CBD	Masters	HL CBD
3 00	Watts	CBD	Selwyn D/c	Corker	P/W	Jenkins
3 15	Meche CBD	Baker	S/set + Brush	Col CBD	Tozer	P/W CBD
3 30	Richmond	P/W	Gladstone	Jennings	HL	Gribble
3 45	CBD	Rickets	P/W CBD	CBD	Smith	Put up
4 00	Hobbs	CBD	Toby	Osborn	CBD	
4 15	Plait	Griffiths	Put up	CBD	Masters	Salter
4 30	Simons	B/D		Adams	P/W CBD	CBD
4 45	CBD	Baker	Curtis	CBD	Tozer	Sadler D/c
5 00	Robins	P/W CBD	CBD	Stevens	HL CBD	Collins
5 15	CBD			CBD		CBD
5 30						
5 45						

Date: Saturday 21 September

 high **Hair**

Wella

Appointments page

for each service, so that you can make appointments accurately and fit in as many as possible. Wasting time and making mistakes when booking clients can be costly. If in doubt, check with the stylist.

Tip

Allow time for client and stylist to confer together before the main service appointments.

Activity

Practise timing your own techniques until they are fast enough to be acceptable.

Apart from the process of managing time and the specific service to be booked, there are other details to be remembered – the client name and contact details, the service required, the date and time of the service, its cost, its duration, and the staff member to be booked. Finally, complete an appointment card with clearly readable details for the client to take away.

Telephone skills

Preparation

Tip

However busy you are, never speak abruptly to a telephone caller, and never rush a call.

1 Always have pencil and paper to hand, so that you can make notes or take messages.

Tip

Never ask a telephone caller to 'hold on' without making sure first that they are willing to wait.

Answering the telephone

2 Answer the telephone promptly.

3 Speak slowly and clearly into the telephone.

4 State the salon's name and telephone number.

5 Ask how you can help the caller.

6 Listen to what the caller says.

7 Write down the caller's name and telephone number.

8 If there is a message, write it down.

9 Complete the call by thanking the caller.

10 Replace the telephone receiver correctly when finished, so that other callers can get through.

11 Keep calls business-like, brief and efficient.

Making telephone calls

- Personal calls may be allowed with permission or in an emergency only.
- Always be brief – others may be waiting to get through.
- Note the call made.
- Record the information received immediately.
- Note further action required.
- After using a mobile phone – return it to the central point.
- Be business-like and efficient without being impolite or abrupt.

Emergency services

You can call the emergency services – fire, police and ambulance – free of charge, at any time of the day or night. Dial 999, then wait for the operator to ask you which service is required. State clearly 'fire', 'police' or 'ambulance', and wait for that service to be connected.

When they answer, be ready to give the salon telephone number if they ask you for it. Give them the full address at which help is needed, and directions to make it easy to find. Speak clearly, and listen carefully. Try not to panic – you will be able to help more if you are calm. Remember to replace the receiver properly when you have finished the call.

Tip

Telephone directories, codebooks and guides to charges provide a great deal of useful information. Read them carefully to make yourself familiar with the telephone services that are available.

Other services

- If you need help getting through to any particular telephone number, dial 100 for operator services.
- If you can't find a telephone number in the directory, dial 192 for directory enquiries.
- If there is a fault on the telephone – if calls cannot be made in or out of the salon – it needs to be reported as soon as possible: any delay could be costly because clients may be trying to make appointments. Call the operator on 151 if you have a residential line or 154 if you have a business line.

- Refer to the telephone directory for fuller information about the services available.

Taking messages

It is important to keep a written note of any messages you take. Use a notebook to record all messages clearly – it may be necessary to refer back to them later.

- Make sure you pass all messages to the people for whom they were intended. Do this immediately, and mark the message book to indicate that this has been done.
- If the person for whom the message is intended is not available, tell others in the salon there is a message waiting for that person. Check later that the message has been received.
- If messages require a reply, or if you have promised to call back, make sure this is done.
- Return calls as soon as possible to avoid unnecessary waiting.
- Listen carefully to the caller, without interrupting, and be helpful and polite in your reply.
- Ensure that all communications are clear, accurate and understood.

The cost of calls is based on distance, time of day and duration of call. Keep calls short, and avoid making long-distance calls at peak time if they are not urgent.

If you need to make a personal call from the salon, note how long it took, the distance you called and the time of day, so that your call can be charged to you.

TELEPHONE MESSAGE

To Suzie   **Date** 15/10

From Ms L White   **Time** 10:45

Number 234 567   **Taken by** Jean

Please call Ms White
regarding
her appointment
tomorrow

Taking messages

Tip

Never leave a telephone caller on the line for longer than a few seconds. Return to let them know what is happening. Being left on the end of a line is frustrating and the caller may hang up.

Handling payments

Tip

Failure to follow salon payment procedures could result in financial loss.

When a service has been completed, you will need to calculate the client's bill. If you have to add up several items, double-check your answer before telling the client how much to pay.

Most salons include **VAT (value added tax)** in their prices. VAT is a percentage of the total bill. It has to be paid to HM Customs and Excise – a government tax collector – quarterly, when the salon's accounts are made up. Make sure you understand the salon's method for calculating VAT, and always ask someone if you are unsure what to do.

Tip

Any tips given by a client should be kept separate from money for the bill. A piggy bank on the reception desk is a good idea.

Tip

Handling payments, calculating bills and giving change relates to key skill Application of Number Level 1.

Payment methods

Clients may wish to pay their bills in cash, by cheque, by credit card or some other way. You must be familiar with all these forms of payment.

Payments in cash

Legal tender is the name given to money that is legal to use in a country. The notes and coins produced in England, Scotland, Northern Ireland and Jersey are legal tender in the UK and may be taken in the salon. The money of Eire is not legal tender, nor is money of other foreign currencies. The local bank will charge the salon for exchanging it, so you can legally refuse to accept it.

The euro

The euro is the single European currency that twelve European countries have adopted to replace their national currencies. The United Kingdom (UK) has not adopted the euro, to us it is simply another foreign currency. Although the euro is not legal tender in the UK some salons may decide to accept payment with the euro currency, particularly if they are situated in a tourist area.

If your salon accepts the euro as payment it will be important to make sure that you are aware of the exchange rate as this may change on a daily basis.

What does the euro look like?

The euro currency will come in the form of notes and coins. Euro notes will be the same across the twelve countries. The coins will be similar in design, they will show the coin denomination and will feature a national emblem and twelve stars which are represented on the European Union flag. Although each country will have a different national emblem on the coins each one can be used within each of the twelve countries.

Activity

To find out more about the euro collect information from your local bank or travel agent.

There are also a number of websites you can visit:

The bank of England – www.bankofengland.co.uk/euro
One currency for Europe –
www.europa.eu.int/euro/html/entry.html
European Central Bank – www.ecb.int

Try to follow a step-by-step procedure each time.

1   Calculate the client's bill and double-check the final amount.
2   Clearly inform the client of the total that needs to be paid.

Tip

Read manufacturer's instructions or manuals so you understand how the equipment such as the till or computer works.

3 Take the client's money, count how much you have been given, and place it on the till, or where the client can see it.

4 Calculate the change required – use a notebook if necessary.

5 State the amount to be paid and count out the change to the client.

6 Double-check the change given and the amount taken.

7 Give the client a receipt.

8 Put the money in the till or cash box.

9 Before the client leaves, make sure that they are satisfied.

10 Check whether further appointments are required.

11 Be courteous and polite throughout.

12 Make sure that takings are recorded, so that the total day's takings can be calculated and checked against the cash in the till.

Euro currency

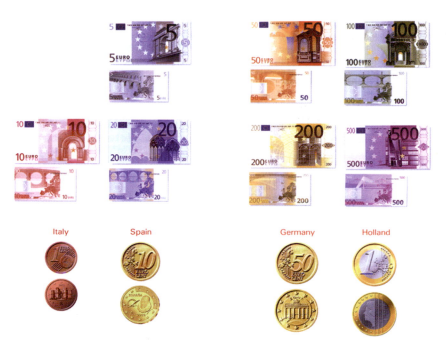

A computerised reception management system

Comp0utilll Ltd

☀ **Activity**

In pairs, practise taking cash and giving change. How can you prevent disagreements about how much cash was handed over and whether the change is correct?

Many salons find it convenient to maintain a **float**. This is a sum of money that is kept to ensure that adequate change is available. The amount of the float must always be carefully noted. Remember, it is not part of the takings. When you are totalling monies, during or at the end of the day, you should deduct the total float sum from the takings, or the monies will not balance.

It will help to keep a certain amount of change in the safe to avoid running short. How much is kept there will depend on how much business is usually transacted each day. It can be time-consuming to look for change, and a nuisance when the salon is busy.

Cash registers vary from salon to salon, and may have a variety of features which deal with cash transactions. These are useful in producing receipts, totalling individual takings and salon takings, and other features too. Make sure you understand how to use the cash register. Always ask if you have a problem or if you make a mistake.

At the end of the day, record the cash register totals in a book, so that accounts can be kept. In most salons the total takings for hairdressing services and sales of other items are listed separately. Records of **petty cash** and other expenses must be kept so that the final totals can be balanced. Find out how to fill in your salon's cashbook accurately. Keep your entries neat and clear to read.

Payments by cheque

Many clients prefer to pay their bills by cheque. This is as good as cash if accompanied by a cheque guarantee card. This card guarantees payment up to a certain amount – usually £50 to £100.

A cheque

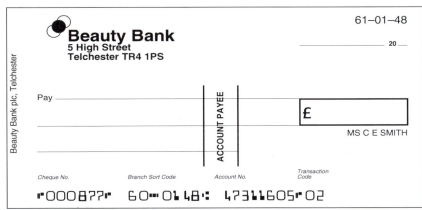

A cheque guarantee/service card

The cheque is an order from the client to their bank to pay to the salon the amount stated, so it needs to be made out correctly. Help your client by making sure the cheque is correct:

1 Know your salon's policy for dealing with payments.
2 Check that the cheque is clearly dated, with the date on which you are receiving it.
3 Check that the name of the salon (or person to be paid) appears on the cheque. If the salon has a stamp for this, offer to print it.
4 Check that the amount to be paid is written both in words and in figures, and that they are the same value.
5 Check that the cheque has been signed by the client, in your presence.
6 Ask the client for a cheque guarantee card, and write the card number on the back of the cheque. Check that the signature on the card matches the one on the cheque.

7 If the bill is greater than the limit on the cheque guarantee card, ask the client for further identification – such as a driving licence or credit card – so you can double-check the signature.

8 Write the client's address on the back of the cheque, in case any problems arise later.

9 Check the date of the guarantee card to make sure that the card is valid. If a card is out of date, do not accept the cheque.

10 Put the cheque in the till and return the guarantee card to the client. Give a receipt.

11 Make sure all cheques are paid into the bank as soon as possible, so that they can be cleared.

Payments by card

Payment by card is equally as popular as payment by cash or cheque. Salons that provide alternative options are meeting the public's expectations of greater choice and wider flexibility. There are many reasons why our customers would prefer to utilise their cards, rather than part with cash. These include:

- availability of cash
- easier accounting for expenditure
- increasing numbers of debit, credit and charge card types
- improved personal cash flow
- increasing numbers of salaries being paid directly into bank accounts.

Look at the number of supermarkets that now offer a cash back service when their customers pay for their groceries by debit card. This shows an awareness by the supermarkets of customer cash availability.

In many respects cash is a liability – with increasing levels of crime it is simpler and safer to reduce cash-holding levels to a minimum, and to maximise on the benefits of other payment options.

Types of 'plastic'

There are three main types of card used for non-cash payments:

- Debit cards
- Credit cards
- Charge cards.

Debit cards

Debit cards such as Switch, Delta, Electron etc. provide a direct alternative to writing cheques. These may be used to pay for purchases in places where an electronic terminal is present. The debit card (which is often a cheque guarantee card as well) enables customers to draw down on available funds within their bank or building society account.

A debit card

Barclays Bank PLC

A credit card

American Express

A charge card

Credit cards

Credit cards such as Visa or Mastercard may be used for purchases in places that accept cards, with either manual or electronic means for transactions. These types of cards are held by those who have applied to operate a credit account. This type of account is different from a personal current account, in that each person has a prearranged borrowing limit to draw against. When charges are applied to a card, the amounts are added to the borrowing balance with an additional interest charge, the APR (Annual Percentage Rate). This interest is charged monthly, proportionally and added to the amount outstanding. When the monthly statement arrives, the card holder has the option of paying some or all of the charged billings, subject to a specified minimum amount.

Charge cards

Charge cards such as American Express or Diners Club provide another alternative for purchases in establishments that offer the payment service either manually or electronically. Charge cards are quite different from the other two systems mentioned above. People holding charge cards have applied to use the facility, for which they pay with an annual fee. This provides them with the ability to purchase goods or services without interest charges. These charges are applied to their card on a monthly basis. When the monthly statement arrives they must pay for all the stated billings.

The cost to the salon

Salons that have agreements with companies such as Barclays Merchant Services, American Express Sales and Establishments etc. offer the facility for card transactions. Regardless of whether the salon (the 'merchant') operates a manual or an electronic payment system it will pay a fee to the card operator for the benefits. Debit cards are charged at a fixed rate, whereas credit and charge cards charge a percentage of the customer's billed amount. The interest amount charged to the merchant is negotiable but dependent upon the turnover of the card.

Card authenticity

The use of cards as a means of payment simplifies till transactions, but as an increasing number of cards are made available it is essential that precautions are taken to guard against card theft and fraud.

The card operator provides full support for the services it offers, and this will include:

- training materials for salon staff
- 24-hour telephone support
- accounting procedures
- advertising and promotional information.

Before you accept a card payment you should make sure that the card is genuine and valid. Within the information pack that is sent out by the card operator to new merchants, you will find a Card

Recognition Guide for each card that is permitted. The guide will contain the following information:

1   *Card symbol* – this logo (e.g. Visa, Mastercard) will appear at the front upper right corner of the card. For charge cards such as American Express, the 'Centurian head' logo will be printed across the centre of the card.

2   *Card hologram* – the card hologram service mark is in the centre right-hand edge of the card. This service mark is etched on to a foil decal which is superimposed on the card's printed background. The service mark on the holographic background (e.g. VISA) will appear as a 'dove' when angled into the light; the hologram changes according to the angle from which it is viewed.

3   *Cardmember number* – the cardmember's number will be embossed on to the surface and across the width of the card. If you use an electronic terminal, always ensure that the cardmember number matches that which is printed on your terminal receipt.

4   *Card validity dates* – the card will show a 'Valid from' date as well as an 'Expires end' date. If the card is not in date then it should not be accepted.

5   *Cardmember's name* – check that the name on the card and the title of the cardmember, if it is embossed, match the presenter.

Card type identification

There is a range of cards now in force – some advertise charities or sponsorships but all will show the service provider's international trademark(s) and hologram(s). Look for these features, also apparent upon the back of the card (debit cards such as Delta and Electron will also contain clearly defined logos and may be used as cheque guarantee cards, but only up to the value shown on the hologram at the back of the card):

6   *Magnetic strip* – this incorporates the data which can be read when the card is used via an electronic terminal.

7   *Signature strip* – check that the signature strip has not been tampered with and that it is flush with the surface of the card.

8   *Cardmember's signature* – the card should be signed on the signature strip.

Extra security features continue to be added to credit and charge cards and you will start to see these new features on recently issued cards. Both existing cards and cards with these new security features are valid.

Processing manual payments by card

Different cards have different sales vouchers. Receipt for payment by Visa or Mastercard cannot be transacted upon an American Express voucher and vice versa. Similarly Switch, Delta and Electron cannot be transacted by manual imprinter, as these are debit cards and require electronic means in order to draw down on account funds.

Procedure for manual transactions

1   Place the card face up on the imprinter.

2   Place the correct type of sales voucher, face up, over the card and operate the imprinter by drawing the rollers (using the handle) across to the right and then back to the left.

3   Check that the details from the card and merchant's stamped plate are imprinted through all parts of the voucher.

4   Remove the sales voucher and card from the imprinter. Write all the necessary details, including the date, the amount and a brief description of the goods, on the sales voucher using a ballpoint pen. Make sure any space boxes for the total amount are struck through if you are not going to enter figures into them.

5   Ask the cardholder to sign the sales voucher. Hold the card and watch the cardholder sign in the box indicated. While holding the card, rub your thumb lightly over the signature strip; it should be smooth and flush with the surface of the card.

6   Check that the signature on the voucher matches the signature on the reverse of the card.

7   Check that the spelling of the surname of the signature corresponds with that embossed on the card and also that the card is in date.

8   Check that the card is not subject to any 'hot card' warnings.

9   Check that the card has not been subjected to any damage or tampering.

If the total value of the sale exceeds your agreed 'floor limit' (that is, a predetermined sum for manual transactions), or if in any way you are suspicious of either the card or the circumstances, you must telephone for authorisation.

If you are satisfied that all the procedures have been completed and that all checks have been successfully carried out, you can detach the cardholder copy of the voucher and hand it to the customer with the card.

Processing payments by electronic terminal

Payments made by debit, charge and credit card by electronic terminals are authorised during the transaction process and provide funds which will be deposited into the business current account on either a daily or a weekly basis. (This excludes transactions carried out in fraudulent circumstances, which might include card theft, tampered/damaged cards and mail order when the customer is not present at the point of sale.)

The electronic terminal is a rented unit which consists of a key pad and card swipe input, with LED display recording each step of the transaction procedure. In addition there is a carbonless two-ply receipt roll, which is connected to the power supply and the card companies via a telephone link.

'Swiping' a card through an electronic terminal

Procedure for electronic payment systems

1   Check that the terminal display is in sale mode.

2   Confirm that a sale is to be made by pressing button *yes*.

3   The terminal will request *Swipe card*; do this while ensuring that the magnetic strip passes over the reader head and that you retain the card in your hand. In some cases the magnetic strip cannot be read by the swipe card reader; in this situation the complete card number must be keyed manually into the terminal. This does not necessarily indicate that there is any need for suspicion, but inspect the card for any signs of tampering.

4   Enter *Amount* by using the key pad to input the total number of purchases. (If you make a mistake, you can clear the figures using the *CLR* button.)

5   Press *Enter*, which will connect the terminal to the card company first by *Dialling* and then prompting the message *Connection Made*.

6   Customer details are automatically accessed and, after a few moments, a message will authorise payment by showing *Auth code*, for which a code number will be printed on to the receipt along with the other purchase details. Conversely, if the transaction is declined, *card not accepted* will show.

7   While holding the card, tear off the two-part receipt and ask the cardholder to sign in ballpoint pen in the space provided.

8   Check that the signature matches the signature on the card and return the top signed copy with the card to the customer.

Seeking authorisation

If the total value of services and/or goods exceeds your prearranged floor limit, or if you are in any way suspicious of the card, its presenter or the circumstances of the sale, you must seek authorisation.

Having ensured that any items, in addition to services, are not within the customer's reach, take the card and the completed signed sales voucher, with a ballpoint pen, to the telephone. Dial authorisation (the service provider's telephone number will be printed on stickers and should be attached to or nearby the telephone) and you will be connected to the authorisation operator. Be ready to provide the following information:

- the number embossed on the customer's card
- the salon's merchant number (a unique number registered with the card-operating companies)
- the amount of the transaction.

Occasionally you may be asked to obtain some form of positive identification from the customer presenting the card.

When the sale is authorised you will be given a code which may include numbers and letters. You must write this code in the Authorisation Code Box on the sales voucher.

If the request is declined, no reason will be given. You should return the card to your customer and ask for some other form of payment.

Code 10 authorisation calls

There are times when it is necessary to seek authorisation for a transaction where it is not possible to speak freely over the telephone – particularly if you are suspicious of the circumstances surrounding the transaction.

To avoid any difficulties, when it is not possible to speak freely you simply state that it is a code 10 call. The operator will understand your predicament and will deal with your call sympathetically. If you are able to speak freely and are suspicious of the circumstances surrounding the transaction, let the authorisation operator know immediately.

Hot card warnings

From time to time notification will be sent to the salon about cards that cannot be accepted. If a customer attempts to purchase goods or services using a 'hot card' you should retain the card and telephone authorisation. The full instructions on how to handle hot cards will be sent with each hot card warning notice to the salon.

Retaining a suspicious card

There are occasions when the authorisation operator will require you to retain a card. When this is so, politely inform the customer without causing embarrassment or putting yourself at risk. Preserve the evidence for further action and take the following steps. With the card front facing you and upright:

- cut off the bottom left-hand corner from the front of the card.
- preserve intact the signature panel and magnetic strip
- handle the card by its edges to preserve finger prints and other forensic evidence
- return both pieces back to the card company along with any sales receipts or voucher
- claim your reward – all card companies want to stamp out card fraud and pay generous rewards for the recovery of wanted cards.

Genuine or forgery?

What to look for:

- Is the card valid? Pay attention to the commencement and expiry dates.
- Condition of the card – check whether the card has any defects or has been altered intentionally. Are the letters of the cardmember's name unevenly embossed? Is the magnetic strip damaged or missing?
- Does the name on the card match the presenter?

Tip

All information regarding clients should be handled in strict confidence. This safeguards all concerned and helps to reduce the possibility of embarrassment and loss of clients.

- Is the presenter old enough to possess the card? (Applicable where cards show member since information.)
- Is the number on the front of the card embossed?
- Is the number on the back of the card printed in black? (Applicable to some charge cards.)
- Compare the signatures.

Other non-cash payments

Gift vouchers are sold by some salons to be used in payment for goods and services. These payments may be treated in the same way as cash or cheque payments. There are different forms of gift voucher; some may be used in other stores. Make sure that you know how to use these.

Traveller's cheques may be offered in payment by some clients. Find out whether or not the salon's policy is to accept these. If so, make sure the client countersigns the cheque in your presence, and check that the signatures match and that the date is correct.

 Activity

Make a list of all the different cards that may be used for payment in your salon, and of the differences between them.

Discrepancies

Inconsistencies, disagreements or differences – invalid currencies being tendered, out-of-date cheque cards or unsigned cheques – should be dealt with as soon as possible. Where a payment card is being fraudulently used or there is a payment dispute, such as a bill totalling more than was previously agreed to, then a senior member of staff should be referred to. Should an illegal transaction be attempted, or even one suspected of being illegal, it may be decided to refer the matter to the police. This should finally be decided only by senior staff members, however. In these instances effective communication is very important, so that everyone concerned understands what is happening.

Computers

Computer systems are being used in very many salons. Many types are available, and you may be required to operate one.

A computer system consists of hardware (the equipment) and software (the programs), and each computer system has its own special features. In the salon the computer may be used in taking cash and issuing receipts, to total each person's takings, for general accounting, client records, stock records, storing information, or taking bookings. As more and more client's use computer systems at

Using a computer system

home to organise their day-to-day activities, the greater the need for the salon receptionist to have information technology (IT) skills. Clients may want to book appointments by sending an e-mail and will expect you to respond quickly and effectively and so on.

Make sure you understand your salon's system and know how to use it. Remember to ask for help if you run into problems – pressing the wrong button could cause even greater problems!

 Activity

Collect information about different software systems that can be used in the salon. Review how they differ from each other and what benefits a reception area would have by becoming a computerised salon.

This activity will work towards key skill Communication Level 2.

!

Health & Safety

Always keep the reception area uncluttered, allowing free passage for clients and staff.

Activity

In threes, use role-play to practise reception duties. One person acts the client, another the receptionist. The third person notes where the duties are done well, and where things go wrong.

Repeat the activity, with the client complaining about the service received.

Reception security

A counter cache

It is important to maintain a safe and secure environment at the reception area. All monies must be secured, and products on display must be safeguarded. All personal details of clients, such as record systems, should be held under cover. If a client sees record cards lying around, they will have little confidence in the discretion of the salon staff. The following points should help to ensure adequate reception security:

- The reception area must be staffed at all times.
- Keep as little money on the premises as possible – enough in the till to give change for a £50 note is sufficient. Keep extra notes that build up through the day in a strong, secure container (counter cache) which is bolted underneath or beside the till.
- Never leave the till drawer open when it is not in use or if you have to leave the reception, even for a moment.
- Check all notes to ensure that both the interlaced 'Queen's head' metal strip and the water mark are present. On a forged note, either or both may be missing.

Volumatic

Keep as little money in the till as possible

- When a client hands you a note, put it outside the till until you have accurately counted the change.
- Never leave money in the till overnight.
- Leave the till drawers open, but emptied, at the end of the day to prevent a burglar from damaging them by forcing them open.
- Large amounts of money should be regularly transferred to a secure safe or bank.
- Visits to the bank should be irregularly timed to deter muggers. If the receptionist normally does the banking (it could of course be any staff member) someone else must be nominated to take the responsibility while they are absent from work. If possible, they should be accompanied.
- Receipts should be given for all payments and bills retained.
- Remember that all bills, receipts and money withdrawn or additions must be noted so that a balance can be achieved.
- At the end of the day all monies must be checked, recorded and either secured in a safe or banked.
- Follow your salon's security procedures at all times.

Assignments – Reception

A practical activity

With the help of your colleagues carry out the following:

1. Practise the different reception duties that you have been shown by your trainers.
2. List any mistakes you made, and what corrections were required.
3. Discuss and make notes on the correct ways of dealing with people.
4. List the different situations that can arise at reception.
5. Think carefully about why there is a need for confidentiality.
6. Make sure you are familiar with the salon's appointment system.

Make careful notes, and keep them in your folder.

For you to find out

Investigate and collect together information concerning reception areas and receptionists' duties. Visit your doctor's and dentist's surgery, or watch other receptionists at work. Explain to them what you are doing before taking notes. Include the following:

- the differences between the different receptionists
- the common aims
- the importance of accurate communication
- ways of dealing with people – new and existing clients, internal and external calls, communicating directly face to face or indirectly by telephone or letter
- the importance of a courteous manner and efficiency.

A case study

A client has asked for an appointment with a stylist who no longer works at the salon. Describe your salon procedures for:

- what you would tell the client

- the questions you would ask
- the alternatives you could offer the client
- what you would do if you could not deal with the situation.

Preparing for Assessment

In preparing for your assessment on reception work the following checklist may be useful. Check that you have covered and now fully understand these items:

- the need to be clean, hygienic and efficient
- using the telephone efficiently
- receiving clients pleasantly, politely and courteously
- finding out, by questioning and discussion, what services and goods a client requires
- operating the salon's appointment system effectively
- ensuring that safety and security practices are followed
- allowing time for consultations before services are given

- clarifying requests made
- communicating effectively
- recording all information received
- dealing adequately with any discrepancies arising from payment transactions
- remaining calm, composed and unflurried throughout all dealings with clients and visitors
- recording messages and passing them on to the relevant person
- ensuring complete confidentiality.

When you feel that you are ready talk to your trainer and arrange a suitable time for your assessment.

By reading this chapter, carrying out the above activities, assignments and case studies, and by meeting the requirements in preparing for assessment you will have worked towards the key skill requirements in Communication Level 2 (C 2.1) (C 2.2) and Application of Number Level 1 (N 1.2).

If you have used a computer to complete your assignments or activities you will have worked towards the key skill requirements in Information Technology Level 1 (IT 1.1) (IT 1.2).

Working effectively

Mahogany

Learning objectives

The following are some of the topics covered in the chapter:

- measuring effectiveness
- developing and improving your performance
- appraisals
- teamwork.

11

Introduction

This chapter is about taking responsibility for your work by constantly trying to improve your performance at work and working well with your colleagues to ensure the salon and your contribution is effective.

Tip

National Occupational Standards can be obtained from the Hairdressing And Beauty Therapy Industry Authority (HABIA) see section on useful addresses page 307.

Developing and improving performance

Tip

Continual Professional Development (CPD) is the term used by professionals who continually update their skills. Your trainer and assessor will undertake CPD activities.

Tip

Use trade magazines and manufacturers' websites to update your knowledge on technical skill activities and new products on the market.

Your ability to meet the expected standards at work is referred to as personal effectiveness. These standards relate to:

- Occupational standards, that is, the levels of skill and knowledge that you apply to the individual activities that make up the NVQ Level 2.
- Personal standards, that is, the care that you take about your appearance and personal hygiene (see Chapter 12 Health and Safety) as well as the overall image that you portray to fellow staff members and, most importantly, the customers.
- Professionalism, that is your ability to conduct yourself in a way that communicates the image of a positive and supportive professional person to clients and fellow staff members.

These statements can be broken down into smaller, specific targets of personal effectiveness which can be achieved over a set term and reviewed periodically during your training programme. This process of evaluation and review is commonly known as appraisal. It can be undertaken in two ways: by yourself, that is, self-appraisal – the way in which you measure your own strengths and weaknesses against set standards; or in conjunction with your manager on a more formal basis.

However you should not wait for a formal review or appraisal. If you are having problems with any aspect of your training or your job you should ask for support or classification from a senior stylist, your trainer or manager. If you have completed the objectives set in your training or appraisal before the due target date, ask for more objectives to be set. This will help you keep motivated by completing your training earlier and increasing your knowledge of the job, enabling you to do higher skilled work.

An appraisal form

Performance Appraisal	
Name:	Jane Manners
Job Title:	Trainee stylist
Date of Appraisal:	5/6/2002
Objectives:	To obtain competence within: Cutting hair layering techniques across the range. Blow drying hair on a variety of hair types and lengths
Notes on Achievement:	Competence has been achieved across the range for all the cutting requirements.
	Competence has been achieved for most blow drying range requirements.
Training Requirements:	Further training and practice is needed within the area of blow drying longer length effects.
Any other comments on performance by Appraiser:	Jane has achieved most of the objectives set out during the last appraisal.
Any comments on the Appraisal by the staff Appraised:1	I feel that this has been a fair appraisal of my progress although I did not achieve all of my performance targets. J Manners.
Action Plan:	To achieve occupational competence across the range for blow drying (i.e. longer length hair).
	To undergo training and practice in perming methods and techniques.
	To take assessment for perming.
Date of Next Appraisal:	4/12/2002

Measuring effectiveness

To be able to measure progress towards training targets as well as overall work contributions, there needs to be clear stated expectations of the performance required. For both training and work activities, this is the standard in which competence will need to be demonstrated.

In training situations you will undergo a programme of training which states:

- what training activities will take place
- what tasks need to be performed
- what standards are expected to be reached
- when assessment should be expected
- when a review of progress towards the agreed targets is to take place.

Job description – Stylist

Location:	Based at salon as advised
Main purpose of job:	To ensure customer care is provided at all times
	To maintain a good standard of technical and client care, ensuring that up-to-date methods and techniques are used following the salon training practices and procedures
Responsible to:	Salon manager
Requirements:	To maintain the company's standards in respect of hairdressing/beauty services

To ensure that all clients receive service of the best possible quality

To advise clients on services and treatments

To advise clients on products and aftercare

To achieve designated performance targets

To participate in self-development or to assist with the development of others

To maintain company policy in respect of:

- personal standards of health/hygiene
- personal standards of appearance/conduct
- operating safety whilst at work
- public promotion
- corporate image

as laid out in employee handbook

To carry out client consultation in accordance with company policy

To maintain company security practices and procedures

To assist your manager in the provision of salon resources

To undertake additional tasks and duties required by your manager from time to time.

In normal, ongoing work situations, **performance appraisal** will be based on the following factors:

- results achieved against objectives and job requirements
- any additional accomplishments and contributions
- contributions made by the individual as compared with those of other staff members.

The job requirements would be outlined in the employee's **job description**. A job description is a written specification of the main purposes and functions expected within a given job. Good job descriptions will include details of the following:

- the job title
- the work location(s)
- responsibility (to whom, and for what)
- the job purpose
- main functions (listed)
- standards expected
- any special conditions.

Standards expected from the job holder will often be produced in a staff handbook – this document will often include standards of behaviour and appearance, the salon's code of conduct and grievance procedure, employee legal entitlements and responsibilities along with Health and Safety requirements. If these have been stated from the outset, the job holder will know what is expected. If you do not have a job description ask your employee/manager if you can have one, so that you know precisely what is expected of you and how your job role fits into or along side other colleagues. You will have a clear guide on your limits of authority. Some large salons will have a staff structure chart that explains everyone's role in the salon and the reporting structure.

The appraisal process

At the beginning of the appraisal period, the manager and the employee discuss jointly, develop and mutually agree the objectives and performance measures (targets) for that period. An **action plan** will then be drafted outlining the expected outcomes.

During the appraisal period, should there be any significant changes in factors such as objectives or performance measures (targets), these will be discussed between the manager and employee and any amendments will be appended to the action plan.

At the end of the appraisal period, the results are discussed by the employee and the manager, and both manager and employee sign the appraisal. A copy is prepared for the employee, and the original is kept on file.

An appraisal of performance will contain the following information:

- employee's name
- appraisal period
- appraiser's name and title
- performance objectives
- job title
- work location

- results achieved
- identified areas of strength and of weakness
- ongoing action plan
- overall performance grading (optional).

Self-appraisal

An important aspect of self-appraisal is having the ability to evaluate and review your own progress. This is done initially by measuring your own strengths and weaknesses. How do I evaluate my own progress? See the exercise below.

Fill in the column indicated below, using the appropriate letters A, B, etc. in the boxes for which you think they best apply. For example:

I can do this very well	A	
	D	
	J	

A. I neutralise perms on short to medium hair.
B. I neutralise perms on long one-length hair.
C. I handle payments by cards at reception.
D. I make appointments for all services.
E. I help, assist and communicate with customers on a routine basis.
F. I prepare the chemicals carefully for the stylists.
G. I recommend products to customers, encouraging them to buy.
H. I conduct salon business over the telephone.
I. I blow-dry clients' hair to help out the stylists.
J. I apply colours for stylists.
K. I am always punctual for work.
L. I am particular about my appearance.
M. I thoroughly clean and prepare the working surfaces.
N. I monitor the usage of stock and materials.
O. I notice when things need doing.
P. I recognise situations where they may be a potential hazard.

Level of ability	Employee fills in this column	
I can do this very well		
I do this OK		
I think I'm getting there		
I find this a bit tricky		
I can't do this at all		

After you have completed the activity of putting the letters A to P in the appropriate box, you may have other additional statements that you want to add to your list. Does your supervisor agree with your responses? Hand this to your supervisor and ask to have your responses checked. Your supervisor can fill in the last column in the same way. Now see if both columns match.

Level of ability	Employee fills in this column	Supervisor fills in this column
I can do this very well		
I do this OK		
I think I'm getting there		
I find this a bit tricky		
I can't do this at all		

Working as a team

Toni & Guy

Always remember that your work colleagues need your assistance to help them do their job. Sharing the work load *is* working as a team. This can be achieved by:

- providing support
- anticipating the needs of others
- maintaining harmony
- maintaining good communication.

In some salons, you might see some staff busy attending to their clients, but others hanging about around reception, flicking through magazines or disappearing off to the staff room for a coffee. Teamwork is about making an active contribution, seeking to assist others even if it is only passing up rollers. It is good for staff morale and it shows a good image to the clients as well as keeping the sales running effectively and keeping client appointments on time. In short make yourself useful, and contribute to the team effort by assisting your fellow workers.

Anticipating the needs of others follows on from providing support. Clean and prepare the work areas ready for use, locate and prepare products as and when they are required. (This will help the smooth operation of the salon.) Cooperate with your colleagues, make a positive contribution to your team by assisting them to provide a well-managed and coordinated quality service. Be self-motivated, keep yourself busy. Don't wait to be asked to do things. If you support others they will always be willing to support you when you ask for or need help. If you have quiet moments in the salon, take the opportunity to practise your technical skills or update your knowledge on products and services.

Maintain harmony and try to minimise possible conflicts. Most good working relationships develop easily; others, however, need to be worked at. Good communication skills will help you work effectively with colleagues and clients (see Chapter 2).

Whatever your personal feelings are about your colleagues, clients must never sense a bad atmosphere within the salon caused by a friction between staff. You will spend a lot of time in the company of people you work with, but you will not always like everyone you meet. People are different: at work, in order to work as a team, a mutual respect for others is more important than close friendships. So remember:

- treat others with respect
- be sensitive and responsive to others' feelings
- show concern and care for others
- avoid actions that discriminate against others or may offend them.

If you ever have a problem or conflict with a colleague that you cannot sort out yourselves, you should report it to your manager who will want to resolve the situation quickly and fairly. If necessary, they will implement the grievance and disciplinary procedure. This procedure will have been set up by your employer and should have been given to you when you started work. It details the actions to be taken if, for example

- you have a conflict with a colleague
- you have been treated unfairly or do not agree with a decision made
- you are asked to do something outside of your job description
- if a colleague has offended you or you have been discriminated against.

The actions taken will depend on the seriousness of the grievance. Sometimes an arbitrator can sort out problems simply. In other cases, it may need disciplinary action.

Tip

Always use your spare time effectively to help others or develop your skills.

Assignments – Working together

A practical activity

This assignment offers you the opportunity to study and assess your professional strengths and weaknesses. The table consists of three columns. The first column contains headings covering personal skills, while the second and third columns are left blank, ready for you to complete.

After completing the table ask your training supervisor to check your answers. If you both agree with your answers, keep the completed document for use in your folder or personal portfolio.

Assignments – Working together (cont.)

Personal skills	*My strengths are*	*My weaknesses are*
Organising myself at work		
Communicating with other staff		
Communicating with the clients		
Helping and supporting others in their work		
Solving problems on my own		

For you to find out

In relation to your salon, find out the following information and record the details along with any drawings, illustrations or photographs in your folder or personal portfolio.

1 What contingency action is taken in respect of the following circumstances?

- services/treatments running later than planned
- clients changing their previously booked services/treatments

2 What things can you find to do when the salon isn't busy?

3 Passing information to clients and staff is all part of maintaining good communication. Review the communication section in Chapter 2. By what methods do you pass on information to management? Make particular reference to:

- handling personal matters
- maintaining the provision of services/treatments
- health and safety issues.

A case study

For this assignment you are required to carry out a self-assessment of your own skills. You will find this activity is easier to do if it is carried out after completing the first assignment in this chapter.

Have a go at completing the checklist. If you do not understand the words used, or if you cannot yet tick all the boxes, ask your training supervisor to help you. Keep the completed document for use in your folder or personal portfolio.

A case study (cont.)

When I'm at work...	Yes, I do this ✓	No, I don't do this ✗	My training supervisor's comments
I discuss my different job strengths and weaknesses with my training supervisor			
I discuss ways of improving my work effectiveness with my training supervisor			
Where possible, I always do jobs without having to be asked first			
I discuss my progress during regular reviews with my training supervisor			
I like to keep abreast of hair fashion and new products and equipment			

Preparing for Assessment

Whilst making preparations for assessment on working as a team, the following checklist may be helpful. Check that you have covered and now fully understand these items:

- getting yourself organised
- the tasks and activities you perform in your work
- providing information to management
- supporting and helping others in their work
- self-appraisal.

When you feel that you are ready, talk to your trainer to arrange a suitable time for your assessment.

By reading this chapter, carrying out the above activities, assignments and the case study, and by meeting the requirements in preparing for assessment you will have worked towards the key skill requirements in Communication Level 2 (C 2.1) (C 2.2).

If you have used a computer to complete your assignments or activities you will have worked towards the key skill requirements in Information Technology Level 1 (IT 1.2).

Health and safety in the salon

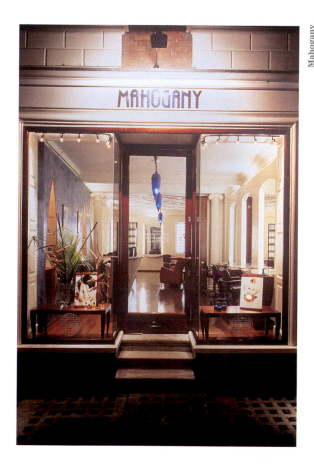

12

Mahogany

Learning objectives

The following are some of the topics covered in this chapter:

- Working safely in the salon
- That your own actions do not create health and safety risks
- Taking sensible action to put things right
- Avoiding hazards
- Dealing with accidents
- Dealing with fires
- Health and Safety legislation.

Introduction

This chapter is for everyone working in the salon, whether full-time or part-time. It is very important that you understand your responsibility for the health and safety of yourself and others such as your colleagues and clients.

Legislation provided within the Health and Safety Act 1974 (see page 295) requires all employers to:

Take reasonable care for the health and safety of himself and any others who may be affected by his actions or omissions... and to cooperate with their employer, so that their employer can fulfil his obligation by complying with the current (UK and EC) health and safety requirements.

Working safely in the salon

You have a duty to your employer and your colleagues to keep the working environment safe. You need to be alert, spot potential hazards to stop them becoming a risk and prevent accidents happening. If the hazard or risk is something you can deal with, quickly and effectively do so, but always follow the salon's policy. However if you have spotted a hazard or risk that you cannot deal with report it immediately to the person responsible for health and safety. You need to ensure you carry out all work activities safely in accordance with any instructions, salon policy and legal requirements.

- A hazard is something with the potential to cause harm.
- A risk is the likelihood of the hazard's potential being realised.
- Almost anything can be a hazard, but they may not become a risk:

Suppose for example that some one had carelessly left a box of recently delivered stock in the reception area by the side of the desk; this would be classed as a hazard. It would be a risk if that box was left in a doorway that someone would trip over or if it was blocking a fire exit.

A trailing electrical cable from a piece of equipment such as a hand dryer is a hazard. If it is trailing across your client's access route there is a risk that they will trip over it, if however it is lying against the wall out of the way, the risk is much less.

Toxic or flammable chemicals such as perm lotion, relaxers, colours and hydrogen peroxide that are used in most salons are a hazard and may by their nature present a high risk. However if they are stored in a secure place and handled only by properly trained staff, the risk is much lower.

A failed light bulb is a hazard. If it is one of many light bulbs in a room the risk is minimal, however if it is the only light bulb in the room or on a staircase the risk becomes very high.

Tip

Health and Safety is continually updated. Make sure that you are aware of the latest legislation.

Tip

Always read your salon's policy guides. It will give you all the information you will need to work efficiently and effectively.

Tip

Always read manufacturers instructions before using their equipment or products.

Always remember to follow your salon's health and safety policy when working – this will help to minimise accidents occurring. The policy should cover:

- How to use tools and equipment safely
- Rules on working practices
- How to use hazardous substances safely
- The salon's rules on eating, drinking and drugs
- What to do in the event of an emergency
- Personal presentation and hygiene.

Avoiding potential hazards and risks

Obstructions

It is dangerous to obstruct areas used as thoroughfares, such as doorways, corridors, stairs and fire exits. In an emergency, people might have to leave the salon, or part of it, in a hurry – perhaps even in the dark. It could be disastrous if someone injured themselves, or fell, in these circumstances.

So always be on the lookout for any obstruction in these areas. If you see something that could present a risk, move it away as quickly as you can.

Spillage and breakages

Take care when you have to clear up spilt chemicals or damaged equipment. First of all find out what has been spilt or dropped. Is this something that needs special care and attention when handling? (See page 298.) Does personal protective equipment need to be worn? (See page 296.)

 Activity

List the things that staff use in the salon that could be unsafe if they are not used in the right way.

Find out what things could be a danger in areas where staff work.

 Activity

Draw a diagram of your salon. During a period of one week identify on the diagram if you spotted and dealt with a hazard/s and write a small report on what you did to rectify them.

Covered waste bins

Disposal of waste

General salon waste

Everyday items of salon waste should be placed in an enclosed waste bin fitted with a suitably resistant polyethylene bin liner. When the bin is full the liner can be sealed using a wire tie, and placed ready for refuse collection. If for any reason the bin liner punctures, put the damaged liner and waste inside a second bin liner. Wash out the inside of the bin itself with hot water and detergent.

Disposable sharps

Used razor blades and similar items should be placed into a safe container supplied by your local authority. When the container is full special disposal arrangements are provided by your local authority. Contact your local council offices for more information.

Design a checklist to cover the safety requirements for your salon that concern fire doors, corridors, exits etc.

Find out what types of waste are generated within your salon, and how each type is disposed of.

General salon hygiene

The salon

A warm, humid salon can offer a perfect home for disease-carrying bacteria. If they can find food in the form of dust and dirt, they may reproduce rapidly. Good ventilation, however, provides a circulating air current that will help to prevent their growth. This is why it is important to keep the salon clean, dry and well aired at all times – and this includes clothing, work areas, tools and all equipment.

A tidy salon is easier to clean. So get into the habit of clearing up your work as you go.

Floors and seating

Floors should be kept clean at all times. That means that they will need regular mopping, sweeping or vacuuming. When working areas

A salon

Hair Express/Regis

are damp-mopped during normal working hours, make sure that adequate warning signs are provided close to the wet areas. (You will notice that this is a standard procedure in fast food chains.)

The salon's seating will be made of material that is easily cleaned. It should be washed regularly with hot water and detergent. After drying the seats can be wiped over with disinfectant or an antiseptic lotion.

Working surfaces

All surfaces within the salon, including the reception, staff and stock preparation areas, should be washed down at least once each day. Most salons now use easily maintained wipe-clean surfaces, usually some form of plastic laminate. They can be cleaned with hot water and detergent, and after the surfaces are dry they can be wiped over with a spirit-based antiseptic which will not smear. Don't use scourers or abrasives as these will scratch plastic surfaces. Scratched surfaces look dull and unattractive as well as containing minute crevices in which bacteria will develop.

Mirrors

Glass mirrors should be cleaned every morning before clients arrive. Never try to style a client's hair whilst she sits in front of a murky, dusty or smeary mirror. Glass surfaces should be cleaned and polished using either hot water and detergent, or a spirit-based lotion that evaporates quickly without smearing.

Salon equipment

Towels and gowns

Each client must have a fresh, clean towel and gown. These should be washed in hot soapy water to remove any soiling or staining, and to prevent the spread of infection by killing any bacteria. Fabric conditioners may be used to provide a luxurious softness and freshness.

Health & Safety

You have a duty to your colleagues and clients to minimise the possible spread of infection or disease.

Hairdressers by the nature of their work are in constant close contact with their customers and need to pay particular attention to healthy, hygienic and safe working practices.

Styling tools

Most pieces of salon equipment, such as combs, brushes, curlers and so forth, are made from plastics. These materials are relatively easy to keep hygienically safe, if they are used and cleaned properly.

Combs should be washed frequently. When not in use they should be immersed into an antibacterial solution. When needed they can be rinsed and dried and are then ready for use.

If any styling tools are accidentally dropped on to the floor, do not use them until they have been adequately cleaned. Don't put contaminated items on to work surfaces as they could spread infection and disease.

Handle non-plastic items, such as scissors and clipper blades, with care. Clean them with surgical spirit by carefully wiping over the flat edges of the blades. Although most of these items are made of special steels, don't immerse them in sterilising fluids. Many of these contain chemicals that will corrode their precision-made surfaces.

Preventing infection

Some salons use sterilising devices as a means of providing hygienically safe work implements. **Sterilisation** means the complete eradication of living organisms. Different devices use different sterilisation methods, which may be based on the use of heat, radiation or chemicals.

Autoclaves

An autoclave

These provide the most effective method of sterilisation. They work on the principles of the pressure cooker. The items to be sterilised are heated with a small amount of water inside a pressurised container to a temperature of 125°C for 10 minutes. The high-temperature steam produced destroys all micro-organisms.

Ultraviolet radiation

Ultraviolet (UV) radiation provides an alternative sterilising option. The items for sterilisation are placed in wall- or worktop-mounted cabinets fitted with UV-emitting light bulbs, and exposed to the radiation for at least 15 minutes. Penetration of UV radiation is low, however, so sterilisation by this method is not guaranteed.

Chemical sterilisation

UV cabinet

Chemical sterilisers should be handled only with suitable personal protective equipment (see page 296), as many of the solutions used are hazardous to health and should not come into contact with the

Ellisons

Barbicide

skin. The most effective form of sterilisation is achieved by the total immersion of the contaminated implements into a bath of fluid. This principle is widely used in the sterilisation of babies' feeding utensils.

Disinfectants reduce the probability of infection and are widely used in general day-to-day hygienic salon maintenance.

Antiseptics are used specifically for treating wounds. Many pre-packaged first aid dressings are impregnated with antiseptic fluids.

Dealing with accidents

If there is an accident within the salon, you must notify the 'Appointed Person'. This is someone who is appointed to take charge in the case of an emergency such as an accident. They will call an ambulance, if required. An appointed person usually has first aid training, but not always. A salon does not have to have a qualified first aider but it is recommended that a member of staff attends a first aid course, such as those run by the Red Cross or St John's Ambulance.

Tip

Make sure you know who the 'Appointed Person' is in your salon. They are responsible for dealing with first aid and accidents.

If you are going to have to deal with minor accidents within the salon, you must have a basic understanding of the use of first aid. More serious injuries *must* be treated by a qualified first aider or a professional medical practitioner. The present law suggests that the ideal ratio for workplace-trained staff in low-risk occupations like hairdressing should be one trained first aider for every fifty employed (or self-employed) staff.

Activity

Find out where the first aid kit is within your salon.

List the contents of the first aid kit.

Activity

Find out how tools and equipment are made hygienically safe in your salon.

What special precautions are taken?

Every salon should have a first aid kit in accordance with the Health and Safety (First Aid) Regulations 1981 (see page 300). Remember that any first aid materials used from the kit must be replaced as soon as possible. All accidents and emergency aid given within the salon must be documented in the accident book (see page 292).

General guidance on first aid

Normally a casualty should be seated, or lying down, when being treated by a first aider.

Mouth-to-mouth resuscitation procedure

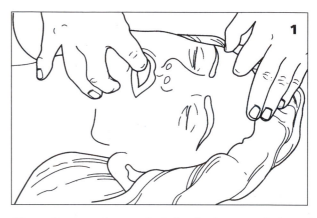

Place the casualty on their back. Open and clear their mouth.

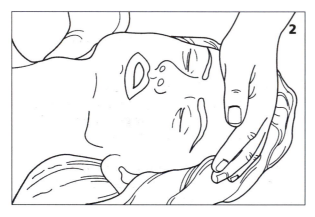

Tilt head backwards to open airway (maintain this position throughout). Support the jaw.

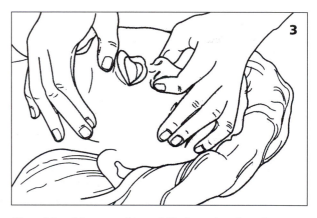

Kneel beside casualty, while keeping head backwards. Open mouth and pinch nose.

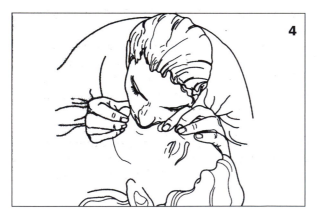

Open your mouth and take a deep breath. Seal their mouth with yours and breathe firmly into it. Casualty's chest should rise. Remove your mouth and let their chest fall. If their chest does not rise, check their head is tilted sufficiently. Repeat at a rate of 10 times a minute until the casualty is breathing alone.

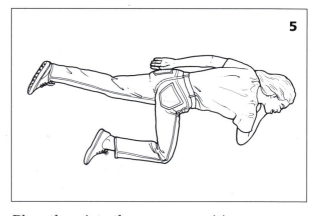

Place them into the recovery position.

Problem	*Action to be taken*
Casualty is not breathing	1 Place the casualty on their back. Open and clear their mouth. 2 Tilt head backwards to open airway (maintain this position throughout). Support the jaw. 3 Kneel beside casualty, while keeping head backwards. Open mouth and pinch nose. 4 Open your mouth and take a deep breath. Seal mouth with yours and breathe firmly into it. Casualty's chest should rise. Remove your mouth and let their chest fall. If chest does not rise, check head is tilted sufficiently. Repeat at a rate of 10 times a minute until the casualty is breathing alone. 5 Place them in the recovery position.
Unconscious	Place into recovery position.
Severe bleeding	Control by direct pressure using fingers and thumb on the bleeding point. Apply a dressing. Raising the bleeding limb (unless it is broken) will reduce the flow of blood.
Suspected broken bones	Do not move the casualty unless they are in a position which exposes them to immediate danger.
Burns and scalds (due to heat)	Do not remove clothing sticking to the burns or scalds. Do not burst any blisters. If burns and scalds are small, flush them with plenty of clean, cool water before applying a sterilised dressing. If burns and scalds are large or deep, wash your hands, apply a dry sterile dressing and send the casualty to hospital.
Burns (chemicals)	Avoid contaminating yourself with the chemical. Remove any contaminated clothing which is not stuck to skin. Flush with plenty of cool water for 10–15 minutes. Apply a sterilised dressing and send to hospital.
Foreign body in eye	Wash out eye with clean cool water.*
Chemicals in eyes	Wash out the open eye continuously with clean, cool water for 10–15 minutes.*
Electric shock	Don't touch the casualty until the current is switched off. If the current cannot be switched off, stand on some dry insulating material and use a wooden or plastic implement to free the casualty from the electrical source. If breathing has stopped start mouth-to-mouth breathing and continue until the casualty starts to breathe by themselves or until professional help arrives.
Gassing	Use suitable protective equipment. Move casualty to fresh air. If breathing has stopped start mouth-to-mouth breathing and continue until the casualty is breathing himself or until professional help arrives. Send to hospital with a note of the gas involved.
Minor injuries	Casualties with minor injuries of a nature they would normally attend to themselves may wash their hands and apply a small sterilised dressing from the first aid box.

*A person with an eye injury should be sent to hospital with the eye covered with an eye pad.

If you are fortunate, you may never need to use your first aid skills. But you should nevertheless be prepared for the following types of incident:

- cuts
- burns
- eye injury
- sprains
- bruising
- fainting
- electric shock
- epileptic fit
- heart attack.

In a serious emergency, you could save someone's life if you knew how to give mouth-to-mouth resuscitation (see pages 290).

Recording accidents

All accidents must be recorded in the accident book. The recording system should always be kept readily available for use and inspection.

When you are recording accident details you will need to document the following information:

- the full name and address of the casualty
- the occupation of the casualty
- the date of entry in the accident book
- the date and time of the accident
- accident details: location, circumstances, the work process involved
- injury details
- signature of the person making the entry.

Fire

Your salon will have set fire safety procedures, which must always be followed.

Raising the alarm

Most salon fires arise from either smoking, an electrical fault or a gas escape. Smoking can cause fires when lit cigarettes are dropped, discarded or left unattended to smoulder in ash trays. Faulty or badly maintained electrical equipment, such as hand dryers or hood dryers, may malfunction and overheat, and even ignite occasionally. Gas appliances, such as ovens or hobs, present a possible risk if they are left unattended. Staff cooking facilities need to be closely monitored to prevent gas being left on, whether lit or not.

In the event of fire breaking out your main priorities are to:

Raise the alarm. Staff and customers must be warned, and the premises must be evacuated.

Call the fire brigade, even if you believe that someone else has already phoned. Dial 999, ask the operator for the fire service, and give the telephone number from where you are calling. Wait for the transfer to the fire service, then tell them your name and the address of the premises that are on fire.

 Activity

Find out the answers to the following questions.

1 Where is the fire fighting equipment in your salon?
2 What does it consist of?
3 What is involved in the checking of fire extinguishers?
4 What is your salon's fire drill?

Fire fighting

If the fire is small, you may tackle it with an extinguisher or fire blanket.

Under the Fire Precautions Act 1971, all premises are required to have firefighting equipment, which must be suitably maintained in good working order.

Different types of fire require different types of fire extinguisher.

Classes of fire

There are four classes of fire:

Class A	Fires that involve solids, such as paper, wood or hair.
Class B	Fires that involve liquids, such as petrol.
Class C	Fires that involve gases, such as propane or butane.
Class D	Fires that involve metals (not normally encountered in the hairdressing salon).

Types of fire extinguisher

All fire extinguishers are coloured red but have different coloured labels to highlight the differences.

Firefighting equipment

Chubb Fire Ltd

Water – Red

These extinguishers are colour-coded red and can only be used for Class A fires. They are usually of 9 litres (2 gallons) capacity and *must not be used on electrical fires or flammable metal fires.*

Foam – Yellow

These extinguishers are colour-coded yellow and are used for Class B fires and small Class A fires. Standard capacity is 9 litres (2 gallons) and *they must not be used on electrical fires or flammable metal fires.*

Carbon dioxide CO$_2$ – Black

These extinguishers are colour-coded black and can be used on electrical fires and burning liquid. They should not be used on flammable metal fires.

Powder (standard) – Blue

These extinguishers are colour-coded blue and can be used on burning liquid and electrical fires. They should not be used on flammable metal fires.

Halon – Green

These extinguishers are colour-coded green and are suitable for burning liquid and electrical fires. The vapours emitted 'starve' a fire of oxygen and are therefore dangerous to people in confined spaces. Halon is no longer manufactured in the EU but, while stocks are available for reuse, it may continue to be used in extinguishing equipment.

Fire escape

All premises must have a designated means of escape from fire. This route must be kept clear of obstructions at all times and during working hours the fire doors must remain unlocked. The escape route must be easily identifiable, with clearly visible signs. In buildings with fire certificates, emergency lighting must be installed. These lighting systems automatically illuminate the escape route in the event of a power failure and are operated by an independent battery back-up.

Fire safety training

It is essential for staff to know the following fire procedures:

- fire prevention
- raising the alarm
- evacuation during a fire
- assembly points following evacuation.

Training is given to new members of staff during their induction period. This training must be regularly updated for all staff, and fire drills must be held at regular intervals.

Health and Safety legislation

This section will provide you with an outline of the main health and safety regulations that affect hairdressers and their work.

The Health and Safety Executive (HSE) is the body appointed by Government to support and enforce health and safety law by checking that businesses are following all guidelines.

Health and Safety is the responsibility of everyone at work. Your employer or supervisor in particular have a greater responsibility for health and safety than you the stylist, however everyone has a responsibility to work in a healthy and safe way.

The Health and Safety at Work Act 1974 (HASAWA) is the main legislation from which most of the following legislation comes and covers the employers responsibility to a variety of healthy, safe working practices and associated regulations:

- Safe equipment and systems at work
- Safe handling, storage and transport of substances
- A safe place to work with safe access and egress (exit) within the salon
- Safe working environment which has welfare facilities
- All necessary information, instructions, training and supervision
- Provision of all necessary personal protective equipment (PPE) free of charge.

The Health and Safety at Work Act

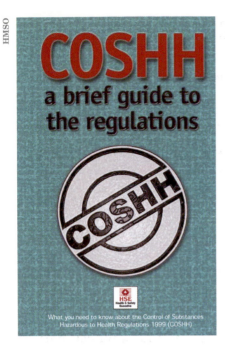

COSHH Regulations

You may not need to know the content of this Act, but you should at least be aware of the existence of all relevant regulations made under its provisions. Those that are applicable at the time of writing are as follows:

Control of Substances Hazardous to Health (COSHH) Regulations 1999

This relates to the control of any substance, particularly if chemical such as perms and colours, likely to affect health and safety but also shampoos, styling and setting products – all the products that stylists work with. It relates to the safe handling, storage and use of products that are, or could potentially be, hazardous. A substance is considered hazardous if it can cause harm to the body. It only poses a high risk if it is:

- In contact with the skin
- Absorbed through the skin
- Breathed in
- Swallowed
- Injected into the body
- Absorbed into the body e.g. via a cut

Your salon will have made a risk assessment of the products held or used in the salon, this will give you specific information on their handling and precautionary requirements.

Cosmetic Products (Safety) Regulations 1989

These regulations lay down the recommended volumes and percentage strengths of different hydrogen based products. The strength of a product will vary depending on whether it has been produced for professional or non-professional use. It is important that manufacturers' guidance material and current legislation is checked when using or selling products. Copies of the legislation can be obtained from Her Majesty's Stationery Office and guidance can be obtained from the product manufacturer.

Personal Protective Equipment (PPE) at Work Regulations 1992

Relates to the requirement of employers to provide suitable and sufficient protective clothing and equipment for all employees to use and for employees to use it.

The PPE Regulations 1992 require managers to make an assessment of the processes and activities carried out at work and to identify where and when special items of clothing should be worn. In hairdressing environments the potential hazards and dangers revolve around the task of providing hairdressing services – that is, in general, the application of hairdressing treatments and associated products.

Potentially hazardous substances used by hairdressers include:

- acidic solutions of varying strengths
- caustic alkaline solutions of varying strengths
- flammable liquids, which are often in pressurised containers
- vapours and dyeing compounds.

There are also potentially hazardous items of equipment and their individual applications, such as:

- electrical appliances
- heated/heating instruments
- sharp cutting tools.

All these items require correct handling and safe usage procedures, and for several of them this includes the wearing of suitable items of protective equipment.

 Activity

Make a list of the items of protective clothing that should be worn when

- handling a range of hairdressing products
- handling a range of hairdressing equipment.

Workplace (Health, Safety and Welfare) Regulations 1992

This act has replaced most of the Office, Shops and Railway Premises Act 1963.

These provide the employer with an approved code of practice for maintaining a safe, secure working environment. The regulations cover the legal requirements in respect of the following aspects of the working environment:

- maintenance of workplace and equipment
- ventilation
- indoor temperatures
- lighting
- cleanliness and the handling of waste materials
- room dimensions
- workstations and seating
- conditions of floor and traffic routes
- falls or falling objects

- windows, door, gates and walls
- ability to clean windows
- organisation of traffic routes
- escalators and moving walkways
- sanitary conveniences
- washing facilities
- drinking water
- accommodation for clothing
- facilities for changing clothing
- facilities for staff to rest and eat meals.

Health and Safety (Display Screen Equipment) Regulations 1992

This states that an employer who has display screen equipment (computers) in the salon should:

- Assess the display screen equipment workstation and reduce any risks that have been found for example the user's posture and seating position and accepted radiation emissions.
- Plan display screen work so that the employee has regular breaks or changes in activity.
- Provide information and training on the equipment.

Display screen users will also be entitled to eyesight tests and to special glasses if they are needed paid for by the employer.

Manual Handling Operations Regulations 1992

These regulations apply in all occupations where manual lifting occurs. They require the employer to carry out a risk assessment of the work processes and activities that involve manual lifting. The risk assessment should address detailed aspects of the following:

- any risk of injury
- the manual movement that is involved in the task
- the physical constraints the loads incur
- the (work) environmental constraints that are incurred
- the worker's individual capabilities
- steps/remedial action to take in order to minimise risk.

Provision and Use of Work Equipment Regulations (PUWER) 1998

These regulations lay down important health and safety controls on the provision and use of work equipment. They state the duties for employers, the persons in control (the users) and the self-employed. In general they affect both new and old equipment alike. In addition to this they cover the selection of suitable equipment, maintenance, manufacturer information, instruction and training. Specific regulations address the dangers that could arise from operation of the equipment and the potential risk of injury.

Electricity at Work Regulations 1989

This requires employers to maintain electrical equipment in a safe condition and have them checked by a suitably qualified person. A written record of the equipment tests should be kept and made available for inspection. It is the employees' responsibility to report any known faulty electrical equipment to their employer or supervisor.

RIDDOR (Reporting Injuries, Diseases and Dangerous Occurrences) Regulations 1995

This regulation requires employers to report to the Health and Safety Executive (HSE) certain work related accidents, diseases and dangerous occurrences. The following must be reported:

- Deaths
- Major injuries, including fractures (other than to fingers or toes); amputation; dislocation of the shoulder, hip, knee or spine; temporary or permanent loss of sight, any injury penetrating or burning the eye, injuries resulting in unconsciousness, requiring resuscitation or more than 24 hours in hospital
- Accidents resulting in more that three days off work
- Certain diseases
- Dangerous occurrences.

Management of Health and Safety at Work Regulations 1999

This regulation requires the employer to carry out risk assessments in the salon to protect the health and safety of employees and clients. The regulations require a competent person to be appointed to assess risks posed by all activities in the salon and take appropriate action to remove or minimise the risk. It requires reviews of assessment to be carried out regularly and always recorded. It requires that employees should be trained and aware of health and safety procedures such as evacuation procedures, and is designed to take account of risks to, for example, expectant mothers and new or young employees.

Smith & Nephew

First aid kits

Health and Safety (First Aid) Regulations 1981

These require the employer to provide facilities and equipment, which are appropriate for administering first aid. In a hairdressing salon a First Aid Box and eye wash equipment should be sufficient. First Aid Boxes should not contain medication of any kind. If an accident does happen in the salon you should always notify the person responsible and trained to carry out the first aid treatment. Do not carry out first aid yourself if you have not been trained.

First Aid Box contents

Number of employees	1–5	6–10	11–50
Content	Quantity	Quantity	Quantity
First Aid Guidance Notes	1	1	1
Individual wrapped sterile adhesive dressings	20	20	40
Sterile eye pads, with attachment	1	2	4
Sterile triangular bandages	1	2	4
Safety pins	6	6	12
Medium-sized sterile unmedicated dressings	3	6	8
Large sterile unmedicated dressings	1	2	4
Extra large sterile unmedicated dressings	1	2	4

The Work Time Regulations 1998

This regulation relates to working hours, rest periods and holidays and covers the following:

- A limit on the average working time per week to 48 hours, although employees can agree to work longer.
- Minimum daily and weekly rest periods – adult workers are entitled to 11 hours consecutive rest between working days. Individuals under 18 years are entitled to 12 hours.
- Rest breaks at work – employees are entitled to 20 minutes rest if the day is longer than 6 hours. Individuals under the age of 18 years and working 4.4 hours in a day are entitled to 30 minutes.
- Paid annual leave – every worker is entitled to four weeks paid annual leave after they have been continuously employed for 13 weeks.

Assignments – Health and safety in the salon

A practical activity

Copy the table shown below. Then find out the information required to complete it. Keep the finished document for use in your portfolio.

To find the necessary information, reread the section headed 'General salon hygiene' in this chapter (page 286). Also ask your fellow work colleagues for help.

Work areas	Potential hazards	Reasons for keeping clean	Methods of keeping clean
Reception			
Styling units			
Drying areas			
Dispensary			
Stock room/cupboard			
Staff room			
Toilets			

For you to find out

With reference to your salon find out the following information.

Record the details. Keep them in your folder or personal portfolio.

- The Health and Safety at Work Act 1994 is the legislation that covers the employer's responsibility and employee responsibility to a variety of Health and Safe working practices.

- Explain the other associated regulations that fall under this act and how you fulfil your obligations whilst carrying out your day to day duties.

A case study

It was Tuesday morning at 'Jenny's Hair Salon'. Jenny had allocated Karen, one of the juniors, to remain on reception whilst she attended to paperwork in the office. Steve, one of the stylists, has clients booked in. Sharon, the other stylist, had most of the morning free.

A well-dressed woman with short greying hair came in and asked Karen if she would be able to have her hair coloured before travelling to London that afternoon. Karen said that Sharon could help her.

Sharon greeted the lady, putting her at her ease and carried out a consultation and colour selection. She asked Claire, another junior, to prepare the client for the service. Claire seated her in the salon, hung up her coat and looked for a colouring gown. There weren't any.

'Use one of the cutting capes, then,' said Sharon, 'the others are still at the launderette. I'll mix up the colour and you can apply it while I collect them.'

A case study (cont.)

Claire had applied colours before but tended to be a little careless. Today her application was sloppy, and she did not bother to wear gloves. Ten minutes later Sharon returned. Horrified, she beckoned Claire into reception. 'You've not only coloured her hair, you've got colour on her neck and even on her jacket,' she exclaimed.

'I know,' said Claire, 'I'll change the gowns over now and ask her to take off her jacket so that it won't get creased. Then I'll clean it without her knowing.' 'OK, but keep it to yourself,' said Sharon.

When the hair do was finished, the client paid her bill and left.

Two days later, Claire told Jenny that she had visited the doctor because of sore, itching and burning hands. He had diagnosed dermatitis and told her it was an occupational disease and should be reported. He'd signed her off for a week.

On Saturday morning, Jenny received a letter from a firm of solicitors. This is what it said.

Re Ms Cane in pursuance of Compensation

Dear Madam

I regret to inform you that my client whilst attending your place of business on Tuesday 11 February did suffer due to the gross negligence of your staff an allergenic reaction following a colouring treatment. There are indications of burns and weeping pustules as well as damage sustained to her attire. We await a comprehensive medical report which we believe will provide the basis for our pursuance in court and recovery of damages. We will be contacting you in due course.

1   List in order the mistakes that were made.
2   What actions should, or could, have been taken to avoid the outcomes?
3   Who were to blame and why?
4   What are the possible short- and long-term effects for Jenny, her staff and her business?
5   How do COSHH and RIDDOR apply to this particular scenario?

Preparing for Assessment

Whilst making preparations for assessment health and safety in the salon, the following checklist may be helpful. Check that you have covered and now fully understand these items:

- safe salon working practices
- how to look out for the potential hazards in the workplace
- how to look after tools and equipment
- how to dispose of salon waste items
- salon policy in respect of emergency procedures
- salon policy in respect of first aid procedures.

When you feel that you are ready, talk to your trainer to arrange a suitable time for your assessment.

By reading this chapter, carrying out the above activities, assignments and the case study, and by meeting the requirements in preparing for assessment you will have worked towards the key skill requirements in Communication Level 2 (C 2.1) (C 2.2).

If you have used a computer to complete your assignments or activities you will have worked towards the key skill requirements in Information Technology Level 1 (IT 1.2).

Assessment

This section of the book will provide you with the background information and explain the principles surrounding the **assessment** of competence.

Before NVQs became available, trainees who wanted to gain nationally recognised qualifications would have to practise the technical skills, study art, science and design and then, after a period of training, be expected to take both practical and theory examinations. Depending how they performed on the day, they either passed or failed. This system is considered to be unfair for vocational qualifications. Some trainees who were expected to pass with flying colours have actually failed because of the pressures exerted by taking the exam. The examination system neither provides a realistic working situation, nor truly reflects the candidate's previous training achievement.

The solution is at hand, however. Continuous assessment of performance provides a suitable option. Monitoring and recording the trainee's progress towards achievement (occupational competence) is now providing the currently preferred route to certification.

Trainees are enrolled with an approved centre and then undergo a period of initial assessment to identify their training needs. Following this assessment, a personal training and assessment plan is devised. This plan will state *where*, *when* and *how* the training will be delivered, *who* will be responsible for monitoring, training and assessing, and *what* will be the expected time scale for training and reviewing of progress.

This detailed plan provides a tailor-made training programme which allows the trainee to:

- practise the required skills, and
- acquire the essential background knowledge.

Then, at the point where trainees can consistently perform the required tasks to standard and can demonstrate that they have the required knowledge, they are deemed competent.

What is the required standard?

Chris Moody

The standard could be described as 'the level of competence required in order to perform the task'. The currently nationally recognised standards have been devised by the Hairdressing and Beauty Industry Authority (HABIA). This organisation is made up of representative bodies within the hairdressing industry. It is responsible for defining the standards of competence at each of the NVQ levels (Level 1, Level 2 and so on). After the standards have been agreed they are submitted to the Qualifications and National Curriculum Authority (QCA) for their approval and subsequent accreditation (accreditation is the giving of the Council's formal approval to the national standards, providing it with a licence to operate).

The standards are written specifications of how certain tasks or functions are to be performed. They are used in two ways to assess trainees:

- By observing their performance of practical ability within the specified conditions of the range
- By questioning candidates to find out their basic understanding and knowledge of the practical task.

Ishoka

Each standard is made up of the following components:

- units
- outcomes
- performance criteria
- range statement
- essential knowledge.

Level 2 in Hairdressing consists of eight mandatory units and one optional unit. The mandatory units are the basic essentials of the NVQ, and they must all be completed. The optional unit groups provide the trainee with a choice of different hairdressing skills or support services. There is also an NVQ Level 2 in Barbering. This consists of six mandatory units and three optional units.

Each unit can be achieved and certificated separately. This means that trainees may accumulate units of competence:

- for specific work-related tasks
- for part-certification
- for full Level 2 certification
- in any order
- at their own pace of learning
- within the workplace or at a training centre.

Java for Hair

Outcomes

Units consist of various numbers of individual standards called outcomes. The outcomes state the function or task that has to be performed competently.

Java for Hair

Barrie Stephen, Hair Envision

Razors Edge

Performance criteria

A standard specifies not only *what* has to be done, but also *how* it is to be done. It sets out a list of **performance criteria** for each task. These are concise statements of procedural functions, the specific steps that should be taken during the performance of the task if the standard is to be met. They are used as a checklist when the trainee is being observed during assessment.

Range statements

To enable the trainee to gain competence in a variety of situations the standard also states the range of circumstances for which competence must be demonstrated. For example, if a trainee were asked to perform a layered haircut on a model with straight hair, the finished cut would look different from the same cut carried out on a model with curly hair. Although the same methods and techniques are required in both situations, the results are by no means the same. The trainee needs to show competence in a broad range of contexts – hair types, lengths, conditions and so on – which imply a wide variety of conditions and complexity for the given task.

Knowledge and understanding

This refers to the trainee's awareness of *why* the task is done in a certain way. For example, in the unit on shampoo and condition hair and scalp the trainee will need to show a clear understanding of:

- the manufacturers' instructions relating to the use of products
- how hair condition and subsequent salon services are affected by the pH value of the products used.

The trainee will need to know the methods of:

- applying massage techniques to differing densities and lengths of hair.

The trainee will need to know:

- the range of available shampoos within the salon
- the suitability of shampooing products for use with different hair and scalp conditions, together with other salon services
- the difference between effleurage and rotary techniques, and when to use them
- the effects of water temperature on scalp and hair
- what may happen if the wrong shampooing product is used
- when the shampooing process should be repeated.

The assessment activity

Why do we assess?

Assessment isn't just a matter of finding out if a trainee can 'pass' a test. There are four main reasons for an assessment:

- to check whether a trainee can perform the job competently to the required national standard
- to identify where further improvement can be made
- to monitor and record progress towards competence
- to maintain accurate records of the trainee's achievement.

How do we assess?

Assessment is carried out by the collection and evaluation of evidence by a wide variety of techniques. But regardless of the technique used, only one of three possible assessment decisions can be made:

- the trainee is competent
- the trainee is not yet competent
- the trainee has provided insufficient evidence for the assessor to infer competence.

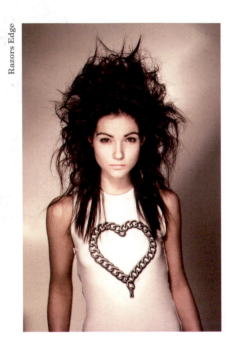

Razors Edge

Observation of performance

A trainee's performance evidence should be sufficient to convince an assessor that it consistently meets the stated performance criteria and that all items within the range are covered. The minimum number of observed competent performances are stated in the assessor's element specific guidance.

In addition to this, *virtually* all the performance evidence must be a result of the trainee's own endeavours and should be a result of real work activities. However, some exceptions for simulated activities will be allowed, for example **Observe emergency procedures**.

Oral questioning

Most of the evidence of competence will arise from the observed performance. However, it may be necessary to supplement this by providing back-up information about the task or answering the specific questions that relate to the Knowledge and Understanding Requirements.

Ishoka

Other supplementary evidence

This may include a variety of sources, such as:

- records of client's comments (if applicable)
- your own notes from your work log
- witness testimonies from responsible people at work
- video recording of yourself at work
- photographs of yourself at work
- extracts from salon systems, if available
- copies of relevant remarks about your work from 'clients comments' book.

Useful addresses and statutory obligations

The organisations listed below should prove valuable sources of information and help to the professional hairdresser. Address any enquiries to 'The Secretary'.

ACAS, LESA. Brandon House, 180 Borough High Street, London, SE1 1LW

Black Beauty and Hair, Hawker Publications, 2nd Floor Culvert House, Culvert Road, Battersea, London, SW11 5DH

Caribbean and Afro Society of Hairdressers (CASH), 42 North Cross Road, East Dulwich, London SE22 8PY (Tel: 020 8299 2859)

City and Guilds, 1 Giltspur Street, London EC1A 9DD (Tel: 020 7294 2468)

Cosmetic, Toiletry and Perfumery Association (CTPA), Josaron House, 5/7 Princes Street, London W1G 0JN (Tel: 020 7491 8891)

Edexcel, Stewart House, 32 Russell Square, London, WC1B 5DN (Tel: 0870 240 9800)

The Fellowship of British Hairdressing, Peel House, High Street, Tisbury, Wiltshire SP3 6PS (Tel: 01747 870 310)

Freelance Hair and Beauty Federation, 8 Willenhall Close, Luton, Bedforshire LU3 3XX (Tel: 01582 593593)

Guild of Hairdressers (GUILD), Unit 1E, Redbrook Business Park, Wilthorpe Road, Barnsley S75 1JN (Tel: 01226 786555)

Hairdressers Journal International, Quadrant House, The Quadrant, Sutton, Surrey, SM2 5AS (Tel: 020 8652 3500)

Hairdressing Council (HC), 12 David House, 45 High Street, South Norwood, London, SE25 6HJ (Tel: 010 8771 6205)

Hairdressing Employers Association (HEA), 10 Coldbath Square, London EC1R 5HL (Tel: 020 7833 0633)

Hairdressing and Beauty Suppliers Association (HBSA), 2nd Floor, Bedford Chambers, The Piazza, Covent Garden, London WC2 8HA (Tel: 020 7836 4008)

Hairdressing and Beauty Industry Authority (HABIA), Fraser House, Nether Hall Road, Doncaster, DN1 2PH (Tel: 01302 380000)

Institute of Trichologists, 5 Belsford Court, Watnall, Nottingham NG16 1JW (Tel: 0870 607 0602)

National Hairdressers' Federation (NHF), 11 Goldington Road, Bedford MK40 3JY (Tel: 01234 360 332)

Scotland Qualifications Authority (SQA), Hanover House, 24 Douglas Street, Glasgow, G2 7NQ

Union of Shop, Distributive and Allied Workers (USDAW), 188 Wilmslow Road, Fallowfield, Manchester, M14 6LJ (Tel: 0161 224 2804)

Vocational Training Charitable Trust (VTCT), 46 Aldwick Road, Bognor Regis, West Sussex PO21 2PN (Tel: 01243 842064)

World Federation of Hairdressing and Beauty Schools, PO Box 367, Coulsdon, Surrey CR5 2TP (Tel: 01737 551355)

Statutory regulations

To assist and benefit clients and staff, there are a number of rules, regulations, laws and bye-laws that must be followed. These underline the main responsibilities of employers and employees. Some of these are listed below. Detailed information of legal requirements can be obtained from your local college, public library and Her Majesty's Stationery Office.

Consumer Protection Acts 1987 (Cosmetic Regulations)

Contracts of Employment Act 1963 and 1972

Control of Substances Hazardous to Health Regulations 1999

Data Protection Act 1984 and 1998

Electricity at Work Regulations 1989

Employer Liability (Compulsory Insurance) Act 1969, Regulations 1998

Employment Protection Act 1975, 1978 and 1992

Environment Protection Act 1990

Equal Pay Act 1970

Factories Act 1961

Finance Acts (annual), current of most interest

Fire Precautions Act 1971, 1976 and 1999

First Aid Regulations 1981

Gas Safety Regulations 1994

Health and Safety (Display Screen Equipment) Regulations 1992

Health and Safety (First Aid) Regulations 1981

Health and Safety (Information for Employees) Regulations 1989

Health and Safety (Training for Employment) Regulations 1996

Health and Safety at Work Act 1974

Manual Handling Operations Regulations 1992

Notification of Accidents and General Occurrences Regulations 1980

Offices, Shops and Railway Premises Act 1963

Pay as You Earn (introduced 1944), Inland Revenue

Personal Protective Equipment at Work Regulations 1992

Provision and Use of Work Equipment Regulations 1998

Race Regulations Act

Redundancy Payments Act 1969

Reporting of Injuries, Diseases and Dangerous Occurrences Regulations 1995

Safety Representatives and Safety Committees Regulations 1980

Sale of Goods Act 1979

Sex Discrimination Act 1975 and 1986

Shops Acts 1950 and 1965

Trade Boards Act 1909

Trade Descriptions Act 1968 and 1972

The Management of Health and Safety at Work Regulations 1999

Employment Rights Act 1996

Employment Act 1989

Employment Relations Act 1999

Social Security Act 1989

Human Rights Act 1998

Work Time Regulations 1998

Trade Union and Labour Relations Act 1992

National Minimum Wage Act 1998

Part-time Workers Regulations 2000

Sales and Supply of Goods Act 1994

Financial Services Act 1986

Value Added Tax (introduced 1973), HM Customs and Excise

Workplace (Health/Safety and Welfare) Regulations 1992

Glossary

accelerator a machine that produces radiant heat (infra-red radiation); can speed up chemical hair processes such as colouring or conditioning

acid a substance that gives off hydrogen ions in water, and produces a solution with a pH below 7

acid mantle the natural protective coating of the skin's surface made up from sweat and sebum

acne a skin disorder, characterised by spots and pustules due to inflammation of the sebaceous glands

action plan document that outlines activities to be completed within a given time scale

activators chemicals used in bleaches or some perm lotions to start or boost its action

Afro-Caribbean hair the very curly hair typical of African people

AIDS acquired immune-deficiency syndrome; a condition in which the immune system is damaged and the body becomes vulnerable to many infections

albinism an inherited condition in which there is no (very little) colour pigment in the hair or skin

albino hair hair that contains little or no pigment; albino hair is nearly white or very pale yellow; the condition is usually present at birth

alkali a substance that gives off hydroxide ions in water, and produces a solution with a pH above 7

alopecia baldness

alpha keratin hair in an un-stretched state

amino acids simple organic compounds which form the basic constituents of proteins

anagen the stage of hair growth during which the hair is actively growing

aniline a colourless oily liquid present in coal tar or crude oil, used in the manufacture of dyes

anterior towards the front

antioxidant a substance that prevents or slows down deterioration due to oxidation

antiseptic a substance that kills disease-causing **micro-organisms** or stops them from growing

apocrine gland a gland whose secretions include a part of the secreting cells themselves (e.g. some sweat glands)

arrector pili the muscles that raise the hair (in humans they are very feeble)

arteriole a very small artery

artery a blood vessel that carries blood away from the heart

assessment judging the worth of something or of the results of a task; evaluation, appraisal

assignment a task or a practical activity

asymmetrical lacking in symmetry, thus creating an uneven balance

athlete's foot see **tinea pedis**

autoclave a device for sterilising items in high-temperature steam

azo dyes are temporary colours that coat the surface of the hair, they are synthetic dyes whose molecules contain two adjacent nitrogen atoms between carbon atoms

backcombing/backbrushing pushing hair back to bind or lift the hair using a comb or brush

backcombing taper hair is backcombed and the remaining hair lengths/ends are then tapered into a point

backdressing backcombing or backbrushing

bacteria a large group of **micro-organisms**, many of which live in or on the human body; a few cause diseases

bactericide a substance that kills bacteria

baldness traction hair loss due to harsh physical and chemical treatments, e.g. tight braids and heavy ponytails.

barbering the art of cutting and shaping men's hair

barrier cream waterproof cream to protect the skin or scalp when using chemicals

beta keratin hair in a stretched state

bleach a substance that removes natural colour; acts first on black pigments, then on brown, red and yellow

bleaching removal of natural colour

bleach wraps individual plastic pockets or foil pieces used to isolate/enfold the section of hair being treated

blepharitis inflammation of the eyelids

block colouring colouring areas of hair in a way that is intended to enhance the cut style

blow-drying drying and shaping hair using a hand-held dryer

blow-stretching (straightening) temporary straightening of the hair by smoothing the hair while blow-drying

blow-waving waving the hair while blow-drying

bob cut a hairstyle in which the hair is cut to a level length around the head

body language communication by means of body actions and/or posture rather than speech

boosters providing additional oxygen speeds up a chemical process

brighteners lightening (bleaching) shampoos or rinses

camomile a plant of the daisy family, with white and yellow flowers, it produces a yellow colour and can be used to brighten blonde hair

canities hair that is without pigment and is therefore grey or white

capillary strictly, a very fine tube; usually used to refer to a very small blood vessel

capilliary action movement of liquid by absorption

castle serrations reducing areas of a hair section with special serrated scissors

catagen the stage of hair growth during which the hair stops growing, but the hair papilla is still active

Caucasian hair the wavy or straight hair typical of a European

cetrimide a chemical found in hairsprays, which helps condition and reduce static electricity

chemical hair treatment a term that includes perming, colouring, bleaching, streaking, high- or low-lighting, frosting, lightening, permanent straightening or relaxing

chlorinated water water treated with the chemical chlorine, usually found in swimming pools it can have a negative effect the condition of hair

clear layer also known as the Stratum lucidum, it is a clear layer of skin found in the epidermis between the horny layer and the granular layer

client a customer or patron of a shop or salon

client care looking after customers, ensuring that they are comfortable and confident, and that they will be satisfied with the service and/or treatment they receive

club-cutting or **clubbing** cutting straight across to produce level ends

coiffure a completed hair style

cold permanent waving (perming) a perming process that does not rely on heat for its activation

colonies micro-organisms in large groups, forming a physically connected structure

colour filling see **pre-pigmentation**

colourants any type of colouring substance used on hair

colouring the process of adding artificial colour to hair

communication giving and receiving information; understanding, and ensuring that one is understood

compensation a payment given to make amends for loss, damage, poor service etc.

compound colourings mixtures of vegetable and mineral dyes

compound henna a combination of vegetable henna and metallic salts creates colour for hair; it is not used in salons because it is incompatible with modern hairdressing chemical products

conditioners products used to correct or improve the state of the hair

confidentiality the maintenance and respect of an individual's privacy, including privacy (secrecy) of information

conjunctivitis inflammation of the conjunctiva (the membrane at the front of the eye)

consultation the process of interviewing a client; includes discussing, conferring, questioning, advising and counselling

contraindication sign that some treatment or service is inadvisable or could be harmful

cornrowing fine plaits running continuously across the scalp

CPW abbreviation for **cold permanent waving**

crêpe hair a man-made fibre used to hold the ends of hair in place when perm winding

crew cut short, spiky style with hair standing straight up

cross-infection the passing of an infection from one individual to another

curl base the parted section of hair that a roller or pincurl sits on

cutting angle the angle at which hair is held and cut

cutting comb a flexible comb designed for use when cutting

cutting line the direction in which cutting is made to follow the contours of the head

cutting method a considered sequence of cutting techniques

cutting technique a special cutting skill aimed at producing a specific result

cysteine an amino acid containing sulphur which occurs in keratins and other proteins

cystine two cysteine atoms when oxidised (joined together) make a cystine molecule

damaged cuticle broken, split, torn hair

dandruff scales of dry dead skin flaking from the scalp

Data Protection Act 1998 legislation designed to protect the clients' right to privacy and confidentiality

depth of colour a measure of how light or dark a colour is

dermatitis inflammation of the skin

dermis the layer of the skin underlying the epidermis; the thickest layer of the skin

detergent a cleansing agent, acting by reducing the surface tension of water and improving its wetting ability

development time the 'taking time' of a chemical action such as tinting

diagnosis identifying a disease or disorder by observing its symptoms

discolouration unwanted colour produced by a chemical

disinfectant a substance that kills disease-causing **micro-organisms**

disulphide bridges keratin bonds that are linked together

dreadlocks long thin plaits

dressing the forming and blending of hair into a finished shape or style

dry cutting cutting hair while it is dry

eccrine gland a gland that emits a secretion to the surface of the body; most sweat glands are eccrine glands

eczema an inflammation of the skin, characterised by redness and irritation

effleurage light, soothing, stroking **massage** movement

elasticity the ability of a material to return to the original length after stretching

emollient a substance used (e.g. in conditioners) to soften and enhance the appearance of hair

emulsion a suspension of tiny droplets of one liquid in another liquid (e.g. of oil in water)

end paper a tissue or wrap used during winding to secure a hair point

ensemble several parts which create a whole look

epidermis the outermost layers of the skin

epithelium a tissue of closely packed cells that covers a surface (internal or external) of the body

eumelanin black and brown pigment in the skin and hair

euro the single European currency

facial a face **massage**

feathering action using scissor points

finger (hand) drying drying the hair using the fingers as a comb

finger waving forming waves in wet hair using the hands as a comb

fish-hook a point of hair that has been bent back during rollering or winding

float sum of money that is kept in the till to ensure that adequate change is available; the sum that should be in the till when business opens each day

folliculitis inflammation of the hair follicles; may be caused by bacterial infection

former a frame around which hair can be would, such as a curler or rod

fragilitas crinium splitting of the hairs at their ends

fraudulent dishonest, false or deceitful

freehand cutting cutting without forcing the hair out of its natural position

French roll a vertical fold of hair, usually on the back of the head

friction a stimulating massage technique used when shampooing; it is a vigorous movement using the pads of the fingers against the scalp.

fringe hair that covers the forehead from side to side

frosting **shading** or **colouring** parts of the hair to enhance the style

fungi a large group of living organisms, plant-like in many respects; many cause disease

fungicide a substance that kills fungi

furunculosis an outbreak of boils and abscesses

germinal matrix the living, reproducing part of the hair

germinating layer (stratum germinativum or basal layer) the deepest layer of the epidermis where cellular regeneration takes place

gift vouchers a voucher has been prepaid and can be used as part of, or for all of a payment

glimmering **shading** or **tinting** parts of the hair to enhance the style

gown protective wrap

graduation the sloping line produced by layers of hair

granular layer (stratum granulosum) the layer of the epidermis between the soft living cells and the harder dead cells; it lies directly above the germinating layer, keratinisation begins in this layer

greasy hair (seborrhoea) is caused by an over production of sebum

guide (for cutting) any feature or previously cut section of hair that is used to indicate where the next cut should be made

hair bulb base of the hair follicle containing actively growing cells; this is where new hair develops.

hair fibres hair which grows away from the surface of the skin

hair follicle thin tube-like space in the dermis in which the hair develops and grows

hair muscle (arrector pili) attached to the hair follicle and the epidermis. When contracted the hair stands up trapping a warm layer of air around the skin

hair papillae found at the bottom of the hair follicle it connect the follicle with the epidermis thereby nourishing cellular activity

hair shaper a razor-like cutting tool

hair-strand colour test used in colouring to check that the colour has developed

hair texture the feel of the hair; fine, medium or coarse

hard water water that contains calcium and/or magnesium salts; produces scum with soap

haute coiffure the latest styles and trends

head-hugging plaits plaits of hair lying close to the head

heat moulding shaping the hair while it is softened by heat (e.g. with heated tongs)

henna (lawsonia inermis) a tropical shrub with small pink, red or white flowers

hepatitis inflammation of the liver

herb a herbaceous plant (one that dies back in winter); often refers to a plant that is used for medical or cosmetic purposes

hereditary passing from a parent to a child

herpes simplex a viral skin infection, the all-too-familiar 'cold sores'

herpes zoster a painful viral infection of the epidermis of the skin and of the nerve endings; usually called 'shingles'

highlighting **shading** or **colouring** parts of the hair to enhance the style

HIV human immunodeficiency virus, believed to lead to the condition of **AIDS**

horny layer (stratum corneum) the top layer (surface) of the epidermis consisting of dead, flat, hard cells

humectant a substance that attracts and holds moisture (water)

humidity the amount of water (moisture) held by the air

hydrogen bonds found in the hair structure, they can be easily broken when styling hair

hydrogen peroxide An oxidising agent used in colouring and neutralising

hydrolysis the chemical breakdown of a compound due to reaction with water

hydrophilic attracted by water

hydrophobic repelled by water

hygiene the practice of procedures leading to cleanliness and the maintenance of good health

hygroscopic tending to absorb water from the air

hyperaemia flushing of the skin due to improved blood flow

hypodermis fatty layer also known as subcutaneous or subcutis layer

illusionary effect a style that seems to diminish or accentuate certain facial features or shapes of the head

immune system the body's defence against disease

impetigo a bacterial infection of the **epidermis**

incompatibility inability to combine or coexist without ill effects

indicator a substance that changes colour at a certain pH value

indigo a tropical plant used as a source for dark blue dye

infectious a disease that can be passed from one person to another

international colour chart A chart that defines hair colour by depth and tone

itch mite the animal **parasite** that causes **scabies**

job description a written specification of what is expected of someone who has to carry out a task

keratin the principal protein of hair, nails and skin

lanolin an **emollient** extracted from wool fat

lanugo hair the soft downy hair of an unborn child

lathering lubricating and softening the beard before shaving, using a foam, gel or cream

layering cutting hair at various angles to produce **graduation**

legal tender forms of money that are legally recognised as valid for making payments

length and density of hair the length above or below the shoulders, the amount of hair on the head and the thickness of the individual hairs

level length *see* **bob cut**

lightening *see* **bleaching**

lighting the effect of natural or artificial light on the environment

limescale hard deposit of calcium carbonate, separating from **hard water** when it is heated

litmus papers *see* (pH papers)

lowlighting shading or **colouring** parts of the hair to enhance the style

macrofibrils the slender fibres, which make up the cells in the cortex of the hair

malpighian cells formed by continual division they contain melanin and are present in the epidermis

massage the practice of moving skin and muscles by rubbing, kneading, etc. to promote relaxation and suppleness and improve blood flow

medulla the inner or central space in the hair

melanin the pigments that give colour to skin and hair

metallic dyes has the sheen of metal or is a derivative of a metal

microfibrils the fibres that form the macrofibrils in the cortex

micro-organism a small living creature visible only with a microscope

mis-en-pli putting hair into set

mixed layer Found in the epidermis immediately below the granular layer, it consists of a variety of cell types

moisturiser a substance that attracts and holds moisture (water)

Mongoloid hair the lank, straight hair typical of Asian or Amerindian people

monilethrix beaded hair

mousse a foam formulation used in setting or colouring

movement the amount of direction the hair can move within a given style

natural colour hair colour produced from the melanin (natural hair pigment)

neckline the line of the hair across the nape of the neck

neutral having a pH close to 7

neutraliser a chemical formulation used to return hair to its normal condition after cold perming

nit an egg of the head louse *see also* **pediculosis capitis**

nitro dyes semi permanent colours that penetrate to just below the cuticle. They are made from substances called nitrodiamines and nitrated aminophenals

normaliser *see* **neutraliser**

observation watching, noticing, studying, recording

outlining marking out the boundaries of parts of the head and face (e.g. neckline, beard outline etc.)

ova eggs of the head louse

overbleaching *see* overprocessing

overbooking making appointments for too many clients at the same time

over-processing leaving a chemical product on the hair longer than what is recommended or required

oxidant an oxidising agent

oxidation reaction with oxygen, as in the neutralising of a perm

oxidising agent a substance such as hydrogen peroxide which reacts with a product to release oxygen

papilliary layer the top layer of the dermis that connects with the lowest layer of the epidermis

parasite an organism that lives on or in another organism, and may weaken it or cause symptoms of disease

partings separate or divide the hair

pathogen a **micro-organism** or **virus** that produces harmful effects such as disease

pediculosis capitis an infestation of the head by the insect known as the head louse

performance appraisal usually carried out with your boss to discuss and record your performance within your job role, to identify training needs and setting targets

perm lotion a reducing agent used to break the disulphide bonds in the hair

permeable allowing other materials to penetrate or pass through

perming or permanent waving the process that changes straight hair into waves or curls that last throughout the life of the hair

pétrissage deep, stimulating, kneading **massage** movement

petty cash cash kept on a firm's premises to meet minor items of expense

pH scale measure of acidity or alkalinity

pH papers (litmus paper) the paper changes colour when in contact with a liquid substance thereby indicating acid or alkaline

pheomelanin red and yellow pigment in the skin and hair

pigments (melanin) found in the hair cortex and give hair its natural colour

pincurling forming hair into curl shapes which are held with pins or clips until dried

pityriasis capitis *see* **dandruff**

plaiting intertwining several sections of hair to form a single structure

plasticisers substance added to manufactured products which can help reduce brittleness and increase support for the hair style

plastics used in setting aids to slow down the absorption of moisture and help new shapes in the hair to be formed when styling

pleat a folded roll of hair

pli shortened form of *mis-en-pli*

point tapering cutting the ends of the hair into a point

polishing shading or **colouring** parts of the hair to enhance the style

polymerisation the creation of a substance through the combination of molecules from more than one source

polypeptides a linear polymer consisting of amino acids which form all or part of a protein molecule

porosity (of hair) the ability to absorb moisture or liquids (e.g. colour or perm lotion)

porous having minute holes/space through which liquid of air may pass

post-damping applying perm lotion after winding rods in to the hair

posterior towards the back

postiche hairpieces added for ornamentation or to disguise hair defects

pre-damping applying perm lotion before or during winding rods into the hair

pre-lightening bleaching hair before colouring it to a shade that is lighter than the original

pre-pigmentation adding a colour to porous hair before recolouring; allows the new colour (often a warm colour) to adhere to the hair and prevents patchy or greenish results

pre-softening technique used to soften the hair cuticle prior to applying a permanent colour

previous treatment history finding out the hairdressing services that have been carried out previously

prickle cells found in the mixed layer of the epidermis, between the granular layer and the basal layer

primary colours
of light: blue, green and red
of pigments: blue, yellow and red

processing time The amount of time it takes a chemical product to develop/work on the hair

proteins long chains of amino acids form proteins which nourish the hair, encouraging growth and repair; the main protein in hair is keratin

protofibrils fibres found in the cortex which determine the strength, elasticity, thickness and curl of the hair

psoriasis a condition that produces inflammation, irritation and scaling of the skin

PVA, PVP chemicals used in setting agents

quasi-permanent colour a long-lasting hair colour that fades gradually over time

quassia South American shrub or small tree with medicinal properties

rake a comb with widely spaced teeth

razor clubbing club-cutting with a razor

reception area where clients are received; the process of receiving people

reducing agent ammonium hydroxide releases hydrogen in the hair, for example, the perming/reduction process. It is then oxidised to stabilise the hair structure

reduction reaction with hydrogen, as in cold permanent waving

regrowth application colouring the hair that has grown since the last treatment with colour or bleach

relaxing the process of removing curl or waves from the hair

resins solid or liquid synthetic polymer used in setting aids to slow down the absorption of moisture

resistant hair hair that resists colour penetration

restyle to completely change the hair shape and style

reticular layer the lower layer of the dermis immediately above the subcutaneous layer

retouching colouring or relaxing regrowth

reverse graduation a cut in which the top layers are longer than those beneath

ringworm *see* **tinea**

root the base of the hair

root thinning cutting the hair to reducing bulk at the root

roller a curler or former around which hair is wound to produce a curl or wave

rotary a circular massage movement using the pads of the fingers over the surface of the scalp when shampooing

salt bonds found in the hair structure, they can be easily broken when styling the hair to give a new temporary shape

scabies a skin rash appearing as a reaction to an animal **parasite**

scalp the skin and subcutaneous tissue that covers the top of the head

scalp plaits *see* **cornrowing**

screeners hair aids that act as protective hair coverings

scrunch drying blow-drying while gripping and squeezing the hair; used to produce full effects

sebaceous cyst a swollen **sebaceous gland**; a wen

sebaceous gland a natural oil gland in the skin

seborrhoea over-production of sebum by the sebaceous glands, leading to greasy skin

sebum oily secretion of a sebaceous gland

secondary colours
of light: yellow, cyan and magenta
of pigments: violet, green and orange

sections the divisions of hair for the purpose of perming or setting; the division needs to be the same size and shape as the perm rod or roller being used

self-appraisal, self-assessment judging and evaluating one's own level of achievement

semi-permanent colouring a hair colouring that lasts through several shampoos

setting placing wet hair into positions that will be temporarily held after drying, e.g. with rollers, pins or curlers

shades numbered system used to refer to varying shades of hair colour

shading the lightening (**bleaching**) of small areas (ends or tips) of hair

shampoos products used for cleaning hair

shimmering shading or tinting parts of the hair to enhance the style

shiners protective hair coverings

shingles *see* **herpes zoster**

shingling cutting a short layered style graduating from the nape of the neck

shrinkage theft of stock by members of staff

sideburns, sideboards names for men's side whiskers

silicones durable synthetic resin found in hairspray which adds a sheen to hair

soft water water that is free of calcium and magnesium salts

spectrum the colours contained in light that we see as white (many people can recognise red, orange, yellow, blue, green, indigo and violet)

stabiliser a chemical added to **bleach** to prevent deterioration

static electricity electric charges on hair, producing 'flyaway' behaviour

steam setting setting hair while dry, then steaming, drying and dressing it

steamer a machine used to supply moist heat to the skin and/or hair

stem the part of a curl which gives direction to the curl and forms the body

sterilisation killing all **micro-organisms** that may be present

stock in hand the stock available; re-ordering takes place at prearranged levels of stock in hand

stock rotation ensuring that old stock is used up before newer stock is brought out

stock taking checking the current levels of **stock in hand**

stratum aculeatum found in the mixed layer of the epidermis

stratum malpighi found in the mixed layer of the epidermis

stratum spinosum found in the mixed layer of the epidermis

subcutaneous tissue the tissue lying immediately below the skin, also known as subcutis

sudoriferous gland an alternative name for a sweat gland

suitability the effect of a style has on the client. When the style enhances the client's look

sun carers used on the final dressing to give protection against the environment

surface tension a force created at the surface of water or a liquid

sycosis a bacterial infection of the hair follicles

symmetrical evenly balanced, the same shape on both sides

symptom a sensation or a change in the body or its functions by which a disease may be recognised

synthetic man-made

tailcomb a comb with an extension that is useful for sectioning and guiding hair

tapering (taper cutting) cutting a hair section to a tapered point (i.e. a point like that of a sharpened pencil)

tapotement tapping or patting **massage** movement

teasing separating strands of hair

telogen the period during which a hair ceases to grow, before it is shed

temporary colourings hair colouring that is washed away by shampooing

terminal hair the long, relatively coarse hair of the head and of men's beards

test curl experiment on a curl to determine the required perm lotion, rod size and processing time

texturising removing small amounts of hair without reducing the overall length

thinning reducing the bulk of hair without reducing its length

tinea a fungal skin infection, often ringworm

tinea capitis ringworm of the head

tinea pedis ringworm of the feet (called 'athlete's foot')

tipping shading or **colouring** parts of the hair to enhance the style

tone the overall visual impression given by a colour

toning the process of adding tint or colour to hair after **bleaching**

traveller's cheque a means of making payment without using cash

trichologist a scientist specialising in the treatment of diseases affecting the hair

trichorrhexis nodosa the development of nodules on the hair, leading to splitting

trimming removing small amounts of hair while retaining the original style

twice over shaving close shaving, shaving twice around the face

utilities the practical services essential to the running of a salon (gas, water, electricity etc.)

under-processing when a chemical product has not been left on the hair for the recommended or required development time

uniform layering a hair cut when all sections of the hair are the same length

VAT (value added tax) a general consumption tax assessed on the value added to goods and services, which applies in principle to all commercial activities involving the production and distribution of goods and the provision of services.

vegetable parasites for example fungus, thrush, candida

vein a blood vessel that carries blood towards the heart

vellus hair the fine, fluffy hair that covers skin; may be visible on the human face

venule a very small vein

verruca a type of wart, especially one that grows on the hand or foot

virgin hair hair that has never been treated by any chemical process

virus a very small particle, visible only with an electron microscope, able to reproduce itself but incapable of existing outside a cell of some other organism; many cause diseases

viscous thick and sticky; slow-flowing

walnut tree which produces nuts; colour can be derived from the shell of the walnut and used as a surface colour

wart a viral infection of the skin

wen *see* **sebaceous cyst**

wet cutting cutting hair while it is wet

wetting agents reduce the surface tension in water, thus allowing water or a liquid to spread easily over the hair and scalp

wraps (end papers) are used to enfold hair ends when winding a perm

Index